Author of *Forgotten Millions*
documentary film-maker Dav
an independent TV productio

By the same author

Forgotten Millions
Psychologists on Psychology
J. B. Watson – the Founder of Behaviorism
All in the Head
Broadmoor
Piaget: Critique and Reassessment
Testing Psychological Tests (with Douglas Shelley)
The Development of Play
The Power of Psychology? (editor)
Soviet Psychiatry
Being a Man
The Development of the Imagination (with Dr Stephen MacKeith)
Essential Psychology

DAVID COHEN

Aftershock

The Psychological and Political Consequences of Disasters

PALADIN
GRAFTON BOOKS
A Division of the Collins Publishing Group

LONDON GLASGOW
TORONTO SYDNEY AUCKLAND

Paladin
Grafton Books
A Division of the Collins Publishing Group
8 Grafton Street, London W1X 3LA

A Paladin Paperback Original 1991

Copyright © David Cohen 1991

A CIP catalogue record for this book
is available from the British Library

ISBN 0-586-09073-8

Printed and bound in Great Britain by
Collins, Glasgow

Set in Times

Contents

Acknowledgements

Lindsay Knight was my collaborator on the film *Encounter: Coming Through Fire* on the King's Cross survivors. Many thanks to her and also to Sandy Lowe, who typed much of the script, and to Nicholas Cohen, Reuben Cohen and Aileen La Tourette.

Introduction

When I started to write this book, I wanted to focus on the psychological consequences of disasters. Since the mid-1970s, psychiatrists have argued that both those bereaved by disasters and survivors of them experience considerable difficulties. The problems of these two groups, however, are different. The bereaved have to face not only the typical ones of loss – denial, grief and anger – but also the shock of its suddenness. Usually when someone dies, their death is not wholly unexpected; there has been some time to prepare. In disasters, it is different. The bereaved are left in a state of shock. They often fret about their loved ones' last moments. Were they in pain? Were they terrified?

Sudden deaths in disasters are also marked by unusual problems. For instance, there are frequently difficulties with identifying corpses. At Lockerbie, to take one example, more than thirty bodies of the 270 dead were never found. Often, only bits of bodies remain. In addition, if there is a criminal inquiry following a disaster, as at Lockerbie, the procedures for getting bodies back can be a macabre, bureaucratic nightmare, for the corpse is, temporarily at least, the property of the state.

All these factors contribute to the grief of the bereaved. Lundin (1984) found that those who lost someone suddenly grieved for longer than those bereaved in ordinary circumstances. Children also often die in disasters and bereaved parents are most prone to depression, despair, guilt and anger. Their child's death is perceived as running against the natural order.

Survivors experience some of these emotions, but not all of them. Many say that they simply feel lucky to be alive, but many also report crippling psychological problems, sometimes as a direct consequence of their injuries. For others, the disaster is a turning point in their lives. It leads them to reassess the way they have been living. Cancer patients have reported similar experiences. Having to face death changed their lives in countless ways, some surprisingly positive.

I wanted, therefore, in this book, to explore in detail different reactions to disasters among both the bereaved and survivors. The more I studied the subject, however, the less adequate the purely psychological approach seemed. It not only ignored the causes of disasters, but it also failed to address a question that's both crucial and fascinating: why do governments, businesses and individuals find it so hard to learn lessons from past disasters and, as a result, to improve safety and security?

An instructive example of this failure to profit from hard-learned experience can be found in the successive oil-rig disasters in the North Sea, the first involving the Norwegian *Alexander Kielland* platform, the second the United Kingdom's *Piper Alpha* installation.

The *Alexander Kielland* was the pride of the Norwegian oil industry. The massive platform stood 200 feet high in the North Sea. Its crew of 240 lived in an accommodation module which had been designed to provide every possible comfort. The external environment might be rough but the platform offered a games room, a cinema, a canteen and a small gym. Early in 1980, there was a routine inspection of the platform. It was declared to be in first-class condition. Its structure was sound.

Those who lived and worked on the platform were used to the sounds of the sea: waves crashed constantly against massive supporting struts extending deep into the sea bed. The crew felt relatively safe.

No one noticed the first signs of the disaster. Many of the crew were in the *Kielland*'s cinema as a small fracture began to creep along one of the struts. The sea was inching its way in, twisting, turning and splitting the metal. At 6.30 in the evening the platform suddenly gave way. There was no warning for those on board. One of the huge supporting legs underneath the accommodation block simply began to move away from the platform and the platform itself began to tilt and dip towards the waves.

Thomas Greenwood, Chief Steward of the *Kielland*, said at the subsequent inquiry: 'The first thing I felt was a shudder, then a screeching of metal. Then the whole kitchen began to tilt. Pots and pans started to slide off the shelves and I heard pandemonium breaking out in the mess restaurant next door, where plates were falling off tables and the furniture was beginning to topple over.'

Ronald Jackson, from Manchester, was in the cinema and found: 'All the chairs and bottles were just sliding along the floor. They crashed into the movie screen and the water flooded through the windows and they just disappeared underneath it. I panicked like mad when I saw electric cables burning and sparking just before the power failed.'

Outside the cinema, Greenwood saw men struggling to pull themselves towards the control room at the end of the corridor. They had almost reached it, when 'a roll of oil from the busted drums on the deck came rushing down the corridor'. They fell back fifty feet, and Greenwood tried to reach the helicopter landing pad at the top of the platform. He did not make it, but he did get to a lifeboat. He managed to winch it down to the sea and to get in, but the lifeboat was too late to save four men. Greenwood then tried to help some of those closest to him, including two men whose lifejackets had caught on bits of metal. One man screamed all the way down to the water. Greenwood said, 'I was against one edge of the platform watching her slowly going over.'

The pressure of the sea water built up in the rooms and corridors, and blew out windows. Greenwood saw lifejackets, quilts, and mattresses and bodies expelled into the sea. Jackson, meanwhile, had made it to the deck, though in the dark he found it nearly impossible to climb up the metal structures of the platform, now tilted to forty-five degrees: 'Steel ropes were flying about, drums of oil were bursting everywhere and the water level was rising. It was a crazy nightmare.' The carefully rehearsed evacuation drill had not prepared anyone for the reality.

Jackson was eventually thrown clear and swam out to a

lifeboat. In all, twenty-eight survivors waited throughout the night for the helicopter that would rescue them. The death toll was 126, making it one of the largest disasters in the Norwegian field.

The Norwegian government had always been very concerned about safety in the North Sea, and it insisted on a very thorough inquiry, introducing a totally new system of assessing safety. Statoil, the nationalized Norwegian oil company, introduced a technique called risk analysis. Instead of referring to rather vague assessments of safety, it started to quantify every aspect of oil production and to measure the risks involved in them. It eventually emerged with an 'acceptable' risk of three deaths every 10,000 man-years worked on oil installations.

The United Kingdom and Norway have developed North Sea fields together. They have close contacts. The Norwegians therefore made available to the United Kingdom all the knowledge they acquired. Though the Department of Energy did not go over to a system of risk analysis itself, it did claim to have studied and used the results of the *Kielland* inquiry. It was convinced that a similar accident could not happen in UK installations.

Then, on 6 July 1988, after a number of previous accidents in the North Sea which had nearly ended in large loss of life, the *Piper Alpha* oil platform in the Brent sector of the Piper Field, north east of Aberdeen in the North Sea, exploded, killing 167 people. Thirty-one of the bodies were never recovered. The final results of the *Piper Alpha* inquiry have not been published but the technical investigations that followed showed that many of the lessons of the *Kielland* had not been applied. There were economic reasons (to separate production and accommodation entirely would be very expensive), but there were also other factors involved.

Man-made disasters typically occur in factories, railways, planes and installations designed by engineers. On the whole, engineers have very little understanding of how people behave in emergencies. It is only recently that psychologists have begun to look at this topic and at how, as a result, environments need to be designed. So far, their insights have tended to be used only in 'therapy' buildings like hospitals and prisons.

The design of a building or vehicle becomes crucial in an emergency. Individuals must know, for instance, how to get out. In the chaos, the information has to be available. All too often, it transpires there is muddle over evacuation procedures; emergency exit lights are not actually visible and deadly confusion prevails.

In the King's Cross fire, Dick Bates nearly became a victim of that confusion. He was travelling home to Finsbury Park and changing at King's Cross from the Northern to the Piccadilly line. It was a journey he did every day on his way to and from the *Guardian* in Farringdon Street, where he worked as a sub-editor. As he started to make his way to the Piccadilly line platform, he noticed smoke. His first instinct was to find the escalator going up, which he imagined would bring him to safety, but it was too hot and smoky to go that way. Dick then searched desperately for a way out. First he tried going down to one of the platforms but there he found a train that refused to open its doors to let people in. Desperate passengers were thumping on the doors and shouting that there was a fire but the tube drivers had been told that it was dangerous to open the doors. Dick then looked for where the emergency exit signs led. Many of these signs were not working. He followed, nevertheless, what appeared to be a route that led to an exit. It went down a tunnel, which led him to an exit in the Pentonville Road at the far edge of the station. By this time he had been joined by a policeman. The tunnel was pandemonium all around them.

The fire got nearer and nearer. Dick began to be convinced he would never get out. When they reached the end of the tunnel, they found that the emergency exit was closed. They banged and shouted as the fire began to close in on them. 'I was sure I'd had it,' Bates said. He was conscious of the flames behind him and of sounds of panic echoing throughout the station. Finally, when he had nearly given up hope, someone came to open the doors. He staggered up into the Pentonville Road.

The Fennell Inquiry into the King's Cross fire concluded that the death toll at the station was certainly made worse by a mixture of poor design, bad maintenance, and less than committed attitudes to safety on the part of both management and staff. Psychologists, therefore, do have something to offer in this area of improving both design and emergency procedures.

Man-made disasters are also seen as points of reference. They symbolize the political and social conditions of a particular moment. Some saw the accumulation of catastrophes in Britain between 1985 and 1989 as a political judgement. They appeared to prove that Great Britain was now only a third-rate power. The years of Tory rule had slashed the amount of investment in the infrastructure, especially in transport. Private affluence accompanied public squalor. Early March 1989 saw such criticism and pessimism increase when the Purley and Bellgrove train crashes followed the Clapham rail disaster. It was claimed British Rail was too poor to be safe. The travelling public had lost confidence in it and badly needed reassurance.

The aftermath of Clapham, Purley and Bellgrove revealed a sorry, but not atypical, history of problems. In November 1988 there had been an incident in Newcastle in which fifteen people had been hurt. There had been signal failures, similar to that at Clapham, at East Croydon, Oxted and Queenstown in the two previous years. As a result there was pressure to improve signalling, but, without fatalities, only gentle pressure. British Rail had in fact commissioned a study from the Royal Holloway College in 1986. This showed that in 1987 there had been 782 cases in which train drivers had gone through signals set at stop. There was also a rise in the numbers of signals at danger from 550 in 1983 to 850 in 1988 (*Railway Gazette International*, 11 March 1990). Clearly this was not encouraging, but the implications of these findings were never adequately followed up. In paperwork between central and regional rail offices, the statistics were buried in in-trays.

After Clapham and Lockerbie, the leader of the Democrats, Paddy Ashdown, suggested in the House of Commons on 6 March 1989 that public transport was at 'breaking point'. He added that 'we must put a stop to the calculated running-down of our public transport system'. Michael Martin, a Glasgow MP, accused the government of 'wanting safety on the cheap'. John Prescott, the Labour transport spokesman, said '. . . the

House wanted to know, if the accident could have been avoided if British Rail had not had in mind meeting the Secretary of State's financial targets. MPs wanted to know if reducing costs was affecting the level of safety.' Clapham thus raised questions about the kind of society that Britain had become. Critics of Thatcherism argued that the spate of disasters demonstrated the dark side of a greed-driven economy, that the pursuit of profit had led to a lack of concern for safety. Marketing triumphed. More money was spent on promotions than on precautions. Moreover, the increasingly familiar spectacle of Mrs Thatcher turning up to console survivors often provoked anger because her policies were seen as the disasters' contributing causes. A starved public sector was forced to ignore safety requirements.

Prescott suggested that Paul Channon, the responsible Secretary of State, should resign. For a week or so, Channon's fate hung in the balance. Some Tories accused Prescott of bad form for 'attempting to make political capital out of these tragedies', as David Evenett (Erith and Crayford) put it. Headlines speculated as to whether Channon was congenitally unlucky, a doomed minister fated to preside over disaster after disaster. This, clearly was not a logical response, but a psychological one. However unlucky or doomed Channon was, how could he *cause* disasters? In the end, however, he was duly sacrificed, an example of how psychological or 'magical' thinking, as I shall argue, often surfaces in the aftermath of disasters.

Magical thinking is essentially a form of superstition. It is the very opposite of the logical analysis the Norwegians went in for after *Kielland*. It reflects our fears about examining in cold detail the technological and investment mistakes that cause man-made disasters, but it is not surprising that it often influences our attitudes. For centuries, the only disasters human beings experienced were natural ones, and one can neither predict nor control an earthquake. The only thing one can do is pray to the gods in advance to keep the environment stable, and pray to the gods again afterwards so that they prevent the earthquake happening again. Freud would have recognized the impulse to remove Channon from office as a kind of sacrifice:

hand over one tainted priest to the gods, and, lo, the dark powers will smile on us again; we will be safe.

It is an irony that such moral panics make us feel better and can reassure us. They are also, however, inappropriate. They do not have any impact on floods and earthquakes and they have none on preventable, man-made disasters. Magical thinking is profoundly conservative, in fact, and it may well hinder our ability to change the way particular industries are organized. The ritual exchanges in Parliament after Clapham, for example, did little to focus attention on what needed to be done to improve rail safety. It is perhaps significant that Mrs Thatcher, in her 1989 reshuffle, gave transport to her favoured 'lucky' minister, Cecil Parkinson.

Freud argued that primitive human societies had to rely on magical thinking because the natural forces around them seemed so strong. There is another reason for its prevalence in disasters. Disasters make us uncomfortable. They remind us of our mortality; indeed they blazon it on the front pages. We prefer not to think about such frightening events, especially when most of us cannot avoid travelling on the tube, trains and planes. It is cosier for both organizations and individuals not to draw the necessary and inevitable conclusions. Airline companies, for instance, often claim that one reason they cannot introduce really stringent security is that most passengers would not stand for the delays, even though these delays might save their lives. I recently travelled through Heathrow on one of those rare days when one in three passengers was being thoroughly checked. The scene was chaos. People were angry; they refused to recognize that this time-consuming procedure was there to ensure their safety. From a sceptical psychological point of view, it looked as if it was more comfortable for them to be angry at the security staff than actually to dwell on the risks of flying. Technically speaking, they displaced (or turned) their anxiety into consumer anger.

Our attitudes to disaster often show up a human tendency to withdraw from disturbing realities. That tendency is particularly evident now that disasters seem random, events without apparent purpose. In the past, victims of catastrophes could at least believe there was a reason, even an Intelligence, behind them.

In the splendidly named *Terrific Register* of 1825, which offered its eager readers a 'record of crimes, judgements, providences and calamities', there was none of the modern shilly-shallying about the 'point' of disasters. God was making His views known. The register states:

Nor can we fail of deriving moral advantage from the contemplation of these tremendous visitations which in the mysterious dispensation of providence are sometimes destined to level in one common ruin the cottage of the peasant and the Palace of the Prince: to sweep whole generations to their grave. By such displays of power, the weakness of man and the might of Omnipotence are so visible and striking that hardihood must be cowed and pride humbled.

The *Terrific Register* thundered impressively in a world profoundly different from ours. In 1825, disasters were earthquakes, floods, hurricanes. They were what the insurance companies still refer to as Acts of God. It was only later during the same century that humans would gain enough technological control to create serious disasters (other than war) of their own. It took some time, however, to slough off the pious attitudes of the *Terrific Register*. Two great poets of the late nineteenth and twentieth centuries both saw marine accidents as divinely created. Gerard Manley Hopkins, the Jesuit poet, wrote a poem called 'The Wreck of the *Deutschland*' on the drowning of five nuns. He ignored such mundane questions as whether the coastguards had been called out in time, concentrating instead on the nuns' vision of Christ in the waves, and asserting that the Franciscans died triumphing in faith. Even more bizarre was Thomas Hardy's lamentation on the sinking of the *Titanic*. This was a spectacular story. It had surprise, hubris, irony, sudden death and enough survivors for the active press of 1912 to obtain many human-interest stories. The ship was on its maiden voyage. The owners claimed it was unsinkable. There were telling images of the last minutes that contributed greatly to the poignancy of the story: the orchestra played as the ship went down; the captain stayed on the bridge; the emblem of the machine age was tilted at forty-five degrees before it disappeared. There were in fact mechanical reasons for the sinking of the *Titanic*, of course, but Thomas Hardy wrote:

I

In a solitude of the sea
Deep from human vanity,
And the Pride of Life that planned her, stilly couches she.

II

Steel chambers, late the pyres
Of her salamandrine fires,
Cold currents thrid, and turn to rhythmic tidal lyres.

III

Over the mirrors meant
To glass the opulent
The sea-worm crawls – grotesque, slimed, dumb, indifferent.

IV

Jewels in joy designed
To ravish the sensuous mind
Lie lightless, all their sparkles bleared and black and blind.

V

Dim moon-eyed fishes near
Gaze at the gilded gear
And query: 'What does this vaingloriousness down here?' . . .

VI

Well: while was fashioning
This creature of cleaving wing,
The Immanent Will that stirs and urges everything

VII

Prepared a sinister mate
For her – so gaily great –
A Shape of Ice, for the time far and dissociate.

VIII

And as the smart ship grew
In stature, grace, and hue,
In shadowy silent distance grew the Iceberg too.

IX

Alien they seemed to be:
No mortal eye could see
The intimate welding of their later history,

X

Or sign that they were bent
By paths coincident
On being anon twin halves of one august event,

XI

Till the Spinner of the Years
Said 'Now!' And each one hears,
And consummation comes, and jars two hemispheres.

The press asked how it could have happened, but did not
explore the inglorious facts in full. Why did the ship not have
enough room in the lifeboats for all the passengers? How many
passengers died in the freezing sea who could have been saved?
It took over seventy years for the full story of the technical
design faults to emerge. These were revealed in a TVS film
which also traced a few of the surviving passengers. Some still
attended seances to get in contact with relatives they had lost
on the ship. Magical thinking tended to prevail. The elderly
survivors glossed over the fact that the *Titanic* sank because of

poor design, the greed of the shipbuilders and less than brilliant seamanship. Rather, they appeared to think with Hardy that the disaster was the will of God, designed to punish hubris, to remind humankind not to overreach itself.

This kind of theological attitude to disasters is now hard to sustain, yet those who live through a disaster have to struggle to understand and make sense of what has happened to them. As well as their emotional reactions, survivors often report that they become fascinated by or obsessed with 'their' disaster. Only in this way can they fully grasp how their lives have been changed. I shall argue in this book that feelings of control, or the lack of it, are vital clues towards understanding how people react. It is also becoming clear that it is no longer helpful to regard all disasters as identical and as having identical consequences. Some are predictable, some are not; some lead to complex legal actions, some do not. The relevant literature is only just starting to recognize the heterogeneousness of its subject.

As an aid to analysis, it is therefore useful to divide disasters into a number of different types:

1. *Natural disasters*: e.g. hurricanes, earthquakes
2. *Ordinary disasters*: e.g. rail accidents, where people don't normally perceive much risk
3. *Technological disasters*: e.g. Three Mile Island and Chernobyl, where a high-tech institution places ordinary citizens at risk
4. *Disasters in high-risk industries*: on oil installations, for example, workers know that they are in a hazardous job
5. *Disasters involving crowd violence*: e.g. Hillsborough and Heysel

After disasters like Heysel Stadium and Hillsborough, reactions to the victims were curious. They were sometimes embarrassed, sometimes excessively pious. When victims are not wholly innocent, when they or their group contribute to the disaster by their behaviour, we seem very uncertain how to react. Both Heysel and Hillsborough were seen in Britain as signs of how self-destructive some parts of society had become. How blame is apportioned in such disasters is an extremely complex issue, but it does throw some light on how our reactions to disaster can become confused.

Any book on disasters must also ask a key question that is very hard to answer: is the frequency of disasters increasing?

Some natural disasters remain completely unpredictable. There was no warning either of the Mexico earthquake in 1985 or of the Armenia earthquake in 1988. In theory, as weather forecasting improves, other forms of natural disaster are more predictable. It has been claimed that, in the developed West at least, the number of deaths from hurricanes and floods has gone down. In 1900, for example, the population of Galveston in Florida was decimated by a hurricane which swept, seemingly out of nowhere, into the city. In the last few years, however, meteorologists have improved the accuracy of hurricane warnings. As a result, residents of hurricane-prone areas on the eastern American coast often have between twelve and twenty-four hours to prepare themselves and their houses. The media have become adept at publicizing such warnings. As anyone who lived in Britain in October 1987 knows, though, hurricane forecasts are far from perfect. The Met Office then confidently but wrongly stated that there would be no hurricane. Despite occasional blunders, the prediction of natural disasters has become more of an exact science and the number of deaths has decreased as a result.

Man-made disasters are very different. First, as technology develops, the potential for man-made disasters grows; there are simply more things that can go wrong. In the last twenty years, for example, there have been a number of toxic waste disasters. In Seveso, a leak at a plant that manufactured Dioxin injured 193 and threatened the health of 30,000; in Bhopal, the final death toll was reckoned to be around 2,800 people killed and a vast number were injured as a result of an error in pesticide production; in Brazil, recently, waste material from a nuclear plant was sold in markets and caused a number of deaths. Such accidents simply did not happen until recently. I have been unable to estimate a figure for such new technological accidents, but they are high, even in the developed world where there is a great deal of safety legislation.

In the field of transport, the figures are clearer. Both airlines and the rail industries keep good international statistics. They show over the last ten years a rise in the absolute number of dangerous incidents, near misses and deaths caused by disasters. In 1964 the number of people killed in air disasters was 871 according to the Civil Aviation Authority and 647 according to *Flight International*. The next year, the figures were similar: 662 according to one source or 1,016 if one included military accidents. The International Federation of Airline Pilots' Associations reported, in 1987, a total of 1,300 civil aviation deaths and, in 1988, a total of 1,650. This rise in the number of deaths, however, has to be seen in the context of a huge increase in the number of passengers carried and air miles travelled. In 1964, the number of people in the United Kingdom who had travelled by air was under 1 million; in 1988, it was calculated that one in every two Britons had flown. The number of air miles travelled worldwide has more than tripled since 1964. A recent American survey showed that the average American male flew 2.4 times a year.

More deaths as people travel or produce X times more is not an inevitable equation. The stress put on safety regulations – and enforcing them – is crucial. It cannot stop all disasters but it can make a difference. British Coal, for example, claimed in the *Guardian* on 20 September 1989 that more focus on safety and better use of technology has meant that the number of accidents fell from ninety-four per 100,000 man-shifts in 1979 to twenty-nine per 100,000 in 1988.

Likewise, an increase in road traffic does not necessarily lead to an equivalent increase in the number of deaths and injuries. In 1964, there were 152 cars per 1,000 British inhabitants (30 per cent of households); in 1988, there were 290 cars (68 per cent). There was not, however, a parallel rise in either the number of road accidents or deaths on the road. This relative improvement could be attributable both to stricter laws on seatbelts and to increased awareness of the risks of drinking and driving, or it could simply mean that cars have become tougher. The precise reasons are not clear.

In the wake of the *Marchioness* disaster on the Thames when fifty-one died as a pleasure craft was run over by the *Bowbelle*, a dredger and a much larger boat, Mrs Thatcher said that increasing prosperity gave people the opportunity to travel more. Accidents were therefore inevitable and in a curious way, she seemed to suggest, proof of economic progress. Her remarks puzzled, even irritated, commentators.

An apparently less murky political issue emerging from industrial and transportation accidents is that involving the classic conflict between safety and profit. It would make the arguments of this book neater if it were true that more investment led inevitably to more safety. Unfortunately, the facts are not supportive of this attractively simple conclusion.

The well-funded French railways network, for example, saw, prior to 1988, rather more deaths than cash-starved British Rail. At Ramstein in West Germany, seventy people died at an air display where most conceivable safety precautions appeared to have been taken. The West German inquiry on Ramstein highlighted the fact that communications during the rescue still broke down and that receiving hospitals were short of some vital supplies. Indeed, they were not in stock simply because no one imagined such a disaster would ever take place. Investment is important, of course, but so are the psychological attitudes that help cause disasters and, often, hamper the most effective action in their aftermath. David Canter, a psychologist from the University of Surrey and an expert on behaviour in fires, has argued that many people die or are injured in fires because they do not assess the emergency they are in quickly or sensibly. Often, they rely on received wisdom to get them out of an emergency, and received wisdom does not fit a high-tech world well.

An interesting illustration of this mix of the human and the economic comes, surprisingly, from an assessment of Aeroflot's performance in 1988. For years, Aeroflot had a reputation in the West as a risky airline. In 1988, all over the USSR 115 people were killed and ninety-three injured in sixteen major air crashes, fifty-eight planes and helicopters were written off by the airline. In analysing these statistics, Rudolf Teimurazoiv of the Soviet Aviation Commission argued that 83 per cent of the disasters were due to human error or faulty devices, while 9 per cent could be blamed on faulty aircraft design.

Aeroflot acknowledged the mixture of causes. In the capitalist world, the debate is too easily polarized. The left blames economic factors almost exclusively; the right dismisses such accusations as 'politically motivated'. There are certainly many examples of companies resisting expensive changes. A number of Boeing crashes late in 1988 and early 1989, however, focused attention on the issue of the age of planes and quality control in manufacture.

In the last four years (since 1985), Boeing aeroplanes have been involved in thirty-six accidents in which there has been loss of life. After the Lockerbie and British Midland crashes, there was considerable concern about a number of issues of aircraft design. It was argued that many planes in the jumbo fleet were now over fifteen years old. They were tired machines. A study showed recently that, of operational Boeing 707s, 720s, 727s, 737s and 747s, a substantial proportion had been flying longer than their original design objectives allowed for. There are, for example, 1,649 727s in service. One hundred and seventy of these have done more than the 60,000 flights they were designed for; 785 of them have flown for more than 50,000 hours longer than they were designed for.

Second, it was alleged that Boeing was the victim of its own success. It was having to fulfil so many orders so fast that its staff was cutting corners on safety and quality control. After the British Midland M1 crash, there was controversy about whether the new Boeing 737 model ought to be taken out of service. The initial investigation demonstrated again how complex the causes of disasters are. The French-built Snecma engine vibrated dangerously soon after take-off. The pattern of wiring that Boeing installed at Seattle gave the pilot incorrect messages. The captain believed that the right engine was in trouble when, in fact, it was the left engine. He shut the wrong engine down and chose to fly not to Luton, the nearest airport, but to East Donington. He seemed to be making it, but three miles from the airport, new vibrations started up and when he desperately tried to start the shut engine, he was unable to do so. Forty-seven people died in the resulting crash at Kegworth. The press's attitude to the captain exemplified the raw emotions that swirl around disasters. First, he was a hero. His brilliant flying of a crippled machine was a miracle. Then, as it became clear that he had shut down the wrong engine, he swiftly became a villain. At the inquest into the deaths, it became clear that the pilots were confused as to which engine had the problem and that two of the cabin staff did not tell them what they knew as they could not imagine the pilots didn't already know.

Boeing denied the charge that it was failing to maintain proper quality control. It sniped that a rival firm had leaked that rumour to the press. Nevertheless, Boeing did put on extra training programmes for staff. In May 1989, it announced that it would redesign some features of the stretched 737 to meet the latest European safety standards.

As the green agenda dominates more of the political debate, such issues are likely to get more attention. Old aircraft tend to be dirty and noisy. Their continued heavy use does not, however, show simply that the airlines will do anything for profit. The airlines are responding to a market. People want to travel and to travel cheaply. The politics that surrounds disasters is often complex. Often, remarkably, nothing at all gets done. Our inertia in the face of repeated disasters remains curious, and I believe it cannot be understood solely in economic terms: companies skimping or the employment of inefficient bureaucrats.

One useful new approach comes from ergonomics. In an authoritative account, W. T. Singleton (1990) argues that studies of disasters reveal a consistent mixture of bad design, poor safety procedures and human error. The reasons for the human error are complex. They can include fatigue, boredom, stress at home, momentary lapses of attention and inexplicable inaccuracy in such procedures as reading altimeters. It is not always easy, Singleton argues, for operatives to perceive something extraordinary going wrong. One of the most worrying facts to emerge from the inquest into the British Midland crash was that the pilots may have found the way information was displayed on the dials confusing. In the 1950s, Donald Broadbent, a psychologist, suggested that confusion about altimeter readings (which indicate the altitude of planes) had contributed to some crashes. The problem then was that the smallest needle on the dial, and so the easiest to misread, showed altitude in thousands of feet, a confusion that could be catastrophic.

Broadbent's work (1961) was much noticed. Yet, here, the problem may have reappeared. Further, most designs allow for credible failures but incredible events do happen. The design of the containment dome at Three Mile Island, for example, was intended to limit predictable damage – not what occurred. Bignell and his colleagues, in an analysis of seven disasters (1976), also demonstrated that most disasters had a complex history: the web of failures only became clear after the event; hindsight is easier than insight. Singleton claims it is vital to understand how human and machine failures interrelate. Only then will it be possible to design safer systems – safer either because they completely prevent disasters happening or, at least, because they incorporate procedures that obviate the worst impact of catastrophe. Despite his interest in the psychology of 'the mind at work', Singleton has nothing to say on an altogether murkier aspect of human attitudes.

Human beings are both fascinated by and fearful of disasters. We find it hard to change the structures and procedures whose inadequacies are demonstrated, yet we relish studying the minutiae of disasters. This paradox needs explaining. David Sturgeon, a psychiatrist who has been involved in counselling the survivors of King's Cross, told me: 'People have disasters in their kitchens every day. Every day people have individual disasters. I'm not sure why we have suddenly become so fascinated by disasters when individual disasters have been with us a very long time.' Major disasters have always made good copy. In his entertaining book, *Deadline Disaster*, Michael Wynn Jones points out that the first English newspaper, the *Oxford Gazette*, thrived on news of the Great Plague and the Fire of London. Certainly, the press relished calamities in Victorian times. Wynn Jones reproduces the gaudy headlines that described the great Chicago fire of 1871: 'Inhuman Incendiaries Caught', 'Men Wolves Hanged to the Lampost', 'A Feast of Death' and 'Robbery Rapine and Famine'. He notes that as early as 1900 photographers had their cameras smashed by irate victims of the Galveston floods. Disasters have been both events that demand explanation or comment and the inspiration for much moving literature.

There are of course many books on specific disasters, some

sensational, some personal, some learned. The recent spate of football disasters has led to a considerable volume of psychological literature which mainly investigates football violence. There has been, however, very little attempt so far to look at the difference between disasters of various types and their implications. A number of different questions need to be raised: first, what is the psychological impact of these different disasters? Do the services we provide for people adequately meet their needs? What can be done to make it easier to absorb the lessons of earlier disasters? Why is it so hard for us to learn? Should there be a national disaster 'service'? The Home Office, after much pressure, has announced that a co-ordinator will be appointed to deal with peacetime emergencies, recommending how to organize services better.

In the chapters that follow, a study will be attempted of how well lessons from particular types of disaster have been learned.

Chapter One examines natural disasters, from the Lisbon earthquake of 1755 onwards. Natural disasters are most familiar to us; they have formed most of our attitudes on how to react and deal with them. But although natural disasters are the most dramatic – the 1988 earthquake in Armenia killed 50,000, outdestroying any man-made disaster – they are no longer the most common.

In Chapter Two, I examine the Buffalo Creek Dam disaster and the Dutch train hijackings of 1975 and 1977. These two very different events focused the attention of psychiatrists and psychologists on reactions to disaster, no longer seen as inevitable acts of God. The reaction of the Dutch authorities in particular provided a model (good and bad) for how to handle disasters.

In Chapter Three, I look at the series of recent transportation disasters in the UK, from King's Cross to Lockerbie, and at what they have taught us both about the way people reacted and about the organization of rescue and counselling services.

In Chapter Four, I look at disasters involving high technology: Three Mile Island and Chernobyl. Such disasters provoke different reactions from those to either natural or ordinary disasters.

In Chapter Five, I look at disasters in industries which are known to have high risks and rewards attached. In the past that was true of mining and now it is mostly true of oil exploration.

In Chapter Six, I look at disasters in which crowd violence – or fear of it – is an important contributory factor. I focus largely on the Hillsborough disaster and its remarkable aftermath of commercial grieving.

In Chapter Seven, I look at Third World disasters. The most devastating was at Bhopal, and the negotiations between Union Carbide and the Indian government show all too clearly that there is one rule for Western disasters and another for the rest of the world.

In Chapter Eight, I look at the way counselling services have evolved in the UK and ask what sort of help holds the best hope of preventing long-term damage.

In Chapter Nine, I examine how British law and legal procedures have changed as a result of the recent spate of disasters. Solicitors and even judges are now being obliged to handle new sorts of cases.

In the final chapter, I ask how we can use psychological insights to learn more effectively the lessons of disaster. Bradford University has recently set up a Disaster Prevention Unit which aims to do just that. There has also been much lobbying for a well-funded national disaster office. But resources cannot be the only answer. The causes of disasters are complex, and preventing disasters will involve the imaginative use of psychological techniques in areas like training. Lessons for the future can and must be learned from what has happened in the past.

1
Natural Disasters

Just before 11 A.M. on 1 November 1755, Lisbon: one observer noted,

I threw down my pen being stunned with a horrid crash as if every edifice in the city had tumbled down at once. The house I was in shook with such violence that the upper stories immediately fell in. I expected nothing less than to be crushed to death as the walls continued rocking to and fro in the most frightful manner and opening in several places. Large stones fell down from the cracks and the rafters started from the wall. The sky in a moment became so gloomy that I could distinguish no particular darkness. It was an Egyptian gloominess.

The anonymous author added, 'I found myself choked to death for nearly ten minutes.' The tremors lasted for ten minutes and ripples were felt as far away as the English Channel. A freak tidal wave hit Dover and Calais. Lisbon had been shattered. The best contemporary estimate was that 50,000 people died. In the eighteenth century statistics were even less accurate than they are now, but some claimed one-third of Lisbon's inhabitants were killed.

The witness of the Lisbon earthquake got out of the house and made for an open space near St Paul's Church. Many of the congregation had been buried inside. He decided, wisely, to get away from the 'tottering houses' in case there was a second shock.

He made for the river where there was 'a prodigious concourse of both sexes and of all ranks and conditions whom their mutual dangers had here assembled as to a place of safety'. This huge crowd was 'on their knees at prayers, with the terrors of death in their conscience, every one striking his breast and crying incessantly to heaven for protection'.

A second shock came in the midst of their praying, finally bringing down many buildings that had been swaying. 'The consternation now became universal; shrieks and cries could be distinctly heard from a certain distance: at the same time we heard the fall of the parish church. Many were killed on the spot.' The force of the second shock was so intense that he 'could barely support himself on his knees'.

Then came the next crisis. Some of the crowd turned and noticed that the River Tagus was foaming. The witness noted: 'I perceived it heaving and swelling in a most unaccountable manner for no wind was stirring. In an instant there appeared a large body of water rising like a mountain. It approached with a roaring and rushed towards the shore with such rapidity that we ran for our lives as much as possible.' He was sure he had saved himself only by clinging on to a large beam.

To the confused inhabitants of Lisbon, who knew nothing of tidal waves, it now seemed that their whole universe was in chaos. The writer went back to St Paul's, from where he saw the ships 'tumbling and tossing about as if a violent storm had broken their cables'. They were whirled round 'with incredible swiftness, several large ones turned keel and all this without any wind'. A number of people actually sought safety on ships and were drowned. The lack of wind felt particularly eerie.

After the tidal waves – and there were a number – evening fell, but it brought no peace. 'The whole city appeared in a blaze so bright that without exaggeration I could see fire in a hundred different places.' The burning continued, he assured readers, for six days and the inhabitants were in such distress that they did little to stop its progress. When the fires subsided, it became clear what had happened.

It was All Saints' Day. After the first shock some inhabitants rushed into the churches to light candles in order to pray to God to prevent more shocks. The second shock upturned these candles and set fire to the curtains and tapestries in the churches. It was truly divine fire that consumed Lisbon. The writer estimated the death toll at 60,000. 'This whole opulent city was nothing but a heap of ruins.'

Devastating though it was, the Lisbon earthquake was far from the most destructive ever to occur. The US Oceanic

Service publishes a list of great earthquakes through the ages which notes that in 1202 A.D. a million died in Upper Egypt; in China an earthquake in 120 A.D. left an estimated 240,000 dead. Even Europe had previously seen earthquakes as devastating as the one in Lisbon. The scale of the disaster did not make Lisbon noteworthy. Rather, it was perhaps the first natural disaster in modern times to provoke extended, international comment. It was recognized at the time as a 'news event'. The reactions to the Lisbon earthquake were interesting and novel; many were repeated in later disasters. In this chapter I also examine more recent responses to natural disasters.

The Great Fire of London did not lead to much metaphysical speculation, perhaps because, since it started with a careless baker in Pudding Lane, it hardly raised deep questions about the meaning of life and the ways of God. No contemporary English philosopher used the fire to raise major issues. With Lisbon, it was different: within a few months of the disaster, Voltaire was writing at length about it in an exchange of letters with the philosopher Rousseau. The earthquake would also provide a background for Voltaire's novel *Candide*. In the book, Candide, the innocent abroad, and Dr Pangloss arrive in Lisbon just after the earthquake, a situation which allows Voltaire to tilt at two particular enemies: optimism and superstition. Candide, Pangloss and their party meet a sailor in the devastated city. His cynical aim is to make the best of the situation: 'The sailor said whistling, "There must be something to be made here."

'"What is the sufficient reason for this phenomenon," said Pangloss.

'"It's the last day on earth," cried Candide.'

Voltaire then describes how the sailor runs into the middle of the debris, risks death in order to find money and, having stolen some off a corpse, gets drunk. He then buys the favours of the first girl he meets among the ruins. Finally, Candide begs Pangloss to find him some wine to soothe his wounds. By the next day, Pangloss is dining with the inhabitants. Eloquently, he proves to them the logical necessity of earthquakes. The earthquake is for the best in the best of all possible worlds. Pangloss tells his hosts, who conjure up dinner in the midst of chaos: 'If there is a volcano in Lisbon, it has to erupt. Things couldn't be otherwise and consequently it was for the best.'

Having mocked optimism, Voltaire then acutely depicts how superstition rules after disasters.

After the earthquake which had destroyed three-quarters of Lisbon, the sages of the land declared that they couldn't imagine a more effective way of preventing a total ruin than to give people a fine auto da fe. The University of Coimbre decided that the spectacle of a few persons, burned slowly, with a great deal of ceremoney, was an secret and infallible way of preventing earthquakes.

So Pangloss and Candide are destined to be hanged either because they had caused the earthquake or, more likely, to prevent the next one. Fortunately, our hero is rescued, but not before he has given Voltaire's readers a splendid insight into how disasters provoke magical thinking.

In the real world, in the immediate aftermath of the Lisbon earthquake the Portuguese government managed to be surprisingly efficient. The King and the Prime Minister, Pombal, ordered all bodies be buried at once. Palaces and churches were used to house the sick. A number of European countries offered help as soon as they learned what had happened. The House of Commons voted £20,000 relief as a donation, then a major sum. A plan to rebuild the city was announced.

Voltaire stressed the injustice of the effects of the quake. In 1755, men did not expect to be able to control nature, that being God's prerogative. In the 236 years since, although our power over our environment has become much greater, natural disasters shock us even more severely, by emphasizing how helpless we really are in the face of the elements. When God dominated lives more, when people did not expect the control we take for granted now, so it was perhaps easier to be submissive before the blows of nature. Indeed Freud argues in *The Future of an Illusion* that primitive humans created religion in order to cope with the anxieties of living in an uncertain world. Natural catastrophes could once be seen as the wrath of God, as part of a deliberate plan to stop human beings getting above themselves, but that explanation carries less conviction in societies which are either agnostic or where God is seen merely as a somewhat nebulous externalization of the liberal conscience.

In the rest of this chapter, I focus on two recent earthquakes. Earthquakes are impossible to predict and can be utterly devastating. Both of these facts have psychological consequences.

Natural disasters remind us of our helpless insignificance on this planet. They cause suffering on a scale unmatched, until this century, by man-made ones. Until the invention of the atomic bomb, nothing humanity had fashioned even began to match the destructive power of natural disasters.

Reactions to two recent earthquakes highlight some of our paradoxical responses to this fact. Most interestingly, they show how the scale of the disaster provokes immediate unity, a human bond. But, typically, that bond does not last long. There is no one ultimately to blame for the quake but, the first shock over, scapegoats are sought and explanations demanded for the minor tragedies that occurred in its wake.

Mexico

During the night of 19 September 1985, the patients in Mexico City's largest psychiatric hospital slept badly. They were, according to their doctor, restless and fitful. Their medications did not seem to be working. It bothered him. It is a pity that he did not record his story before 7.19 A.M., because at that moment a tremor which reached 7.8 on the Richter scale hit Mexico, and it is hard to be sure that the doctor recounting his extraordinary experiences was not simply being wise after the event. There have, however, been stories of animals sensing an earthquake in the offing. In 1976, in Tientsin, cattle and dogs were said to have fretted, moaned and acted oddly for hours before the quake which killed 750,000 people. This is a rough estimate, since proper figures were never made available by the Chinese authorities; the Chinese did not let foreigners in either to observe or to help. Physiologists suggested the animals' magnetic sense might have been disturbed. If psychiatric patients had had similar premonitions it would be significant

and interesting, but as it is, the psychiatrist made this announcement to the press five days after the earthquake. The accounts
of the devastation tended to dwell on the impact on Mexico
City but the earthquake first hit Mexico's Pacific coast, tidal
waves slamming against it from Ecuador in the south to
California in the north. Around 1,500 people were killed
outright in the town of Atentique when a mountain literally
collapsed.

Within Mexico City itself, there was panic. Tourists rushed
out of luxury hotels dressed only in their underwear. Señor
Juvenito Benito de Hernandez had gone to work as usual that
morning. When the tremors started, he rushed back to the
apartment block where he lived. 'I called for my children but
there was no answer,' he said. Rescue workers thought they
might have heard crying from his two-year-old daughter but
they were sure that his two sons were dead. Hernandez sobbed
outside the apartment block, now reduced to rubble. His wife
clutched a Bible that she had somehow managed to rescue from
the devastation.

Other survivors were terrified partly because the quake was
a total surprise. One woman, Ruth Azuara, had been staying
in a hotel. 'It was like the end of the world,' she said. 'As we
were coming down the staircase, it was swaying.' Her hands
still hurt from the force with which she had had to grip the rails
to save herself. Different individuals had different ideas of how
to cope most sensibly. Many felt that the safest thing to do was
to stand under doorframes, which might offer a measure of
protection. One woman kept reassuring her children by yelling
'It will stop,' even though clearly this confidence had no effect
whatever on the earth. The first tremor lasted at least three
minutes, but, as in all earthquakes, there were many aftershocks.

The total surprise and the huge devastation seem to have
dominated the first reactions. In the first few hours, two-thirds
of the country's telephone exchanges were out of order. There
was a smell of gas on the streets and the government appealed
to people not to light matches. The electricity supply ceased.
Worse, because it was late summer, the water supply became
contaminated and, for days afterwards, it was not safe to drink.

Only gradually did the scale of the damage become clear. One-third of all the buildings in Mexico City had been damaged. The city itself is built on what is basically the Texcoco basin. When the Spanish first conquered Mexico in 1500 they found there was a dried-up lake by the site of the future city. Mexico City was built on that lake, a dried-up bed of slush 300 foot deep made up of alluvium and muddy sediment. This slush provided not only uncertain foundations but, according to many geologists, an ideal medium for amplifying the shockwaves of any earthquake. It was like a jelly. As a result, the city was tragically vulnerable, though mysteriously some buildings survived virtually intact next to others that were totally devastated.

A measure of the devastation was the way in which the whole infrastructure of the city, and with it that of the country, crumbled. The bureaucracy suffered badly. The Mexican government tried to claim that only 2 per cent of the city had been destroyed, but what had been destroyed was an important 2 per cent, for it included many ministries. The roll call of the mighty fallen was apocalyptic. Most of the files in the Ministry of Justice were destroyed. The central court records disappeared under the rubble. Documents vital for prosecution cases against major criminals, including drug dealers, were wiped out. The Ministry of Labour also disappeared. The Ministry of Commerce fared somewhat better: it did not fall down but all its windows were blown out, leaving it an eerie pockmarked ruin. Its databank was buried. The Ministry of Agriculture was the quickest to recover and get its bureaucrats back at their desks, taking over a large villa on the outskirts of town.

There were some political benefits, however: at the time of the earthquake, Mexico was in major difficulties with the International Monetary Fund. After it, the bankers had to postpone a demand for $950 million. Partly this was due to international sympathy; partly it was attributable to the fact that much of the paperwork had sunk, literally, into the earth. President Reagan sent his wife to the disaster, bearing a $1 million cheque.

The bureaucracy was not the only institution to suffer. Many churches were razed to the ground, as they had been in Lisbon in 1755. Twenty-five people praying in a church in Gaudalajara were also killed, local radio offering an indication of how this news was received. 'Mexico has been hit with the force of a mighty blow from Hell,' announced one station.

Disposing of the dead was a major public-health problem. Sports stadia were used, and one baseball stadium was full of putrefying corpses – a sight the authorities did their best to hide. Averting panic was a priority, especially when, within twenty-four hours, there were aftershocks. Morale became an acute problem. A number of foreign workers decided that enough was enough and took the first plane out to Miami. They were wise. In the aftertremors, hundreds died, including some at a large hospital treating the injured.

Eventually it was calculated that 20,000 people had died and that 310,000 square miles of the country had been devastated. Guzman, Mexico's fourth largest city, was decimated. These figures, while not so large in historical terms, easily outstrip the largest man-made peacetime disasters, demonstrating that nature has no rivals when it comes to inflicting casualties.

International agencies offered help, particularly with heat-seeking devices and sniffer dogs to find people buried in the rubble. There were some dramatic rescues. One official of the Ministry of Labour, Señor Ruben Rodriguez, stayed alive for nearly six days before being pulled out. He said that he had managed to survive by drinking his own urine and putting a small stone under his tongue to stimulate the flow of saliva. A medical student was applauded as he was rescued, since everyone believed he had been trying to help the injured when he was buried alive.

The most dramatic rescues from the rubble were of fifty-eight new-born babies, who had managed to survive eight days in the city's main maternity hospital. In an attempt to explain the babies' stamina, doctors claimed that 'the lack of the psychological factor' had pulled them through. New-born babies buried in rubble simply did not realize that they were in a stressful situation. They did not suffer from claustrophobia and they did not panic. As a result, they did not use up precious energy and calories by worrying. Given our knowledge about how new-born babies react if they are taken away from mothers and carers, the theory was odd, but its very production showed that, early on, there was interest in psychological factors.

The city found itself in the middle of a public-health crisis and a law-and-order crisis. There were fears of typhoid. There was no clean water. Armed looters took to the streets. Some donned Red Cross uniforms and smashed their way through roadblocks to rob jewellers' and other stores.

In the wake of these internal problems, many international criticisms suddenly erupted. The Mexican government was blamed for not asking for help early enough. The relief agencies were criticized for being slow to react; it had taken them four days to send in the sniffer dogs and heat-seeking equipment. Despite the enormous publicity the rescue of the babies received, experts pointed out that ecstasy might be premature. In 1980, there had been an earthquake in the Italian town of St Angelodi Lombardi. A thousand people had been injured. Some 500 of these subsequently died, either from crushing injuries or because of dust inhalation. The moving pictures of dramatic rescues might therefore be misleading.

Mexico is a Catholic country, and the Pope issued a statement in which he offered sympathy and prayers. He did not, however, address the key theological issue: why does God permit earthquakes, and allow innocent adults and children to be horribly killed and mutilated? Such questions do not appear to have answers, and so we tend to avoid them by focusing on smaller issues. Why did the government react so slowly? Was its apparent tardiness another sign of its corruption? Such questions clearly do matter, but the fact that they surface so soon after natural disasters reflects our need to make sense of events. The metaphysical dimension prompts us to ask unanswerable questions, so we focus on the little, explicable things. The world's huge media circus, paid to inform and comment, does just the same.

The behaviour of people in communities at risk baffles psychologists. The residents of Tokyo and much of California know they live on fault lines which are likely to give way at any time. San Francisco had a great earthquake in 1906; Tokyo was devastated by its 1923 earthquake. Since then, each city has

had many minor quakes, San Francisco experiencing a relatively serious one in 1989. In both places scientists have worked
hard to produce a formula for predicting earthquakes, yet the
best that American geologists have come up with is the information that, in recent geological history, the Andreas fault
'blows' in a major way at intervals of between sixty and 400
years. There is excellent detailed analysis of events after they
occur, but earthquake-forecasting remains too vague to be of
practical use. Given the known risks, one would hardly expect
Tokyo, San Francisco and Los Angeles to be desirable resi-
dences. Yet real estate prices in Tokyo and Los Angeles are
among the highest in the world. Surveys repeatedly show that
the sophisticated citizens of these cities do not deal rationally
with the risks of living there. They go on living there by not
acknowledging the dangers, surviving on cosy assumptions –
the earthquake will only be so bad; it will not strike them; their
houses are secure; or, simply, it's just one of those things.
There is no evidence that after the 1989 San Francisco earthquake (in which sixty-six people died) people have modified
their attitudes or behaviour much. Rather, since the initial
death toll was rumoured to be much worse, California has
treated the fact that there were only sixty-six deaths as a minor
triumph. Earthquake analysts, however, have warned that
often in history tremors occur in clusters over a few years. The
Andreas fault may not have 'blown' all its stresses away. Some
recent geological work suggests that the 1989 earthquake was
not 'the big one'. It registered only 6.9 on the Richter scale.
Despite these findings (*New Scientist*, 10 May 1990), there is no
sign of any change in public attitudes or actions. Estate agents
are still doing well in LA. The survey findings are a telling
reminder of our ability to ignore the threat of disaster. In
Japan, whose culture emphasizes the need to accept the blows
of nature and values endurance in the face of suffering, such
attitudes are at least rooted in tradition. In California, values
are very different. California is the land of the encounter
group, of twenty-four-hour therapy, where people are obsessed
with taking the right exercise and eating the right health food.
It is remarkable that a culture that is so narcissistic should
completely blank out this major threat to its very existence.

Armenia

Armenia also has a long history of tremors. A particularly destructive quake occurred in 893 A.D., when an estimated one million people were killed. Like all historical estimates, this figure is rather hard to confirm, but clearly the event cast a long shadow.

The recent earthquake took place on 7 December 1988. News of the earthquake was first broken, improbably, by the Islamic News Agency of Iran. In Edinburgh, the British Earthquake Research Centre recorded a tremor of 6.9 on the Richter scale. There have been many stronger quakes so, for the first few hours, the scale of the destruction was not obvious. Communications were slow, but the first press reports suggested that perhaps 200 had died. It is indicative of the different ways in which we measure natural and man-made disasters that a figure of 200 dead in an earthquake would not have been deemed a major disaster, a point that will surface later in examining the reporting of the 1989 San Francisco earthquake.

The December tremor hit an area covering most of Armenia. The Armenian capital Yerevan was not badly affected but a number of fairly large towns, including Spitak (population 70,000), and Leninakan (population 200,000), were near the epicentre. Survivors described extraordinary scenes. In some places the earth opened up and whole buildings were swallowed into the bowels of the earth.

Our awareness of disasters now comes most memorably through television. Glasnost allowed Soviet television to broadcast, fairly quickly, pictures of the devastation. It was awesome. Almost the whole town of Spitak was destroyed. Seven of the eight schools were razed to the ground. In nearby Leninakan, there was not a building more than eight storeys tall that did not topple. Appalling as the television pictures were, survivors agreed that they did not convey the full horror of what they saw. The pictures themselves could not take in in one sweep the whole end of life there. It was estimated that perhaps 55,000 people died in Spitak. The stench of decomposing bodies was gruesome.

Local people who survived, and the emergency services who

went in to help, were horrified. They heard screaming coming
from many buildings. Soldiers and volunteers clawed at rubble
to try and get people out. The Soviet press abandoned its
conventional and rather formulaic reporting of natural disasters. It discovered a graphic, truthful style. Even the staid Party
newspaper, *Pravda*, reported that in Spitak 'we have people
screaming from beneath the ruins. Every hour the screams get
quieter.' *Pravda* also noted that 'helpless sobbing people clambered on the wreckage of an apartment house from which can
be heard heart-rending cries for help'.

The experiences of many survivors duplicated those of the
man in Lisbon who felt that his entire universe was in chaos.
Mrs Anna Pogosyan was with her niece on the fourth floor of a
block of flats in Stepanavan. She heard a noise and the building
began to shake. She tried to open her door but was unable to
do so. The next thing she knew, she was lying on top of a pile
of rubble, quite unaware of how she had come to be there.

Two factors prompted the rest of the world into action: the
scale of the tragedy and the fact that it clearly could only be
described, depending on one's ideology, either as an act of God
or a fact of nature. No one could be blamed for it. The West
offered unprecedented assistance, far more than at Chernobyl
in 1986. The American Red Cross rushed medical supplies in.
President Reagan offered unconditional help. From 6 A.M.
onwards the London branch of the Moscow Narodny Bank had
calls from people offering help. One man handed in a dollar
cheque for the equivalent of £109,000. The London Fire
Brigade flew in three specialists with heat-seeking equipment
to detect signs of life in rubble. The equipment was badly
needed. From inside many buildings rescuers heard voices. One
said faintly: 'I can see the light. Seven people are here and the
dust is falling.' Men from Kent Fire Brigade also went out with
their own heat-seeking equipment. They found conditions
gruelling. It was not easy to co-operate either with the Soviets
or with emergency services from other countries: there were
endless language problems, the conditions under which they
had to work were stressful and there was not enough food.
Bizarrely, at one point, the Kent firemen had to beam a report
back to their headquarters in Maidstone and set up a special

satellite radio transmitter to do so. In normal circumstances, Westerners setting up a private radio transmitter would have seemed very suspicious to the Soviets – especially as they chose to do it near a military installation – but no one interfered with what in other circumstances could have been mistaken for a spying mission.

The Armenian earthquake, ironically, helped bring the USSR back into the international community. The Soviet Union's new willingness to accept help, its honesty about the scale of the disaster, seemed to confirm it was changing. Here was glasnost in action.

The Soviet authorities were worried that there might be an epidemic. They sent nine medical control teams to the area to make sure that survivors and rescuers had the drugs they needed. Confusion among the rescue services, however, added to the survivors' feelings of helplessness. There was, the Soviet news agency Novosti noted, anger that food was being badly distributed and that there were traffic jams on the roads into Armenia as many Soviet enterprises sent supplies – and especially cranes – to help.

As the scale of the disaster became clear, President Gorbachev hurried home from New York, cancelling his visit to Britain. He flew straight to Armenia and was obviously shaken by what he saw there, saying, 'What I have seen is a terrible tragedy. It is unbearable to see so many people suffering. I find it difficult even to talk about it. Good organization is vital. There are still people alive under that rubble.'

Natural disasters, as the *Terrific Register* noted, can sweep away the hovel and the palace of the prince alike. They are great levellers and, as a result, they provoke an immediate emotional, generous reaction. This immediate generosity was evident both within the Soviet Union and outside. In the new climate of perestroika, religious comment on the disaster was allowed. Voltaire's questions, however, were not addressed. Vazgen I, Catholicos of all the Armenians and in effect head of the Armenian Church, spoke of 'the blind rampage of the elements', noting that people were almost too sad to weep. 'The power of reason is frozen. Almost all of us are the same. We can't think why this disaster came on. We can't even weep.'

As a Christian bishop, he could not give in to the grave sin of despair, but he was clearly struggling against it.

Many children were orphaned in the disaster. The Soviet press made much of thirteen boys and girls from Stepanavan Boarding School no. 21 who saw the walls of their buildings collapse and their fellow inmates perish. The survivors were moved to the Armenian capital Yerevan, ten were reunited with their parents and the rest had to pick up their lives as best they could. Soon, however, conflicts developed surrounding the fate of children who had been orphaned. Within a week of the quake, Armenian nationalists accused the authorities of using the disaster as an excuse to airlift orphaned Armenian children out of Armenia. They would be fostered by Russians, and would therefore lose their Armenian identity. The race would be diluted. Gorbachev reacted angrily to that accusation: 'What kind of people are they? Do they have no morals?'

All kinds of other accusations were made. The so-called Karabakh Committee, a committee of Armenians who wanted the return of Nagorno Karabakh from Azerbaijan, was accused of exploiting the situation. Certainly the night after the first earthquake there were morale-sapping rumours that there would be another one, but rather more sinister were rumours that a nuclear bomb had been triggered near Leninakan. In fact the nuclear power stations in Armenia functioned perfectly well. The Karabakh Committee also claimed that relief had not been properly organized. On 10 December they held a rally in front of the Writers' Union building in Yerevan. They called for Armenia to reclaim Nagorno Karabakh. To many Russians this action seemed highly exploitative. The Communist Party was worried, however, and the Karabakh Committee was accused by Miroslav Buzhkebich in *Pravda* on 16 December of doing absolutely nothing constructive and of 'spreading outrageous lies, scaring those who have not yet recovered from the shock caused by the death of their kin'. He added that many Armenians thought that 'all grudges should be forgotten' because of the tragedy. This theme was taken up in *Sovietskaya Rossya*, which, in a single day, had received 3,000 letters offering help. One reader with thirteen children offered to adopt baby orphans. Families offered accommodation. The paper noted that the Armenian earthquake offered common pain, felt throughout the Soviet Union. It was against this background that the fury was felt at Armenian nationalism, especially since the Karabakh Committee's allegations were expressed in so-called anonymous letters.

This attempt to exploit the situation, once the first shock is over, is typical of the response to many disasters. The initial reaction in Armenia was very similar to that experienced after the Lisbon earthquake. It was frightening and had to be accepted. For centuries humankind had been prey to natural disasters. You prayed that they would not happen. If they did, they were mysterious acts of God. They could only be endured. You could ask God why He chose to allow them, you could rail at Him as Voltaire did, but there wasn't much point in blaming Him. Much of that feeling was experienced in Armenia, but what was telling was that soon the emotion became focused; it became essential to pin blame on some group, if not for the original disaster, then at least for subsequent developments.

In later chapters, I will argue that people's reactions to disaster are conditioned by two main factors. The first revolves around how much they blame themselves for the disaster, even if only for being, at that particular time, in the particular place. The second concerns loss of control. Could they have exerted any control over what happened? Can they influence events so that it will not happen again? In many recent non-natural disasters, survivors and the bereaved have tried hard to use the legal process not just to get compensation but to get change. Natural disasters present different problems: they are beyond blame, beyond control. Oddly, as a result, they seem to have fewer long-term effects. Baum (1987) suggested there was some evidence that flood victims recovered relatively quickly. The trauma that seems to occur for some people after man-made disasters is apparently deeper and longer-lasting, though it has to be admitted the evidence is a little skimpy. It is certainly true that even where people know there is a risk of natural disaster, they do little about it. They simply adopt a fatalistic attitude. Neither the citizens of Tokyo nor those of California are selling up. Even insurance companies, who should know the cold odds, do not seem deterred from investing there. All this reflects the way we treat natural disasters as great imponderables.

Predictability raises different psychological issues. Human beings like the familiar. We frame our everyday experiences according to our expectations. Singleton (1990) argues that good safety design is very tolerant. It allows errors to be absorbed, monitored and corrected quickly. Often, in the inquiries that follow disasters, engineers and other experts express how amazed they were that no one spotted that a disaster was in the making. All the signs were there: the dial readings were odd; the machine was behaving bizarrely; the smell was wrong. Why didn't the operators on the spot act on the danger signals in good time? Investigators often blame individuals for fatal complacency. They are right, but often too judgemental. It is hard for human beings to be constantly vigilant and, in an increasingly complex industrial world, constant vigilance is vital. Secondly, in crises, human beings are often let down by the systems that are meant to provide the essential information they need. Perrow (1981) found that at certain times during the Three Mile Island disaster the computer printout telling operators what was going on in the crisis-ridden plant was running ninety minutes late.

Singleton stresses the need to train personnel to monitor and interpret unexpected data. He has provided a list of desirable management and training practices which ought to be applied. This distinguishes between procedures that should reduce errors, and ways of coping with emergencies. To reduce errors, Singleton recommends:

1. Good selection procedures which ensure that workers will not react in a pathological way. Subsequently, their health should be monitored and there should be awareness of the need for good group interactions.

2. 'Optimize arousal conditions,' Singleton suggests. The work environment should provide stimulation. Avoid boredom. In all industries, giving workers the information they need is vital. The higher the technology the more the information is needed.

3. Good training. Singleton states that it is especially important to think out effective procedures for dealing with what he
calls 'interface design'. In his book, he provides a useful list of
the different kinds of tasks men and machines do best.
Accountants often cannot see the return on safety training and
it is therefore given low priority, especially when industries are
under financial constraint, as, for example, in the transport
industry. Singleton argues that this is very short-sighted.

4. Good procedures for allocating work. Employees should
have some variation in their work-load, good feedback on their
performance, and regulations that recognize the reality of
fatigue. Tired and stressed workers are more prone to make
mistakes.

5. Strict policies and attitudes towards safety. Singleton's
research has enabled him to draw up a portrait of the kind of
organization that is sensible about safety. It has a general
awareness of the risks involved in an enterprise; there are
'boundaries' that are accepted by its workers. 'Some things are
simply not done because they are unsafe.' Industry is not a
game in which you accept 'dares' as the Chernobyl workers
did. Equally, some things are done because they are necessary,
such as routine checks and general tidiness. Singleton claims
that in safety-conscious organizations there is a consensus that
'when working in a team it's a disgrace if action, or failure of
an action, puts another team member at risk', and there is
pride in coping with potentially hazardous situations. Like all
descriptions of climates of management, Singleton's is a little
vague. But in all the disasters studied in this book, many of
these 'rules' were broken.

Candide, *The Terrific Register* and *Deadline Disaster* illus-
trate our traditional fascination with disasters. Yet even Voltaire ended *Candide* with the axiom that we shouldn't brood
too much on calamities but rather cultivate the garden – grow
cucumbers rather than become too introspective. This long-
standing lack of interest in the psychological impact of disasters
now seems strange. It may have been due to a kind of religious
resignation. Judaism, Christianity and Islam saw disasters as
the will of God, as punishment for grave sins. The Egyptians
displeased Jehovah and were smitten with ten plagues, after

all. The Church throughout history has accepted disasters as inevitable. People probably deserved them. Eastern religions did not see disasters as divine retribution but rather as part of the great cycle of nature. Neither view paid much attention to man-made disasters. So when the Industrial Revolution created technologies powerful enough to cause disasters when they malfunctioned, no one perceived these as any different from natural disasters. There were thousands of deaths due to new technology, from the collapse of the Tay Bridge to railway accidents to the sinking of many 'ironclad' ships. Yet no one studied their after-effects; stoicism prevailed. What makes this even odder is the fact that throughout the nineteenth century psychiatry was developing rapidly. As early as 1848 there was, for example, a learned journal dedicated to those who owned and worked in asylums. Psychiatrists and psychologists began to take an interest only when they came to see that survivors of disasters had symptoms strangely like those of shell shock. To understand much of the current psychiatric interest in disaster victims, one has to go back to 1918, when the countries of Europe were dealing with the wounded of World War I.

2

The Discovery of Psychological Effects

It took nearly a century from the construction of the first railway for man-made disasters to be seen as crucially different from natural ones. The railways, shipping lines and mining companies had a vested interest in families who were bereaved and injured victims seeing disasters as acts of God, and it was not until the eighteenth century that the law in Britain recognized the right of an accident victim to sue for compensation. By the end of the nineteenth century, it was firmly established that those who offered transport services had a duty of care to their passengers.

It thus became possible for victims to sue, either directly or through their unions, but they had to show both negligence on the part of the company and how much their physical injury had cost them, in terms both of suffering and of loss of earnings. Physical damage was crucial: if you lost a leg, for instance, you could hardly continue your career as a dancer. The notion of *psychological damage* did not exist, in legal terms, as something for which a victim might seek compensation.

In this chapter, I want to look at how the notion that disasters have psychological consequences came to be accepted. I shall argue that one reason for our persistent tendency to consider all disasters as having similar effects is the fact that natural disasters offered, for a long time, the basic framework for understanding disasters. Moreover, the law on psychological damage is itself relatively new, its origins lying in the 1914–18 war. The ferocity of the battle in the trenches shocked the world. Harold Macmillan, the British Prime Minister, who fought at Ypres, noted that he felt a great sense of relief when he was wounded: he no longer had to pretend to be brave, or that the noise, threat and stench did not matter. For, during this most brutal of wars, men had to serve weeks, even months in the trenches. Many simply could not take it. The British Army contained a number of doctors interested in psychiatry and many of them noted how soldiers less privileged than Macmillan snapped under the stress.

When the war ended, Europe suddenly contained thousands of sufferers from shell shock. There was no clear way to treat them but many observers, Freud among them, swiftly realized that they were witnessing a profound reaction to the conflict. Indeed, treating a few shell-shocked patients made Freud change one of the fundamental concepts of psychoanalysis. Until 1920, he had argued that the life force, *libido*, motivated human behaviour. Confronted by the atrocities of the war, Freud acknowledged both our instinct for aggression and the paradox that we seek to die quite as much as we want to live. All organisms apparently yearn for a state of inertia, of tension-free Nirvana. Freud claimed that our desire to return to this state showed up as a death wish.

Freud saw only a handful of shell-shocked patients; British psychiatrists dealt with hundreds. Millais (1924) began to study their symptoms in some detail and to devise ways of treating them. He helped generate interesting new techniques, such as getting those who had been in the trenches to talk of their experiences, taking them through traumatic events step by step and sometimes using a drug, sodium amytal, to 'dis-inhibit' blocked memory. Millais, like Freud, assumed that some of these memories of war were so terrifying that they would be deeply repressed and that the ex-soldier would remain ill until he got the memories – and, especially, the linked terrors – out. To speak of them was to begin to overcome them.

By 1939, 'war neurosis' was a well-established condition. It was seen as affecting soldiers, however, not civilians. The possibility that civilians might suffer from similar conditions was first raised after John Hershey, in the *New Yorker*, reported in 1946 on the devastated city of Hiroshima. He was aware not just of the enormity of the event but of the psychological consequences of it, emphasizing that Hiroshima was in shock. The Japanese seemed to have lost the will to live. While the Hiroshima museum shows the sheer fragility of things

– shredded clothing, charred bowls, twisted bits of metal – and the landscape around Hiroshima was reduced to rubble, a more uncomfortable memorial might have been effected by simply leaving the shattered city in its 'lunar' condition. The normality of the Peace Park suggests that we recover. Such attitudes may be too optimistic. Research on Hiroshima's bomb and its after-effects started the moment the Americans occupied Japan. Initially, doctors were much more interested in the physical diseases of radiation, an understandable reaction, given the sheer scale of the pain. It was only in 1951 that Robert Jay Lifton began to explore the mental damage. The survivors suffered, he found, from chronic anxiety, depression and, often, a sense that life was not really worth living. Lifton was surprised by the extent to which people had failed to recover.

Hiroshima, the Holocaust and the experience of prisoners of war at the hands of both the Nazis and the Japanese were human dramas so extreme that psychiatrists thought they had uncovered a new kind of trauma, something beyond Millais' 'war neurosis'. Jan Bastiaans, then Professor of Psychiatry at the University of Leiden, studied Dutch prisoners held in Nazi camps. While most had not been treated quite as badly as the Jews, gipsies and homosexuals had been, Bastiaans neverthe-less argued that they suffered from the KZ syndrome, the concentration camp syndrome. In the 1950s and 1960s, he had many patients who were depressed, unable to sustain relation-ships. After the war, they had suffered, and that suffering was not recognized because Dutch society simply preferred to forget. Bastiaans told me in 1976: 'After the war the Dutch wanted to believe that normal life could resume, but I saw many patients who had *vita minima*, minimal lives. They went through hell. For example, there were many people who were forced to witness executions, even decapitations of comrades and friends. With the SS watching, they could not express their feelings of hatred or their horror. It had to be repressed.'

Bastiaans wears impeccable suits and does not look at all like a member of the counter-culture, but he gave LSD to patients who could not recall events to flush memories out. He claimed the drug worked better than anything else with some patients. His work with war veterans has made Bastiaans prone to make too few distinctions between scales of disaster, but he was, nevertheless, a key figure in putting on the clinical agenda the difficulties experienced by victims in picking up the thread of their lives once the traumatic events themselves had ceased.

Hiroshima, Nagasaki and the concentration camps were unprecedented phenomena, much more like natural disasters than man-made ones in terms of casualties. As a result, they were studied intensively, and it was out of this intense study that the idea that trauma followed extreme stress came to be accepted. Post-traumatic stress disorder is first mentioned, in different language, as a symptom in Freud's essay on melancholia.

Nevertheless, stoicism and heroism continued to be expected from those involved in disasters in the 1950s and 1960s in both Britain and America. It was thought brave to carry on living and rather shameful to dwell on the tragedy. Such social pressures simply added to the problems of many survivors. Few supposed that they might need professional help, and it was only in the 1970s that psychiatrists began to be interested in what might happen to those who had been involved in relatively minor disasters, and to link their difficulties with the sorts of trauma diagnosed in battle, or bombing, or other forms of large-scale destruction.

Buffalo Creek is a mining valley in West Virginia. On the night of 26 February 1972, a tidal wave of sludge and black water rushed through it, virtually destroying the village. The collapse of a slag waste dam at the top of the valley had caused the wave; it left 125 dead and over 600 injured.

The preparation for litigation required survivors to describe that night as fully as possible. One man said, 'Down below there was a huge amount of water. It looked like a river passing by. It was going so fast I couldn't believe it. I could see houses – some were broken up and some looked like whole houses still in good shape just floating down on this water.' Some people spoke of grabbing the children and starting blindly up the hill out of the way; others actually got caught in the flood and yet managed to survive. One man told how he ran to his front porch and tried to picture where the sidewalk was beneath the black water. He was felled the moment he started to walk; the current knocked him off his feet. He was amazed he did not drown but somehow, he could not remember how, he surfaced again. Others were unable to leave their houses and had to wait, terrified, as the water fell on them and their world disintegrated.

With their villages devastated, the survivors were moved into refugee camps all over the valley. The move itself would add to their problems.

It is unlikely that we would know much about the psychological effects of the Buffalo Creek dam disaster were it not for the fact that the 654 survivors decided to sue the Buffalo Mining Company which owned the dam. Their lawyers decided to seek damages not just for physical injuries and loss of property but also for psychological trauma, and to this end they retained psychiatrists, psychologists and case workers from the University of Cincinnati to do a pilot study of fifty survivors. The federal court, however, was not satisfied with this arrangement, ruling that extrapolations which assumed that the fate of these fifty was typical would not be satisfactory, given the novel nature of the claim. It therefore directed the Cincinnati team to study each of the 654 plaintiffs.

The evidence thus obtained was startling. Over 90 per cent of the survivors showed disabling symptoms. Many had developed personality changes. The two psychiatrists in charge, James L. Titcherner and Frederic Kapp, were convinced that people were not exaggerating their symptoms to bolster their compensation claims; indeed, many were extremely reluctant to discuss their problems at all. While the survivors found it hard to control their emotions, paradoxically they were often incapable of feeling anything, experiencing a 'flatness' like that reported by Bastiaans' patients. Sleeping became difficult. Many reported phobias about wind, water and rain. Anything that reminded them of the disaster could make them anxious. The wife of one community leader never slept while her husband was asleep; one of the couple had constantly to be awake and on the alert. When it rained, survivors frequently phoned one another to check that there was not a new slide on the way.

The survivors reported that nothing motivated them, that

they found it hard to be interested either in their work or their leisure. Titcherner and Kapp called this effect 'psychological conservatism', a kind of survival weapon in extreme circumstances, similar to Bastiaans' *vita minima*. Many survivors felt Buffalo Creek itself had changed. One man told the court: 'Only people who were in the flood realize that it's not rudeness when you have to ask them to repeat something simply because you weren't listening, your mind was somewhere else.' Difficulty with attentiveness, however, was the least of it: another plaintiff said, 'My nerves have been and are so bad. Sometimes I feel I hate myself. My body is one big pain, so stiff when I get up in the morning. And I feel like I am going to fall. I feel like the flood has brainwashed me.' Kai Erikson, a teacher of sociology at Yale, was approached by the law firm of Arnold and Porter to investigate the effect of the disaster on survivors. He found that victims also suffered cognitive damage. Often, they couldn't remember a friend's name or address. Many lost their sense of direction and, even though they had lived in Buffalo Creek most of their lives, often got lost running the most basic errands. Their sense of time was also distorted.

At the time of the study, the concept of survivor shame was not well articulated, despite the Holocaust studies. Titcherner and Kapp found that many survivors blamed themselves for still being alive. It was an irrational feeling, of course, when the valley had collapsed round them, yet it was a strong and genuine one. Many had, actually, behaved heroically. They still felt guilty, and most felt that they had been diminished by being in the disaster.

Titcherner and Kapp also noticed a paradox: many survivors felt rage as well as guilt. The reason, the psychiatrists concluded, was that the disaster was not an act of God; it was man-made and had even been predicted. For years, there had been a rumour that the dam was unsafe but people nevertheless continued to live in its shadow, just as they had continued to live in the shadow of the slag heap at Aberfan. Titcherner and Kapp were surprised by this finding as nothing had prepared them for it. Yet it is clearly an important issue: are reactions affected by premonitions of disaster? Does the fact that a disaster has been predicted make it more damaging when it happens? Do people then blame themselves for doing nothing?

The Cincinnati team found that survivors felt helpless and that this helplessness had changed their personality. They became the sort of people who did not mind, or were fatalistic, about being powerless: 'Since we lost everything,' one man said, 'what's the point of trying?' Even those who had been safe all along and never in danger of being engulfed by the sludge showed similar changes in attitude and behaviour. Kai Erikson suggested that the way the survivors had been treated made their situation worse. Buffalo Creek, like many mining communities, was a close-knit one, yet the refugee camps were scattered all over the valley. As a result, people lost contact with each other. To some extent, the victims were resigned to this isolation, since they had lost heart and faith, but it highlighted how the community had failed. Erikson wrote: 'The community (what remains of it) seems to have lost its most significant quality – the power it gave people to care for one another in moments of need, and the power to protect one another in moments of danger.'

Social scientists use basic measures of social trouble and disharmony. In Buffalo Creek, they found that, subsequent to the disaster, there was more theft, more delinquency, more divorce and more difficulties in marriage. The sludge even became a metaphor of doom. Erikson found that people spoke of moral decay slipping into the area just as the sludge had done.

The thoroughness of the research impressed the court. It granted psychological damages of between $7,500 and $10,000 to each individual and lawyers even won damages for those who had been away on the night of the disaster, but who had come back to find their community had been swept away.

The research also impressed the editors of the *American Journal of Psychiatry*. They devoted the whole issue of April 1976 to the disaster, because they saw that this was a major piece of innovative research. Indeed Buffalo Creek has remained a key frame of reference for studies of subsequent disasters and stress situations like the Dutch hijackings, Three

Mile Island, the Japan Airlines crash in 1984, and even Chernobyl.

Some months after I had reported on Buffalo Creek, I read a snippet in the *News of the World* which said that all those who had been held hostage in the Dutch train siege of 1975 had gone mad after the experience. Since it was not the kind of story I expected to find in the *News of the World*, I was interested, especially because it seemed to resemble the experiences reported from Buffalo Creek, I therefore persuaded Richard Creasey of ATV to let me make a film about those who had been hijacked, and I set about tracing all those who had been in the train and the psychiatrists who had treated them. The picture to emerge, however, was to be very different from that of Buffalo Creek.

On 2 December 1975, the morning train from Groningen to Amsterdam had reached the outskirts of Assen, which, like much of north Holland, is surprisingly desolate, given how small the country is. At Assen, the railway line is surrounded by fields. A small road crosses the track to two large houses; otherwise, the country is deserted. The communication cord was pulled and, in all the carriages of the train, a number of masked men suddenly brandished guns. The hijackers then moved through the train and herded passengers into two carriages at the back, telling them to put their hands above their heads and to wait. Hans Prinz, who was eventually to emerge as one of the toughest of all the hostages, said that, initially, there was chaos and terror.

Some of the passengers thought they were all going to be killed. In the first minutes the hijackers took one man, forced him on to his knees and shot him at point-blank range. They also shot the driver dead. One passenger was in army uniform: Jan Bies had been doing his national service and thus became a focus for the hostility of the hijackers. Once the driver had been killed, they yanked Bies into the cab of the train, tied him up, and made him sit there, isolated, for eight hours. Bies later told me: 'They were afraid of us. They thought that soldiers were quick and knew about guns, which wasn't true. I had all the time a gun at my head. I had only to say one word and that was it. I was afraid.'

Gerhard Vaders was bald and tall; he described himself once as 'a big old editor'. In fact, he was the editor of the largest local newspaper in north Holland, the *Neusblad von het Noorden*. As a journalist, Vaders' reaction was mixed. He was frightened, like all the other passengers, but he saw at once that the ordeal was also an opportunity for him: the greatest story he would ever cover – from inside. Like Bies, he was treated roughly: 'They made me stand up on the first day, tied up in the gangway, for six hours.' He too had a gun aimed at him. 'As a journalist,' Vaders told me later, 'I saw it as a challenge, and I began to take down notes.' He was careful at first, however, not to let the hijackers see him writing. He wrote frantically in the toilets. 'I knew I took a risk drawing attention to myself.' Gradually, however, such precautions became less necessary, though Vaders always retained a certain anxiety that his writing would mark him out.

There was no doctor on board. The person with the closest to a medical qualification was a biologist, Hans Prinz. Prinz is very tall, rather gaunt and bearded. His size gives him a natural air of authority. On the first day of the hijack, Prinz was nearly killed three times by Eli Hahuri, the leader of the hijacking, 'the most hostile and the most volatile of them all'.

The hijackers were South Moluccans, a group almost unknown until they took over the train, but who regarded themselves as victims of the process by which the Dutch had abandoned their empire. The Moluccas are a group of islands lying in the Pacific between Indonesia and Java. The Moluccans claimed that the Dutch had promised them independence when they withdrew from Indonesia in 1952, since the Moluccans did not wish to form part of the Indonesian Republic. A document signed by the Dutch government in 1951 did indeed apparently promise a separate independence to the Moluccan islands, but when the Dutch left Indonesia they did not implement this agreement. The islands became part of the Indonesian Republic, an outcome unwelcome to the Moluccans especially as thousands of them had served in the Dutch Army, under an arrangement similar to that involving the Gurkhas in the British Army. Their loyalty to the Dutch thus made the Moluccans hated by the Indonesians, a muddle common in colonial wars at the end of empires. To the government in Amsterdam, the fate of the Moluccans did not seem particularly serious. Most Moluccans chose to remain in the Pacific, but some twelve thousand, mainly soldiers and their families, were allowed to stay in Holland. The Dutch authorities considered they had acted with honour; old soldiers were given accommodation in Holland and the chance to start a new life in the West. But the dream of an independent Molucca did not fade. The Moluccans were moved to villages in north Holland. Here nostalgic old NCOs set up organizations that aimed to reclaim their old homeland. Once every year, they held marches to ask the Dutch government to give them back their islands. The Dutch government, with a certain condescension, received petitions from the marchers requesting action the Dutch were completely unable to take. They did not even press internationally for what little might have been achievable, such as a UN review of the Moluccans' case. The leaders of the Moluccans, who tended to be military men, typically ex-sergeants with a curious faith bred in colonial times that Holland would see justice done, were essentially deferential. Years passed, however, without any progress. Moluccan children were born in Holland and, for them, the Moluccan islands were a fabled paradise, the promised land in the Pacific.

The Dutch government had assumed that all the Moluccans would be assimilated. In theory, the dark-skinned Moluccans had the same rights as the native white Dutch, but, in fact, there was substantial racial discrimination. Most of the Moluccans were housed in separate villages in the poorer parts of Holland. By Dutch standards, they lived in slums. The young Moluccans tended to do badly at school and many of them were unemployed. They did not think Holland had been fair to them.

The effective leader of the hijack was Eli Hahuri, a man with a record of violence. He had assembled a group of six others who agreed with him that the old soldiers' deference would never succeed. It was Eli who, brandishing a gun, told the passengers that from now on they were under his command. Even Prinz, who soon lost his initial terror, was somewhat frightened of Eli's irrational outbursts.

The Dutch government reacted to the hijacking very quickly. Troops and units of the special police force were sent to isolate the train. A security cordon was thrown around the whole area. When the world's press descended on Assen, it was kept miles away. Cameramen had to use extremely long lenses to get any pictures of the train. The news media could do little but show the occasional picture of sinister masked men moving around the train. The government was in no mood to compromise. Since they had always regarded themselves as kind to Moluccans, a sense of outrage made them respond harshly. They let it be known that there would be no quarter given to the hijackers, and at first, there was even little practical help for the hostages. The government did, however, establish a command centre at Assen for the police and military. They also called in psychiatrists and psychologists to help, among them a Dr Muelder and the aforementioned Professor Jan Bastiaans from the University of Leiden. Muelder immediately tried to establish a rapport with Hahuri and to get the hijackers talking.

Although no one detected an underlying sense of guilt in the early stages of the affair, later analysts would wonder if some of the Dutch decisions did not betray the paradoxical defensiveness of the white-liberal conscience concerning colonialism. The authorities were often unyielding when flexibility, or even a bare acknowledgement that they understood the frustration of the Moluccan community, might have defused a dangerous situation.

This lack of flexibility did not help the hostages, who received no food for forty-eight hours. When food did arrive there was nothing to eat it with and it took, Prinz claimed, endless phone calls to get the command centre to send cutlery. Even when that arrived it was not adequate. Only plastic spoons were sent, so that people had to cut cold meat or cheese with spoons. There was also no heating in the train. In addition, many of the women had periods, but the government at first refused to send in clean underwear. When they finally did so, it was all the same size, 'a size', sniped Prinz, 'that would have fitted a six-year-old girl'. This lack of concern made the hostages feel that the outside world did not care what happened to them, that all the train's passengers, hijackers and hostages alike, had become pariahs. Prinz noticed that many of the passengers became withdrawn and frightened. Jan Bies felt this sense of abandonment acutely: 'We felt that they didn't care. They didn't care if we were killed. I felt only hate for all the people outside the train.'

Bies' rage may help explain a mystifying phenomenon. In 1975, some psychologists suspected that, during hijackings, strange emotional reactions took place. Patti Hearst, for instance, the American heiress who had been taken hostage by the Symbionese Liberation Army, became very involved with one of her hijackers, although this may have been due to duress. Then, during a siege in Stockholm Bank in 1976, a hostage had started to have an affair with one of her captors. Those who lived through the Stockholm affair said no duress was involved in this case. In Britain, after the siege at the Spaghetti House in 1975, one of the victims had visited their captors in gaol. In an attempt to explain this phenomenon, psychologists drew on an old psychoanalytical concept. Anna Freud argued that there was a mechanism of 'identifying with the aggressor' and that this happened in such cases. In Assen, there was never any hint of a sexual relationship, but Vaders and Prinz both noticed a definite shift in atmosphere as the siege progressed. They themselves were affected by it. Feeling isolated from the rest of the world, hijackers and hostages became not really friendly but definitely involved with each other.

'We had to listen to them,' Vaders said. As they waited for the Dutch government to decide what to do, the hostages heard the Moluccans' side of the story. Even to a sceptical journalist like Vaders, it was clear that the Dutch did have a case to answer. Why had not the government honoured its obligations? And worse, why did they not accept that the return of the Moluccas was an issue worth raising at the United Nations? Prinz too became convinced that the Moluccans did have a case, and although he did not claim that it justified the hijack, he did assert that the background to the siege made it impossible to see them as vicious terrorists.

Both Prinz and Vaders became sceptical about the intentions of the government. Official actions confirmed their scepticism.

The hijackers demanded a bus to take them to Schipol Airport. Once there, they promised to release all but six of the hostages in return for a plane to fly them to a destination of their choice. NOS, the Dutch television station, showed pictures of a coach that had been prepared, stripped as the South Moluccans demanded, which suggests that the authorities had agreed to such a bargain. Prinz also insist d that there had been such an agreement. But, on the third morning of the hijack, with everyone on the train waiting, the coach did not come. The government then denied that it had ever agreed to the hijackers' demands. Such confused and dashed hopes made the hostages feel frightened, and the hijackers too became aggressive again. The failure of the coach to arrive affected how Prinz saw the situation. He had been talking to the emergency centre on the phone and was, he told me quite definitely, promised a bus. He was angry and bitter about this betrayal: 'The hijackers could have thought that this was a product of my imagination and killed me.' Bies too became bitter as the bus failed to arrive, seeing it as another indication of the way the world outside the train did not care if they lived or died.

The next day, the hijackers sent a new ultimatum to the government, demanding that a statement of their demands be read on Dutch radio. If the statement were not read, they would kill a third hostage. When Prinz telephoned this demand through to the local commanders, he was told that it would be dealt with promptly. The Dutch authorities then kept the intermediary – a Mr Passeron – waiting for forty-five minutes, before they would even listen to what the hijackers wanted. The hijackers first became irritated and then grim. If they did not carry out their threat, they would lose face. It was, Prinz said, a quite criminal delay. Eventually, the authorities said that they would transmit the hijackers' demands on the radio only if they first released all elderly and sick passengers. The hijackers refused to accept that counter-ultimatum. Hahuri moved through the carriages and seized upon Bert Bierling as the one to be killed. 'They were terrible moments for us all,' said Prinz, 'including the hijackers.'

The world's press saw, far off in the distance, a man made to kneel at the door of the train, then being thrown out. At such a distance, there were no sounds, but it was clear a man had been shot. This cold-blooded murder of Bierling made it impossible for the government to negotiate anything but the surrender of the hijackers, but inside the train it felt very different. Prinz said: 'The shooting of Bert Bierling was carried out by the hijackers but it was indirectly caused by the Dutch government.' Five minutes after Bierling's body was thrown out of the train, the government caved in: the hijackers' demands were broadcast.

The murder of Bierling had, Prinz felt, a curious impact on the Moluccans: 'They were almost coming to the point that killing was too much. They didn't want to kill any more.' Outside the train, however, there was no sense of that shift – a shift that was eventually to lead to the surrender of the Moluccans. Outside, in fact, the murder only made the masked men seem more frightening. Vaders, particularly, could guess only too well that the press would be depicting them as monsters; they would be, he smiled wryly, black men doing black things. But for those on the train, the hijackers had started to be human, to be individuals. Thirteen days spent together in great tension had resulted in the hijackers not being perceived as stereotypes of evil.

After Bierling had been killed, the situation on the train became tense and fearful again. But then, on 5 December, there was an accident on the train: one of the hijackers accidentally fired his gun, wounding two passengers and one of the hijackers. 'There was panic,' said Prinz, 'and the panic was calmed down not by the hijackers but by the passengers.' Prinz took the lead in getting transportation for the wounded. 'We also got out the wife of one of the wounded passengers. During that period, it was as if the hostages had taken over the running of the hijack.' Prinz himself had every chance to escape. When the transport was being arranged, he was outside the train. He could have returned to 'normality'. He did not. He even had to knock to get back in to the train.

The whole balance of power within the train changed. 'Initially, all the power was theirs,' said Vaders, 'and you were just a bit of fluff in their hands which they could blow away. But we also, as it progressed, got power over them.' Then, on the thirteenth day of the hijack, there were clear signs that things were changing. The government's negotiating tactics seemed to be working, especially as the hijackers could see no way out. The end came remarkably suddenly. On 15 December, Moluccan negotiators approached the train and agreed with Hahuri and the four remaining hijackers (one having been wounded) on the terms for the end of the affair. Inside the train there were bizarre scenes: many hostages shook hands with their hijackers. Even Bies, who now admits to hating the hijackers, said, 'I shook hands with them.' Shaking his head in astonishment at the memory, he is still puzzled at his own action: 'Why? Never do such a thing again. Why shake hands with people who had murdered? I never explain it.' He supposed that many hostages knew that the hijackers would get long prison sentences, but Bies himself regretted shaking hands: 'No, I've got to wash my hands.' Prinz thought it was: 'almost an empty feeling. You had been through very strange, very terrible experiences but now that was all over.' He did not realize that, in many ways, it was only the start of the affair.

For there was little idea in the mid-1970s of the best way to handle such 'endings'. There had been, at that time, no hijack in which anyone had been held for such a long time. In his book *A Time of Terror*, John Bowyer Bell lists a number of plane hijacks, but these tended to be relatively short. There were no long-term sieges. The experiences of the Dutch passengers on the train had been strange, novel and frightening. Now that they were free, the hostages found they had entered a new, and often uncomfortable world. Bies' experience was sobering. He found his family did not understand how frightened he had been, experiencing fears that were simply not going to vanish. No one, however, connected the passengers' experiences with those of victims of either natural or man-made disasters.

The hijackers walked out first with their arms up above their heads. The moment that they had been taken into custody, a swarm of rescue services descended on the train. There were ambulances, policemen, militia. Hundreds of people descended on the train. Prinz commented: 'Tanks, police, helicopters came. We hadn't seen anyone for a fortnight. Now several hundreds. I thought they might as well have stayed away.' It was all very confusing. Vaders wanted to walk but found that there was a helper on hand with a stretcher. An old lady was also bundled on to a stretcher in spite of protesting that she wanted to walk. Vaders intervened. Prinz found that there was more help available than they wanted. Vaders came out of the hijack wearing a superfluous blanket. As soon as the ex-hostages got to the medical centre, they found that plastic tags were put around their wrists. 'I didn't realize it then, but these were the labels the army and Red Cross use to put on dead bodies,' Prinz commented wryly. Hostages merely wanted to go home and return to their families, and most felt perfectly able to do so, yet the bureaucracy of 'debriefing' and the assumption that they were ill prevented them. The authorities acted as if it were wartime. The motorway between Assen and Groningen was closed and a fleet of ambulances shuttled the hostages at what Prinz said was dangerous speed to a hospital they did not need to go to. 'I just wanted to go home,' Prinz remembered, adding that a Surinam student saw the way the hostages were treated after the hijack ended as being another hijacking.

Once they reached hospital, the ex-hostages were faced with a barrage of questions and 'care'. Prinz was vitriolic about it and insisted on leaving. Vaders also insisted on leaving, since he had an urgent story to write. Both these men were confident, successful individuals who knew well how to deal with the Dutch 'system', but even for them it was a huge struggle to assert their rights. Vaders eventually managed to get out a version of his diary, which appeared in the next day's paper. For a man psychologists assumed must have been in deep shock, this was a remarkable performance. The other ex-hostages I talked to later were not so angry about the way they had been treated but they, too, felt it had been assumed that they were more helpless than they were.

Vaders' diary was critical of the way the government had handled the whole episode. Prinz, in a series of interviews, was even more so. Both men also said that Dutch honour required they should pay some attention to the claims of the Moluccans. As the old imperial power, Holland had a moral responsibility to do this. Both drew attention to the government's failures during the episode. Three days after the end of the hijack, the Dutch cabinet dispatched one of its members to meet with the hostages at Assen. He told them that he understood how stressed they had been by their ordeal and assured them that everyone realized their judgement was warped. It was, as Bastiaans had warned, as if they had gone off their heads.

When I first started to report this story, two years after the end of the hijack, I was told by journalists in Amsterdam that many of the ex-hostages had become disturbed as a result of their experiences, that being seen as the only explanation of the fact that they did not hate the Moluccans. Prinz, who became the most involved with the Moluccans, was singled out as especially bizarre, because he publicly stated that it was important to understand why the Moluccans felt so strongly.

It is important, however, not to exaggerate how friendly people became towards the Moluccans. Jan Bies reacted in a quite opposite way, coming to hate Moluccans. Many of the ex-hostages, while not so vitriolic, did attribute their relative friendliness towards their captors during the hijacking to stress. One of the women hostages told me that she had felt persuaded by the Moluccans in the train but that those friendly feelings had evaporated soon after they had escaped from their ordeal.

The accounts that the ex-hostages gave of the immediate impact of being free were thus full of paradoxes. Vaders said that it felt marvellous to be free, but that there were also problems. He could not sleep. He had nightmares for nearly a week. He lost his memory and he found concentration difficult. 'Also, I became so fascinated with the affair that I lost interest in my job. I gave the appearance of being the old editor but I wasn't that interested.' He felt anxious. These symptoms lasted for months, but having been held a hostage had some positive consequences as well. Being so close to death had made him realize some basic truths about his marriage. 'It was the first time we had talked deep into the night for months,' Vaders told me. He realized that his family had had to cope not just with the fear but with a total lack of information, with not knowing what was going on in the train, a state of suspense Vaders believes might have been even worse than his ordeal.

The hijack had created intolerable stress for the families and, as a result, many of them were eager to help in subsequent situations.

For Prinz, the feeling of having survived was heady. He drove very fast down motorways. He felt he could survive anything. He too experienced the kind of anxiety Vaders described but, in his case, it was not the most important after-effect. The ordeal had changed him politically: he had always been interested in left-wing politics but he now felt he almost had a duty to the Moluccan cause. Yet this feeling did not make him forget those who had paid dearly. When I first met him, he insisted on taking me to see Bert Bierling's widow, and he continued to blame the Dutch government for being so stubborn about reading the statement the hijackers demanded, for playing games with people's lives.

In many ways, one of those to suffer most was Jan Bies. The army sent him to be interviewed by a panel of five psychiatrists, at a time when he was suffering recurrent nightmares. 'Bad dreams. Always black faces with guns.' Bies was young and ingenuous. He showed his anger. The army doctors concluded that he was not fit to handle a gun. Bies said he was told that they were afraid he might take revenge and start shooting Moluccans, commenting: 'If they keep telling you these things, you start to believe them.' He spent eleven months at home while the army decided his fate, and found it very embittering that being a victim had made him lose his position in the army. I drove with Bies through the flat countryside of Fries and saw that he carried a gun in the glove compartment. He was only too aware of his own continuing hatred, but he felt he had every right to hate Moluccans. He felt directionless. Almost too symbolically, he started to lose his way when he worked as a bus driver after the army discharged him: 'I knew where I wanted to go but I took wrong turns.' He shook his head, puzzled at his own irrational behaviour. But of course it was impossible to know if he might not have been predisposed to irrational behaviour anyway.

Both Vaders and Prinz felt that the hijack had changed their lives, not simply because it had made them disturbed, but because it was a crisis that had forced them to reassess the way they had been living. Vaders decided that he would give up the daily routine of editing a newspaper: he would write a column for his paper and see more of his family. As a columnist, he could work from home. Prinz continued to maintain contact with the Moluccans. He was particularly interested in seeing what help could be given them, and he did not want to see a second hijack. His attitude puzzled many Dutch, who attributed it to a form of breakdown.

There was indeed a second hijacking at Assen in 1977, when Moluccans took over another train. The authorities, however, had learned something from the first one: there was no delay in sending food in; the authorities made sure that the families were gathered together in a centre at Assen. Vaders and Prinz became involved in this second crisis, too, though in different ways. Vaders at once flew back from Sweden, becoming active in the centre for the families. He found that he could be helpful to them, since he could tell them exactly what he had been through. He made no attempt to intervene politically. Vaders was most struck, however, by the reaction of his wife, telling me that she became extremely aggressive towards Moluccans: 'All Moluccans should be killed,' she said. It was as if it was now safe to explode with all the fury that she had not dared express while her husband had been at risk.

Prinz was politically the more active, immediately offering himself as a mediator. The government were, he believed, not pleased by his offer since he now had a pro-Moluccan reputation. 'It took them twenty-four hours to reply to me. Then they said that they couldn't let me do it because of safety. I might be risking my life.' Prinz scoffed at their sudden concern; it seemed to him that they had not cared too much for his life while he had been a hostage. 'And this time I would be doing it voluntarily.' But he found that there was no way of persuading the authorities to let him become involved.

The second hijack was in many ways more civilized than the first: food was sent in hot, with correct implements to eat it; there were supplies of underwear. But if the government had learned to manage such an incident better, so too had the hijackers learned. They were led by a man called Max Papilia, whom Prinz had got to know. Prinz was convinced that Papilia was not the kind of man to kill, and he turned out to be right: Papilia remained relatively calm. For thirteen days, the situation was a stalemate; in the train, there were no casualties.

The government did allow in negotiators as long as they were Moluccans. A leading role was taken by a Moluccan doctor called Tan who lived in the nearby town of Entschede. As the crisis developed and it became clear that the Dutch would not put a plane at the disposal of the hijackers, Tan worked out a solution: he would put it to the government that in return for a swift surrender, Papilia and his friends would get light sentences. It seemed likely that the government would agree, Tan told the hijackers on his last visit to the train. 'The last thing Max said was that they [the hijackers] would think about it.' Tan left the train satisfied that the hijackers were not in an excited state; as a doctor, he could be expected to be a reasonable judge.

The Dutch psychiatrists thought differently, even though they had not been in the train. They believed that everyone was exhausted. Dramatically, Bastiaans said that both the hijackers and the hostages were physically and mentally at breaking point, 'though we do not have recorders on the train'. The psychiatrists were less open, according to Vaders, about their own reactions. They were disturbed by the sophistication of the hijackers, who were being subtly wooed, urged to talk, to confess their fears, to trust the man at the other end of the phone, a ploy which had met with some success in the previous Moluccan hijack. Vaders said that when a psychiatrist working for the Dutch government, Muelder, tried to talk to Max Papilia like that 'he was mocked. Papilia said, "don't try to play the psychologist with me. I'm something of a psychologist too." And Muelder didn't like it.' The unease of the psychiatrists played into the hands of hardliners in the Dutch cabinet, Vaders believed. His information was that the cabinet was split. The Prime Minister Van Acht was for talking; the Minister of Interior was for taking a hard line. The hard line won: after thirteen days, Dutch Air Force jets dropped stun grenades on the train as the tanks crashed in. The train was peppered with bullets, deliberately, Prinz believes: the government was intent on making an example of the hijackers. The idea was to kill all the Moluccans, so as to bring hijacks to an end. All six hijackers were killed and so too were two Dutch citizens.

The impact on the Moluccan community of the deaths of the young men was enormous: the dead became martyrs, heroes. A quarter of the Moluccan community turned out for the funerals. In some villages they were jeered, but the Dutch authorities decided that the best way to prevent repetitions of these incidents was to provide money for social reforms. Considerable money was therefore spent on housing and social programmes in Moluccan areas. Initially, the tactic failed: there were two brutal incidents in which schools were taken over. Since 1978, however, there have been no further acts of Moluccan terrorism.

The story of these hijackings had a profound impact on how we view disasters and post-traumatic stress. Vaders was convinced the experience changed the lives of all those who lived through it. In addition, the changes were far more multi-faceted than the ones discovered at Buffalo Creek. Prinz, for instance, believes that a major change for him was that the siege made him more radical and questioning of authority than he had ever been before. As we shall see, this is one of the less attractive consequences of disasters as far as governments are concerned.

There was not much objective evidence of distress on the second train, nor any evident call from the ex-hostages for help. Nevertheless, the Dutch authorities were wedded to a psychiatric model. They set up a formal programme which employed nurses, social workers, psychologists and psychiatrists. They duly visited all those who had been on the train and asked if they needed 'social assistance'. Elisabeth Hoogerhad, a psychologist on this team, was frank about its contradictions. Many of the ex-hostages wanted no help; indeed, for some, the worst aspect of the ordeal was the stigma they suffered when their friends began to treat them as if they were psychiatric cases. The publicity that made them out to be for ever affected did not help either. Many were extremely angry. Hoogerhad conceded that there was not much solid evidence that these hostages were at risk or that the programme was being effective, but she persisted in thinking that it was useful. These controversies were to surface later in Britain, as disaster victims sometimes complained of being overwhelmed by counsellors.

None of those who studied the train hostages paid attention to an important point Vaders, Prinz and others made to me: they felt they were a group – a group, sometimes, which included the hijackers. This feeling offered them a measure of security. A recent study by McGurk (1989) of prison officers who have been taken hostage showed that, even ten years later, many still suffered. McGurk interviewed a small sample: twenty-two, of whom 86 per cent had had short-term psychological problems of the sort familiar to hijack victims. Ten years on, however, 45 per cent still reported a significant number of these symptoms. This percentage tended to have been involved in longer incidents, to have felt more threatened while it was going on and to have had less experience of working in prisons. Two years after the hijacks, few of the Dutch had these kinds of feelings. Not feeling isolated during such a crisis is clearly important.

The Dutch train crisis renewed interest in ways in which to handle violent incidents. Those findings were put into use in subsequent sieges and hostage incidents round the world. It was harder for psychologists to accept one obvious conclusion. If a disaster involves acute short-term stress, reactions to it will be individual. They will reflect not only levels of stress but also how well adjusted the person was previously. No simple formula will apply to every victim.

Before Buffalo Creek and the Dutch hijacks, the psychological consequences of disasters were not discussed, even by experts. Ten years later, as Britain was to learn in the spate of disasters from the Bradford fire onwards, victims were known to suffer far more than physical injuries. And everyone anticipated that; it was an unexpected triumph for psychology.

3

Recent British Disasters and Their Lessons

King's Cross

On 18 November 1987, Mariella Santello was with her fiancé, who had come from Italy to Britain to celebrate her twenty-first birthday. 'I was coming on the Piccadilly line from Wood Green,' Mariella remembers. She had to change at King's Cross. 'When I got off the train, while I was going up, I smelt smoke. I thought it was children who were playing a joke. Then, between the first and second escalators, I saw a policeman telling people to go up. I didn't realize what was going on till I got up. There were a few flames and, then, I went up into the ticket hall.' It was 7.53, soon after Mariella reached the ticket hall, that the smouldering fire reached flashpoint and exploded into flames. Mariella was wearing a plastic jacket, and she noticed it was melting. 'I couldn't see because there was smoke, there was a light that went off suddenly. I found my hands against a wall and I realized my hands were boiling.' She became separated from her fiancé. Like most people in the King's Cross disaster, she experienced terror and confusion. Ron Lipsius, an American musician who knew the underground system well from his days as a busker, said, 'At moments like that you do panic and think only of breathing and getting out.' There was by this time a veritable inferno in the ticket hall. By 8 P.M. a major disaster had been declared by the fire brigade and the ambulance service.

King's Cross was the third major incident in three years, and raised substantial issues of transport policy in Britain. Had public services been so starved of cash as to make them unsafe? Since 1985, with the fire at Bradford City football ground and fifty-five dying in a plane fire at Manchester, Britain has suffered a relentless succession of disasters, each of which has led to some sort of official inquiry. The survivors have often been critical of initial reactions by emergency services and of how their cases were handled later, both medically and legally. The organization of services to handle emergencies is essentially local; the police, the fire brigade, ambulances and hospitals are all local services. The allegation that 'public squalor' in Thatcherite Britain has made disasters even more damaging, has thus been complicated by the fact that there is no national body to co-ordinate these local efforts in peacetime disasters. Consequently, it has been hard for services to hand on to others the lessons of each disaster. Casualty doctors, for instance, recently complained bitterly of this, at their conference in the Isle of Man. In 1989, the Home Office finally announced that there would be one official whose job it would be to develop national disaster policy.

Travelling by boat and rail have traditionally been perceived as safer than travelling by air, yet there have been more rail and shipping disasters than air crashes since 1985. The most devastating was the capsizing of the *Herald of Free Enterprise* in March 1987, which resulted in 187 deaths. The number of deaths due to rail accidents and crashes was seventy-one in 1983, seventy-six in 1984, seventy-four in 1985, seventy-two in 1986 and 104 in 1987. But then in November 1987, the fire at King's Cross killed thirty-one people and, while the inquiry was sitting, on 12 December 1988 two trains crashed into each other at Clapham. Some of the thirty-five passengers who died were killed when they got out from the crashed train and wandered on to the line, mown down by a second train. On 5 March 1989, strangely enough again as the inquiry into Clapham was sitting, five passengers were killed at Purley as a local train went through a red signal. The next day in Scotland, a suburban train from Glasgow crashed at Bellgrove and two passengers died.

There had been concern about safety on the underground ever since June 1985 when there was a fire at Oxford Circus tube station in which one person died. The subsequent inquiry recommended there should be no smoking anywhere on the underground and noted, with some alarm, the lack of staff training in dealing with emergencies. The National Union of Railwaymen had been worried about safety, and the lack of training for their staff, but claimed they had not been able to persuade management to take action.

The timetable of what happened at King's Cross eventually became clear. At 7.30 an escalator began to smoke. There would subsequently be fierce controversy about whether the fire was caused by an arsonist (London Transport's first hypothesis), by a burning cigarette or, as later came to be accepted, by a cigarette which had fallen through on to the escalator. That burning cigarette ignited a load of fluff, skin particles and accumulated grease – used to clean the escalator – beneath. There had already been some thirty small fires of a similar sort at King's Cross. The first alarm was raised just after 7.30 by passengers who went through the station and warned staff of a small smouldering fire. At first, as in many fires, there was neither panic nor alarm. At the inquest, Philip Squire, a financial consultant, said that he first noticed the fire when he was about one-third of the way up the escalator. A lit cigarette seemed caught in the wooden tread. Soon, however, it became obvious to him that smoke was coming up from the gap. He saw a ball of white sparks like a firework sparkler, then smoke started to come out from inside the escalator and pour down it like dry ice. The sparks were intense but there was no perceptible heat. Squire raised the alarm at the ticket office. An official telephoned, but 'people didn't seem very concerned', Squire added. Passengers took little notice and continued to pour down towards the platforms. Other passengers also testified to a widespread initial reluctance to take the alarm seriously.

Sarah Hall, who was trying to get from the Circle line platforms to the ticket hall, did not notice at first that she was near a dangerous fire. She was moving through a crowd of commuters when she suddenly felt 'a huge heat. It was almost as if the door of an oven had been opened. There was smoke hanging over the ticket hall like a cloud.' She stopped to work out what was happening. 'Everyone was calm. There was no sign of a fire, no bells going, no one shouting fire, no people running away.' There was no sign of any planned evacuation, either. Sarah Hall told the inquiry that she decided that the fire must be deep down, and by implication, that the safest way to get out was by going up. As we shall see, the assumptions that people made about the best way out turned out to be disastrously wrong. Andrew Jones, a design engineer for British Rail, was walking towards the ticket hall when he saw smoke. He confirmed that there was no official guidance as to how to get out.

This apparent calm was tragic, but not unexpected. In his study of how people behave in fire, Canter (1979) has found that at first, typically, no one believes there is any serious risk. People become seriously alarmed only once the fire has taken hold, by which time it can be too late. On this occasion, people were still going into King's Cross and even down on to the escalator when the fire had taken hold and was burning fiercely.

Thomas Saegling, an American student, was three-quarters of the way to the top of the escalator when 'a wall of flames erupted which I could only describe as the way in which a small fire would look and sound when someone poured a can of gasoline on it. There was total panic as everyone tried to get down, away from the flames. I could hear screaming coming from the concourse at the top.' Saegling escaped by train, with a man who was extremely distressed by what was happening, shouting at transport officials, 'You bastards. You've sent them to their deaths. I saw a woman and baby burning.'

Mariella had fallen over in the dark. She remembers screams. 'I couldn't breathe. I thought I was going to die. I was feeling sorry for my parents. Then, somehow, I stood up and I found the stairs and then I found my way to the exit.' Sheer luck had saved her.

A number of factors contributed to the extent of the horror. The flames were blown up the escalator and towards the main platform booking hall. Normally, there is a sprinkler system available in the hall, but it was encased in building works. It later emerged that there were too few staff on duty at the station and that it had been many months since any of them had had any fire drill training.

Ron Lipsius is a regular underground user: 'When I travelled the tube, it was almost like a playground. I used to busk in the tube too. I used to sort of know the way it was down there. Know the people who worked down there, too. And it never, never occurred to me that something could happen to me down there.' He was cool and had, he said, 'been down in the tube when it was smoky before'. Initially, therefore, he did not think that the smouldering was dangerous, so carried on up the escalator. When he reached the top, however, the flames were getting more intense and there was suddenly an immense fireball. He thought he would die: he could not breathe, and his hands literally felt on fire. He saw some skin peeling off them. He bent down in order to breathe a little, but the smoke kept getting into his lungs. He felt the wall behind him glowing hot.

Dick Bates looked up the escalator but decided that it would be better to try and find another way out. His hair was on fire when he reached the bottom of the tube, and he was lucky that someone threw water over him. His hands had been badly burned. He moved along the platform towards an exit that promised to take him out on to the Pentonville Road. Behind him, he could hear sounds of screaming and the smell of fire. When he got to the exit he found it locked. 'I was sure I was going to die,' he said. He waited and shouted for help.

The first call to the fire brigade was made at 7.42 and by 7.53 there was a fire engine on the scene. The first fireman to go down was Colin Townley. He could hear the screaming from inside the booking hall, but he wanted to assess the situation as quickly as possible and so he went down without putting on his breathing apparatus. This was against regulations. It was a brave but tragic decision. At the inquest, Mrs Sinder-Parmar, a London housewife, explained how she looked up the burning escalator only seconds before the fireball swept through the ticket hall. She saw a fireman at the top of the escalator trying to rescue a woman who was burning. That fireman was prob-ably Colin Townley. Mrs Parmar said: 'The fire was blazing. I could see orange flames about five or six feet in height. The flames seemed to be moving straight up. I looked up and saw a woman who seemed to be on fire. Her hair at the back was on fire, so was her coat. This woman was screaming. I thought to myself "Oh, my God, I can't believe it." I heard the first

fireman shout out, "It's all right, love, it's all right." He was
trying to reassure her.'

Theoretically, the evacuation procedure for any railway or
tube station is laid down and agreed by the fire brigade, the
British Transport Police and London Transport. Most factories
need to get their fire escapes 'passed' by the fire brigade; the
railways and the underground, however, as nationalized industries, have been privileged. As a result, the London Fire
Brigade could only recommend improvements after the Oxford
Circus fire. It could not close down King's Cross as, in extreme
circumstances, it could close down a factory, for example. The
fire brigade had told London Transport on a number of
occasions that they were not happy with the fire escape procedures but had no powers to compel change.

There was an evacuation plan, however, which called for
passengers to be evacuated by trains. The staff on the station,
therefore, decided that the best thing to do was to direct
passengers away from the fire and down on to the platforms
where trains would carry them to safety. This plan did not work
for a number of reasons. First, people's natural response
underground is to go up in order to get out, because feeling
entombed is frightening. Also, the Transport Police decided
that it would be too dangerous for trains to stop at King's
Cross, a decision taken not on the spot but a mile away, at the
British Transport Police operating centre in Tavistock Street.
At 7.50, therefore, an instruction went out on the tube drivers'
radio ordering them to move through King's Cross without
stopping or opening train doors. As a result, terrified passengers found themselves with flames behind them and trains in
front of them which refused to open their doors, passing them
by on the platforms. This muddle was inexcusable, as British
Transport Police should have known that this was the only
evacuation plan. Passengers beat on the windows of trains in
panic, but the drivers obeyed their radios.

Those who chose other escape routes were a little more
fortunate. Dick Bates was eventually heard. The Pentonville
Road exit was unlocked. He felt his hands burning when finally
the ambulance arrived. 'There was a man in the ambulance
with me and he was bleeding badly and pretty rough. When we

got to the hospital, I kept screaming for water because that did give my hands some relief. The nurses got soaked pouring it over me. Then they gave me an injection and it gets a little blurred. But it was quite a while before I realized that I never saw again the man I'd been in the ambulance with and I realized he'd died.'

Mariella remembered: 'When I got out, I was screaming and crying. Two gentlemen stayed with me and calmed me down.' She had no idea what had happened to her boyfriend. 'When I reached the hospital, I couldn't breathe. All I could say was to give them the phone number of my friends. Then, straight away, they put me on the ventilator.'

The arrangements for taking the dead and injured to local hospitals did not work as well as might have been expected. The Fennell Inquiry eventually concluded it took fifteen minutes for fourteen ambulances to arrive and that all the wounded were not removed till 9.32. The inquiry congratulated the emergency services, but noted these problems in the speed of getting to the accident. There were also difficulties in communication. These were problems that would recur at Clapham.

At University College Hospital, casualty teams were alerted at 7.50 P.M. The hospital warned the ambulance service that it could not cope with all the wounded, so some patients were taken to St Bartholomew's. A few others were sent to other north London hospitals, like Mount Vernon. According to the consultant plastic surgeon, Michael Brough, there were the largest number of deeply burned patients to deal with that he had ever experienced.

For many staff, the scene was traumatic, like a war emergency. It was not like anything they had been prepared for in their disaster exercises. One anaesthetist, who was used to seeing horrific burn injuries, had the job of sorting out the living from the dead. She coped splendidly at the time, but went home and collapsed in tears. It was not the gruesome nature of the burns but the sheer number of dead that overwhelmed her.

As at Ramstein in West Germany, the first problem was that no one expected an accident on such a scale, and as a result some crucially needed supplies were scarce. Resources were also limited. University College Hospital operating theatres were stretched to the limit; other hospitals had to be used.

In the immediate aftermath of the disaster, Mrs Thatcher visited UCH at midnight. Her visit, intended to comfort, irritated some of the staff, especially since they felt government cuts to their NHS budgets had made their task much harder.

David Sturgeon is one of the consultant psychiatrists at University College Hospital. He went to the hospital on the night of the disaster, but there was not much he could do. In the next few days, however, it became clear that psychiatry would have a major role to play. 'Michael Brough, the consultant plastic surgeon in UCH's burns unit, asked me and my colleagues to see a number of patients who were in distress.' There were two reasons for this request. First, burns are, according to Sturgeon, 'one of the most difficult kinds of pain to bear'. Second, 'many people were in an intense state of shock'. Survivors were confused and frightened. Many felt guilty, Sturgeon explained, because they had been travelling with a relative or a friend, and they had survived, while their companion had died. Further, 'Many people experienced intense flashbacks in which they imagined that they were back in the middle of the fire and living through it again. They had terrible dreams.' They also had vivid hallucinations, such as seeing the hospital surrounded by flames. 'The experiences reported by Zeebrugge survivors were similar. Such involuntary flashbacks were very upsetting,' Sturgeon said.

Mariella was put on the ventilator at once. She had suffered 42 per cent burns to her legs, hands and face. When patients suffer 33 per cent burns, their chances of survival are not good. She lost consciousness and had the oddest of dreams, although gentler than those of many others. In one of them, Mariella saw friends playing with matches.

Ron Lipsius's hands were atrociously, deeply burned. For him, the dreams were ghastly. 'It was like a tape loop. Then I would wake up and be physically kicking and jolting. Then, later on, people I knew would be playing some of the parts and it was very bizarre.'

Psychiatry can offer important but limited help, according to Sturgeon. His role in the hours and days after the fire 'was just to be there and listen to what they said. In many cases, it was important to get some of these powerful and very intense feelings out.' In the face of such distress, the reaction of relatives and of ward staff is very natural. Sturgeon explained: 'If people were tearful and crying, relatives and staff often tried to console them and to stop them crying.' But the psychiatrist had a very different purpose: catharsis, not comfort. 'We had to help them cry, to facilitate that.' Previous work, especially the experience of Zeebrugge in March 1987, suggested that if 'these strong feelings stayed bottled up inside they become even more intense'. They fester and then burst out as anxiety and depression. The guilt of the survivors was not vague or self-indulgent. Sturgeon said: 'Many of the victims had had to step over bodies of people who were dying or dead to get out.'

Mariella was unconscious and on the ventilator for twenty-four days. At some moments during that time, she surfaced into semi-consciousness. She saw shadows in front of her and slowly began to recognize them. They were her mother, her sisters and some friends. Only one shadow was never there: her boyfriend. 'I knew that it meant he must have died.' As she became conscious, she felt 'terribly guilty towards his family. He had come to Britain just two days before to celebrate my birthday.' She believed that if only she had done something different, if she had been heroically strong and clung on to his arm in the flames, she would have managed to pull him to safety. The 'if only' feelings survivors have are very powerful: if only they had chosen a different time to travel; if only they had gone down towards the trains rather than up to the booking hall; if only they had run at the first sign of smoke.

Sturgeon believes that 'what you can do is to acknowledge those feelings and to talk about them'. Survivor guilt, however, was very intense for some but not others. Dick Bates, for example, said he felt a great deal of grief for people who had died unnecessarily, but that he could not feel guilty over the deaths of people he did not know.

Not all of the survivors wanted to accept counselling. Some were so angry that they clammed up. Ron Lipsius did not object to being asked to see a psychiatrist: 'I knew I was mentally shaken. I thought it astute of the hospital to have one.' Nevertheless, he did not really want to talk about the disaster. In his case, it was not so much the macho reaction that real men do not put on the agony. Rather, he sensed his fury: why did it have to happen to him? 'Of all the people affected, I felt I was the one who used my hands most. Since I was a kid, I'd used them.' As a musician, his hands were utterly necessary to him. Sturgeon did not nag him to speak. 'He didn't bully or demand. He has a very passive technique. He'd let a pause of ten minutes go by,' Ron said. Sturgeon's willingness to give his time seems to have prodded Ron into speaking.

Initially, Dick Bates was also not keen to speak: when counselling was offered to him, he reacted with a certain suspicion. It was an attitude that would soon change. For others, the decision to reject counselling had other causes. Some passengers saw the disaster as an act of God and their survival as a deliberate divine decision. One woman was sure that Jesus had saved her from the inferno. Ron Lipsius found her reaction incomprehensible. Just why did Jesus allow thirty-one to die? What had they done to deserve it? 'I did mention Jesus the moment I got out of the hospital, but there was a swear word between the Jesus and the Christ.' Voltaire's questions about Lisbon continue to matter and perplex.

Psychiatrists worry about individuals who reject counselling, even though Sturgeon concedes, 'It's a natural reaction. Some people deny it happened and shut it out. It's a natural defence mechanism. Psychiatrists worry about that if it's very extreme.' He adds that research on post-traumatic stress disorder suggests that denial is not very helpful in the long run.

The pain was also a major problem for most patients. Ron found it terrible: his tendons were exposed inside his hand, and his fingernails had been burned inside.

For the families, the initial reaction was shock. Sally Lipsius, on the night of the fire, had 'a strange sensation' that her husband was involved in it. That was not so strange, perhaps, since he had busked at King's Cross, but as soon as she heard about the accident on the ten o'clock news, she knew. By 2 A.M. she had got a friend to drive her down to the hospital, where she learned that her premonition had been correct. In the first few weeks, coping was not that hard: 'You'd sometimes go into a room to cry.' But after three months, it had become clear 'that it wasn't going to be a quick thing. It was tedious.'

It is tempting to divide the aftermath of a disaster into discrete stages, but soon after the initial shock passed and people realized that they were going to live, many of them had to confront the fact that life was never going to be the same again for them. Sturgeon noted: 'Some became intensely angry. They wanted to blame someone. Who caused it?' Others were more philosophical. Ron Lipsius was not ashamed of his anger: 'I'm the kind of person who feels there is a need to point the finger.' He thought it was very therapeutic, especially as it became clear there would be a major legal battle. London Transport offered most survivors and bereaved families an immediate payment of only £2,500. For Ron, the initial meanness of London Transport was a shock, an additional burden, a feeling echoed by the group that the families themselves set up.

Dick Bates agrees that 'by common consensus, London Transport have acted less than honourably'. He thinks that 'it's indicative that I've never received any communication of any kind from London Transport'. I asked if they had not even expressed regret. Dick answered, 'No. I've not had a letter, a phone call, anything.' The government had also been uncommunicative. Dick had a letter from Paul Channon, the Transport Secretary, 'saying he'd been commanded by the Queen to express his regrets and what have you, but nothing other than that'.

The survivors filed claims against London Transport. The legal process has been complicated. Dick said: 'It's taken endless meetings, endless phone calls, endless letters. Paltry sums were offered in the beginning and I think that was an insult, really. London Transport at the very beginning said they would admit that they were wrong. People don't have to prove liability.' As a newspaperman, Dick could analyse their strategy. Admitting liability, London Transport knew, 'was terrific for the headlines but in reality they weren't very keen to actually put the money up front. And I think that's upsetting for people who have already lost wives, girlfriends, sons and daughters to be subjected to that kind of pressure.'

The media can add, often with good intentions, to that

pressure. Early in 1989, a television programme, 'World in Action', looked at a number of cases in which people had acted heroically. Many of the victims of King's Cross, and Sturgeon too, were not pleased by the programme. To be a hero in a disaster meant eternal depression, it seemed to say. Knowingly or not, the programme made many of the sweeping generalizations Bastiaans had made about the Dutch hijacking in 1975. Yet, at King's Cross, as after the Dutch hijacking, the later lives of the victims would be far more various than any simple theory could predict.

Sturgeon came slowly to recognize this complexity. 'I think that having survived an experience like this will always be with them. We need to help them get back to some sort of normality, to get them to adapt to life as it will now be for them,' he said. Certain consequences are obvious: 'They will be much more vigilant. Much more aware of danger and of their own fragility.' Fire would clearly continue to make them anxious. Research after the Buffalo Creek disaster showed that survivors often feared that the same thing would happen again; the survivors of Zeebrugge remain fearful of the sound of running water. Similarly, in the wake of King's Cross, the most normal and best adjusted suffer from highly specific anxieties about fires and tubes. Some, like Dick Bates, insisted on learning to use the tube again – though he avoids King's Cross itself. It is important not to exaggerate these problems. Sturgeon has been surprised by how many have managed to use the tube again. Ron Lipsius said he now has 'the greatest respect for fire'. Now, he would never linger round fire. The sound of crackling has remained with him, though with time it did not intrude into his thoughts as often. But fire, nevertheless, remains awesome to him.

After six weeks, Sturgeon stated, 'I've been very encouraged by how well the people I've seen have coped.' I asked him if there was any evidence that the better integrated people were, the better they coped and the less post-traumatic stress they suffered. He replied, 'People who are seemingly well integrated can develop intense psychological reactions.' He believes that being allowed to express feelings of loss, fear and confusion, in all their intensity, is a key to preventing stress: 'It minimizes damage.' Ron Lipsius felt that nearly everyone who had been through the fire and its resultant trauma 'would say it was helpful to be allowed to vent it'. He added a rider: 'Even so, I'm angry. I want retribution. I want to be able to point the finger. It's quite a complicated issue and a lot of blame has to be apportioned. I don't fool myself I'm not angry.'

If some coped miraculously, others, for reasons not altogether clear, became intensely depressed and helpless. They acted as if they would never recover and would be left with very little in their lives. Sturgeon found that there was no point in trying to rebut those fears: 'I don't think you try to be rational. You just receive them.' In the medium term, survivors had, it seemed, anxieties, connected mainly with their injuries. How long would the pain last and when would the burns heal? What would they look like when they had healed? What would they be able to do? How would the injuries affect the rest of their lives?

Ron, his hands swollen as skin grafts were trying to hold, alternated between being chirpy and aggressive. Mariella was resigned. She had undergone far more extensive surgery than the others. The first operation had been done while she was unconscious. The second had been on her forehead. They were now waiting to work on her legs because they did not know where to take the skin from to do the grafts she needed. After four weeks, Dick Bates went home. He found himself changing in ways that he frankly admitted surprised him. Living so much at home, so close to his wife, brought them very close even though at times he was very angry and she felt there was nothing she could say. He resented the physical helplessness enormously, but he believes that he was helped by the fact that he could return to a structure. His job as a sub on the *Guardian* was waiting for him. His life was there for him; it would clearly have been much, much harder to resume life without that anchor.

In describing the immediate impact of the disaster, Sturgeon emphasized that it was all too easy to concentrate on those who had ended up in hospital, for many of the victims had spent only a little time there and then been discharged; they too continued to suffer.

The second group that Sturgeon thinks must not be forgotten is the hospital staff. None of them had seen the kinds of injuries that were routine on that night. Sally Ann Wrench, a sister, found that many of the student nurses were deeply affected. University College Hospital offered the staff counselling and many of them took it, but for some, there was still a considerable stigma attached to accepting such help. Sally Ann Wrench found that, like Dick Bates, she became philosophical: 'It means that I worry much less about the little things in life, like not having enough money. The main thing is that I'm happy and my family is. Health and happiness.' Sturgeon argues that it is common for people's sense of values to change. Like a brush with cancer, a brush with death confronts us with our own mortality, compelling us to question our value-systems, if not to change them. But the changes are not always the same. Personality, past history, and the sort of disaster and how it is handled determine what changes occur.

I have argued throughout this book that we are now seeing different kinds of disasters which bring in their wake various psychological consequences. The King's Cross disaster made many people realize that travelling by tube or train was not necessarily safe. Anxieties were reinforced by the time lapse before the King's Cross inquiry: it took a year for the Fennell Inquiry to report. By that time there was considerable public anxiety about the underground's safety defects, such as the muddled evacuation plans, the lack of well-trained staff, and the fact that, under pressure to cut budgets, management had reduced maintenance. All this pointed to poor organization at management level.

Despite the national publicity, University College Hospital was short of resources. Ron Lipsius noted: 'I've become an observer of the National Health Service. The hospital is meant to be clean but it's dirty. Often the cleaners don't have time to do much more than edge the broom round the door.' The nurses, too, were stretched. 'I'm not blaming them because they are busy. The medication doesn't come on time. You have to look at your pills to make sure what you're taking. You often have to ask for a dressing change.' He claimed that often there was confusion after handovers between one shift and the next.

For Ron, the worst time had been being left alone after he had come out of intensive care: 'You just want to burst out crying. It's usually a card someone you don't know has sent,' he said, 'that provokes it.'

Progress in recovering from burns is slow. Ron had a series of disappointments in the first three months. The graft on his left hand worked quite well, so a similar procedure was followed for his right hand. Three months after the fire, however, it was not doing too well. It was very red. His fingernail beds had been burnt out and were still very painful. He was complaining bitterly about the pain and the disappointment. 'You feel lonely,' he added. It had also taken him some time to realize the full extent of his injuries: 'I was under the impression that when my hands came out of the bandages, they'd be OK.' But they were not: 'My hands wouldn't move. My joints had all stiffened up.'

At the time of doing the graft for the second time, under anaesthetic, his hands had been manipulated to see how far back they would bend. The manipulation had not worked perfectly. Ron had been supposed to leave hospital that day and go home, but the manipulation had added to his problems and it would be a further six weeks before he returned home. The strain on him was very evident. He and Mariella were to be the last to leave hospital.

Eighteen months after King's Cross, Ron Lipsius still suffers from considerable pain. He wears gloves on his hands because the sequence of operations has not yet finished. He has to go every day for physiotherapy. When I talked to him, he was also due to go back into hospital. The intrusive nightmares had diminished, but he suspected that was because of more positive changes. On 10 March 1989, he became a father, and he relishes his new role, spending most of his time at home. Sally has returned to work in advertising. Together with his mother-in-law, Ron takes care of the baby.

The marriage has changed: 'I don't think it really put a burden on the marriage. It wasn't a burden that was driving a wedge. It was just a burden requiring a lot more commitment

and concentration, which in the end made things even better.'
He saw a side of his wife that 'I probably may never have
experienced or realized before'. Sally felt that they had both
grown up as a result of what had happened: they were not as
likely as they used to be to have flare-ups as a result of little
rows. But she admitted that he was often still 'very bad-
tempered', and that he had to rely on painkillers.

Ron has been determined to retrain his hands. He goes to
physiotherapy regularly but finds it frustrating, yet he has
considerable achievements to his credit. He has been busy with
friends redecorating his house. His ground floor is a strange
sight. All the floorboards have been removed, painted green
and the spaces in between filled with sand to provide some
sound-proofing. Ron is building a music studio which he hopes
will allow him to compose music. He has given up hope,
however, that he will ever get back enough sensitivity in his
hands to play a musical instrument really well again. That is
painful: nothing will ever replace for him the joy of making
music. He tests himself, though: he insists on still trying to
water-ski. His grip is much weaker than before but he can
manage to do it reasonably well.

Ron laughs at the notion that he has become a deeper or
more spiritual person. His problem is, as Sturgeon surmised,
simply getting on with his life. Yet the treatment he is receiving
keeps him in limbo: physiotherapy is slow, and in August 1989
Ron still had to wait for the next operation to be done before
he really knew how much function he was likely to recover in
his hands. Sally also noted that he never left the house without
gloves.

Many of the survivors say they want to forget, but they also
recognize it is impossible. Those who spent time together at
University College Hospital have become friends, and one of
the burns unit nurses has arranged a number of dinners – the
most recent of which took place in what they all decided was a
really unsuitable Greek restaurant which was so noisy that they
could not hear themselves speak. These dinners are a way of
staying in contact. They offer support but there is also, according to Dick Bates, a certain competitive element: 'You want to
see just how their hands are getting on. If he's gone back to

work, then you think you ought to manage it. It's friendly rivalry.' It is also a chance for them all to discuss the progress of their cases against London Transport, cases which are taking a long time to settle.

Perhaps journalists like Gerhard Vaders and Dick Bates are particularly prone to analysing the way they have changed. Dick thinks the disaster has had a much greater impact on him than he reckoned it would. He always saw himself as an ordinary bloke and he is pleased that his progress has shown how such an ordinary man can survive successfully. He spent something close to nine months off work, and in that time he came to be much closer to his wife. They were together in a way they had not been for years. He was never a man for five-year plans, as he put it, but he began to realize that family ties and that time spent with his wife were the most precious things in his life.

Very openly, Bates admitted the value of therapy. He found it helpful to know that he could call on David Sturgeon if he could not face the tube or if he needed to discuss anything at all: 'That safety net is very reassuring.' He was sure that the structure of a settled family and work had also helped him enormously; surviving without those basics to fall back on would have been much harder.

Both Ron Lipsius and Dick Bates had reactions to dent cynicism. They found it exceptionally helpful that people had sent cards from all over the country. They did really make you feel, Dick Bates said, that people cared what happened to them. Some people even sent money, to Ron's complete amazement.

Some survivors have also had to cope with the problems of serious long-term injuries. Mariella has had to wear a mask ever since she left hospital. The mask is to protect the grafts on her face, but it does, of course, make her look odd. She was walking across Gower Street one day when she heard two men in a lorry laughing at her, so she walked over to them and said, 'King's Cross did this to me.' It shut them up and she was glad she had found the anger to say it.

For David Sturgeon, what has come through is the importance of making counselling available for victims as and when they want it. The timetable must not be determined by the professionals; help has to be there on tap. The organizational consequences of that 'insight' are frightening, of course. Sturgeon has nevertheless succeeded in making his patients feel that he will be there when they want him and otherwise that he will not intrude. University College, moreover, has not found it too much of an administrative nightmare, partly because of Sturgeon's personal commitment and partly because relatively few patients were involved long-term. But if we are really serious about learning from disasters, it is the kind of flexible response that needs to be made. At present, it is only if there is a real enthusiast available that it is possible. Sturgeon's research on the psychiatric outcome of the disaster is still carrying on. It is a project whose findings need to be made widely available.

One sign of the increasing awareness of disasters in 1989 was Leonard Cheshire's decision to mount an appeal for the victims of disaster worldwide. On Friday 8 September, victims gathered at many disaster spots round the globe to blow a whistle and have a minute's silence. Ron Lipsius arrived late at King's Cross, with just a few minutes in hand. He paused in the company of a black churchman who had rushed to the station the night of the accident and had tried to comfort the injured and bereaved. Ron blew the whistle and told the man it was just the second time he had been back. The place did not look the same; in many ways, it was worse. London Transport had insisted on installing automatic ticket barriers, which would make it hard for people to get out quickly, though they claim there are emergency override arrangements. Ron said being back just made him think of all the people who had died there.

The organizers of the Leonard Cheshire Appeal told me that they had also asked victims of the Clapham rail crash to blow a whistle at their site, but that none had been willing to do so: their wounds were too raw.

Clapham

I want now to examine a second British disaster, at Clapham, from a slightly different angle: what caused the crash, and why, when so many people knew such an accident was likely, so little was done to prevent it.

On 12 December 1988 one of the many morning trains from Basingstoke, driven by J. McClymont, approached a green signal outside Clapham Junction. About one and a half coach lengths away, the signal suddenly went red. Signals are not supposed to switch from green to red without passing through amber and double amber, but McClymont applied his brakes, stopped the train and began to report what had happened at signal WF 138. The drivers' rule book requires them to reverse to the faulty signal, a procedure McClymont did not follow; ironically, his failure to follow the rules was to lessen the number of deaths.

As McClymont got out of his cab, the Poole train was approaching on the same line behind his. The first sign passengers had that anything was wrong on the Poole train occurred when the emergency brakes were applied. The Poole driver must have done that as soon as he saw the other train, when he rounded the bend. He could see 300 yards ahead, according to the best estimate. Driver McClymont did not see or hear the Poole train approaching as he rang in. He did not get through to the signal box at once; there was a problem on the phone. When he did get through, he complained about the signal going red suddenly and said he would make out a report. He then put back the phone and turned to walk back to his train. It was then that he heard a terrible crash, and saw his train move some six feet in front of his eyes.

Even though its driver had applied the emergency brakes, the Poole train crashed into the Basingstoke train at a speed experts calculated as between thirty-five and fifty-five miles per hour. One of the passengers who survived described the impact as follows: 'It was a perfectly normal journey until we pulled up into a siding up against a concrete wall. Within thirty seconds, God knows what went on – there was an almighty bang like an explosion. The carriage went up and we flew over and over. We ended up on the embankment halfway up the bank. Strangely enough, no one panicked. Everyone just looked at everyone else.'

Greg Fold, in the first carriage of the Poole train, was half-asleep when it happened: 'Suddenly there was a big bang. The next minute there were people thrown all over the place. People started screaming. I had to get up and help them. When I got up, I found I was lying on somebody. I saw there were a couple of people dead on the other side of the carriage.' He saw one woman pinned down by a shaft of metal, which had splintered off during the crash.

Paul Fellich, another passenger, noted that he did not know how he had survived in the midst of all the twisted metal. The passengers in the front coach of the Poole train had little chance of surviving and, given how badly it was damaged, it was a miracle that any at all survived. Travellers in the buffet car also suffered particularly badly because loose furniture fell on them as it careered about the carriage. The report of the counsel to the Clapham inquiry, David Latham QC, noted that: 'The evidence of all the survivors shows a consistent pattern. Whether they were on the Poole train or the Basingstoke train, they were all seriously thrown about and a significant number were hit by flying luggage of one sort or another.' Briefcases fell on passengers, for instance, and a Mr Hague Holmes was struck by an interior coach door which came off its hinges and became a projectile.

In retrospect, everyone, including the survivors, praised the work of the emergency services. Yet there were problems with the rescue, the first one concerning the electric current on the track. No one was sure whether or not it had been turned off and, therefore, if it was safe to go on to the line. Latham stated that 'there is no doubt that the emergency services felt inhibited by uncertainty as to whether or not traction current had been switched off or cut off'. This was the first of many managerial muddles that were to be revealed at the inquiry.

Publicly, everyone unreservedly praised the courage and ability of the fire brigade, the ambulance service and the casualty departments. Communications, however, were something of a problem – especially between the London ambulance service and St George's Hospital, which took the majority of the casualties. St George's initially did not realize there had

been a major incident; the switchboard there did not understand the codes that the ambulance service uses for different
scales of disaster. As a result, when the ambulance service
declared there was a Yellow Alert, St George's did not grasp
that this meant a major alert, and so it was a few minutes
before the accident and emergency teams realized just how
large the accident was. In addition, St George's did not have a
phone line dedicated to deal with the emergency, so all relevant
calls had to use the general switchboard number, competing
with normal traffic. It was argued that these problems did not
mean that anyone who could have been saved, died, but the
sense of muddle was not comforting. Casualty doctors noted
that most of those who had on-the-spot amputations at Clapham later died. That was worrying; casualty specialists at their
annual conference on the Isle of Man in 1989 suggested that
there had indeed been serious problems, including the fact that
all the patients went to just one hospital which was, as a result,
overstretched: patients had to be treated in corridors.

The London Fire Brigade argued to the inquiry that one way
to prevent such confusion was to revise the Fires Act of 1947 to
give the fire service pre-eminent control at disasters. The Chief
Officer of the London Fire Brigade had the support of all other
chief officers in this demand, but, not surprisingly, neither the
ambulance service nor the Metropolitan Police considered
giving the fire service total control desirable.

Important evidence of the cause of the disaster got lost, or
never materialized. There was an absence of photographic
evidence. The actual bit of the relay wire, which may have been
crucial in causing the accident, was destroyed – not to falsify
the record, Latham agreed, but it was still a regrettable loss.
These confusions at the scene suggested that no one had drawn
together the lessons of King's Cross, even though British Rail
had specifically tried to learn from that disaster.

King's Cross might have been expected to alert the railways
to safety dangers in their own operation, and so, according to
David Latham, it did. He noted: 'Fortunately, if that is not the
wrong word to use, the King's Cross fire had directed the
attention of British Rail very clearly to safety issues. It is to

their credit that it did not restrict its analysis of its operations merely to matters of fire.'

The review of safety arrangements that British Rail set in motion after King's Cross took place, however, in the middle of a quite separate exercise: renewing the antiquated signalling system that controls the lines out of Waterloo. Parts of the signalling system on Southern Region date back to 1930. British Rail planned improvements from 1978 onwards. Though the decision to rewire was taken in principle by September 1981, in practice, there was little urgent action. Then, in May 1984, research showed that there had been 26 per cent more signal failures in the south east than in the two previous years.

Finally, on 19 December 1984, British Rail approved major resignalling works. This work was to be carried out in a series of stages over a number of years, and it is a measure of the unhurried pace of the project that, three years later, the plan had just reached Clapham Junction. The plan of stage 7b, which affected the Clapham signals, was put forward by a Mr Callender at a meeting on 11 February 1987. Callender was not a senior BR executive, but it had been left to him to break down the work required into a consistent programme of mini-stages. From the beginning of July 1988 to the end of November 1988, signals in the Clapham area would be converted and modified. On paper, the plan made engineering sense. The problem was that the management skills to carry it out were lacking; there was no clear control of the operation. It was not just engineering difficulties that the resignalling project faced. A large amount of overtime would be needed. Senior BR managers knew this in theory, but did not plan for the consequences. Overtime was accepted as a necessity, but no one asked tricky questions about the stress or the careless work that excessive overtime might lead to. The concept that stress might cause careless work had simply not entered management vocabulary. Counsel for the inquiry noted: 'Nowhere is there any indication that this aspect of the matter was considered at any level in the management at all.'

Only after the crash did the calculations come. Twenty-eight per cent of the BR engineering staff were working seven days a week over two months. The managerial confusion was remarkable. Resignalling of a large area of Clapham Junction, one of the great junctions in the British Rail system, was not anyone's formal responsibility; there was no controlling project engineer. Responsibility was split between the project engineer, who handled contractors and budgeting; the works engineer, who handled operations on the tracks; and the design office, which provided the plans and working drawings. British Rail called this 'lateral management'. Latham sniped that lateral management sounds democratic, but the problem is that it results 'in no one person having overall responsibility'.

Those who were used to such a system did not struggle against the lack of a clear structure; it was accepted as one of those things. Callender became the central figure, installing and testing the new signals at Clapham, but he took that role by default. He told the inquiry that he did not think he was in charge of testing or of implementing the regional plan for improving the testing of signals, which was called 'SL-provisions'.

Ironically, it would have taken confident inspired management to handle all the difficulties of resignalling. First, trained manpower was short: British Rail did not pay well enough to compete for signal engineers in the marketplace, average take-home pay being £12,000! Second, the design office felt under pressure and so did not provide testing copies of the relays unless specifically asked to do so. Much evidence claimed that they were not asked for any. Latham claimed that 'those concerned with arranging the work did the best they could with the workforce that had volunteered itself for work on the list put up between the Thursday and Tuesday preceding each given weekend. Without the discipline of a plan which would identify precisely how many trained men of what particular skills would be required, it was possible for those in charge to be tempted simply to make the best they could with what they had got rather than take a firmly based decision as to what work could or could not be done.'

The local problems were considerable, but so were the central ones. Effective management ensures that staff learn from mistakes; no one drew the lessons from three incidents which had happened previously on the network, though, tell-ingly, a number of people nearly did.

Two kinds of signalling failures need to be noted: signals passed at danger, and wrongside failure. A wrongside failure is where the fail-safe system does not function. There had been a number of these from 1985 onwards in the Southern area, notably at East Croydon, at Oxted and at Queenstown Road. The incident at Queenstown Road had been put down to bad work by a bad worker. At Oxted, since there had not actually been a fatal accident, it had not been reported to BR HQ but dealt with at regional level. The defects of the signalling system were thus clear and known, but no one acted upon them. The Oxted incident in particular showed the need to make sure that when the wires in signal boxes were installed, the ends of the old wires were properly insulated and 'deaded'.

On 25–6 November, some seven engineers set about rewiring the junction. The job numbers and requirements had actually been set in August 1987. From that time on, though, there had been a review of safety but no update of what would be needed. The actual planning near the time consisted of one walk through the area before the first weekend of November by three supervisors. They asked for seven staff from the Eastleigh depot to do the job. The shift was split into three gangs. A Mr Winwood supervised the work in one area, but the central figure was a technician called Brian Hemingway. He was respected: he had designed and installed the terminations for forty-eight core cables connecting the Clapham relay room and the lobby. He was always willing to do overtime, needing the extra money to earn a decent wage. He thus arrived for work on 26 November having had only two weekends off in two months.

Brian Hemingway was given a technical assistant, named Dowd, to work in the relay room. Hemingway had no confidence in Dowd, but never told Bumstead, the overall super-visor on that day. There were not enough people to do the actual work, however, so Bumstead acted as a senior tech-nician, and, consequently, could not supervise work. As a result of these haphazard arrangements, no one felt it was his job to make sure the work was being done properly. The irony was that in the room next to where Hemingway was putting in the new wires, there was a man whose management role included supervision. This man was Mr Dray, the regional testing engineer, perfectly qualified independently to check Hemingway's work. But no one had planned for him to carry out checks, and it did not occur to Dray to do it on his own initiative.

Brian Hemingway could not remember how he had carried out the particular work in the relay room. To understand the problem, it is necessary to explain how the signal box works: there is a relay end and a fuse end. Cutting off the 'eye' of the wire lessened the danger if the insulation was not carried out properly, but Hemingway could not remember just how he had carried out that particular piece of work. Nevertheless, he agreed that he would have removed the old wire, removed the insulation from the new wire and put it over the eye on the old wire. Then he would push the old wire back through the rack and out of the way and finally terminate the new wire. Latham argued that the crucially deficient parts of his practice were that 'he never cut off the eye or cut back the wire in any other way; and second, that he always reused the insulating tape. Moreover, Hemingway reused it in what has been described as a "flag fashion"; this meant that he finally never did anything by way of securing the redundant wire other than pushing it out of the way.'

Hemingway was not following accepted practice in doing this. Yet because no one was checking his work, there was no one to point this out to him. He also failed to carry out a formal wire count. Hemingway told the inquiry that he accepted that he could not have secured or insulated the wire properly. Latham suggested that 'a lack of care in applying the insulating tape could well have resulted in it falling off'. There was no way of knowing if Hemingway did put insulation over the eye and it dropped off or if he forgot to put any insulation over it at all, since the eye itself was cut away in the hours after the disaster.

Hemingway rejected the idea that he was muddled by the instructions in the wiring diagram for the fuse end. The work might have been done by an assistant, however. Whoever did it, it certainly was not checked. Mr Dray, the regional testing engineer, was in the signal box all day and 'knew full well or had the means of finding out easily that nobody had been in to carry out an independent check of Mr Hemingway's work'.

After the work of 26 and 27 November, the signals appeared to function normally; there were no incidents on the line. On the night of 10 and 11 December, however, there was work done on an adjoining relay, and it seems likely that this new work dislodged Hemingway's wiring. The insulated wires were then pushed together. On the morning of the 12th, strange errors crept into the signalling, and a number of drivers who were not happy with the signal sequence they saw reported the matter. Drivers felt, however, that no one paid very much attention to their complaints. The signal confusions drivers reported early on the 12th should have suggested clearly that something very peculiar and worrying was occurring, but there was no structure that allowed for some kind of 'signalling alert' to check how the system was operating, and it was only after the crash that checks were carried out. When they were, the results were alarming.

In the Clapham Junction signal box A, some ten to twenty wires were either uninsulated or unsecured. An audit in the south west of the Southern Region found that there was evidence that redundant wires were not always disconnected at both ends. The final Hidden Report on the accident noted that there were serious flaws in the way British Rail tested signalling. Instructions about new wiring were confusing, as the same document dealt with handling both old and new wires. As a result, it was not clear whether or not engineers knew what procedures they were meant to follow.

Latham argued that Hemingway was a basically good workman who had got into a number of bad working practices. He had been a senior technician for ten years without a single refresher course, and his standard of qualifications would not be accepted by BR now. Hemingway, however, did deserve better from his superiors. His immediate supervisor, Bumstead, knew that Hemingway was likely to follow bad practice because he had spoken to him about his habit of reusing old insulation tape. Bumstead sensed, however, that the whole signals hierarchy was not sufficiently rigorous, and that he would have no reason to suppose that anyone would be critical of his failure to supervise, especially as he had decided to work as a senior technician that day to make up numbers. Latham argued that there was simply no sense of direction in the department. Two of the men directly responsible for the new signals work were, in different ways, less than effective. Mr Lippitt, who was the regional works supervisor, was looking forward to retirement. Mr Bailey, while more energetic, spent most of his time at the Eastleigh depot.

Given this lack of management initiative, the failure to test the system properly before it was commissioned was not surprising. At the time of the accident, British Rail instructions said a wire count was one of the vital checks which had to be carried out as part of the testing process, but good testing requires imagination; it involves trying to catch the equipment out. Railwaymen have thus tended to see testing not so much as a procedure, but rather as a skill. A series of British Rail documents did emphasize, from 1986 onwards, the need for new signals to be properly tested, and the incidents at Oxted and East Croydon reinforced their concern. Nevertheless, Latham concluded: 'Despite this evidence there is little impression of a concerted management drive as a matter of urgency to carry the messages both in relation to good practice and good testing down to the workforce.' There was confusion in Clapham, and testing just happened to be carried out rather than being properly structured. Yet Dray did not carry out a wire count. Callender, his predecessor, would not have carried out a wire count either. Again, it was not the case that no one perceived the need for change, simply that no one managed to impose a sense of urgency.

With access to all the statistics at BR HQ, it should have been apparent that something was seriously amiss. The number of signalling incidents on Southern Region was high. At the regional level, Mr Hale, the regional engineer, did have a sense of the need to reform testing practices: in November 1985 he identified seven factors as making up good testing practice, and

issued the instruction SL53 which outlined the need for different engineers to have proper individual roles. Hale also stressed
the need for independent checking, but he failed to launch the
instruction in a sufficiently energetic way. He did not see that it
would take some dramatic symbolic action to get a rather
complacent department to pay proper attention. It needed,
perhaps, a seminar to persuade the engineers that their testing
procedures had to change. Instead, SL53, his 'reforming'
document, merely landed on people's desks, as more bumf. In
some cases, the Inquiry was told, it did not even land on desks.
It was not, for instance, distributed downwards to the supervisors at Bumstead's level. In sum, nothing brought home to
the staff that this was, as Latham put it, 'a document of the first
importance relating to a matter of safety'. As a result, it was
not hard for those who did not like SL53 to bypass it. Latham
alleged that Callender, either through obstinacy or simple
thoughtlessness, put SL53 on one side, as it was, in his view,
unworkable. Many other testers were not convinced by it
either. When doubts were raised, BR senior managers did not
respond with any urgency. As a result, the instruction was not
properly supported, so that, in effect, it 'appears to have had
rather a token existence', as Latham noted.

BR was undergoing a reorganization and there was much
talk of the need for training. In theory, adequate training and
certification procedures for installing new signalling should
have been in place by autumn 1988. But they were not. None
of these omissions and examples of thoughtlessness could be
guaranteed to have prevented the Clapham crash, but no one
was alert to an accumulation of small lapses, so that, in the
end, no one spotted a crucial, fatal error.

It would be wrong to focus entirely on mistakes of local
management; at board level, BR did place safety high on its list
of priorities, but it did not really will the means to make the
practical implications of this priority possible. The world of the
railways is changing. Historically, from before the time of the
Armagh disaster of 1889, the railways have relied on their men
having pride in their work. The 'culture' of the railways
reinforced that pride. To be a railwayman made one proud.
The railways had a certain status. This is no longer the case.

It seems unlikely that many of those involved in the Clapham Inquiry had read that bizarre but eloquent book, *Notes from Overground*, a commuter's diary. This eloquently chronicles the decline in railway culture. The commuter's routine is made almost unbearable by the decay of the railways. The narrator, Tiresias, curses the 'them' who run Paddington, uncaring bureaucrats of the tracks who love to inconvenience 'us' and relish causing misery and delays, and wreaking general psychological mayhem. David Latham was more prosaic in dissecting the change to railway culture. Modern attitudes to work undoubtedly make it hard to maintain the old railway culture; hence, effective management techniques become all the more important. The management muddles which were revealed at the Inquiry suggest that the BR board did not realize what was going on, that the drift in which no one felt responsible or saw inadequacies had become routine.

The need for clear, efficient management was reinforced by the fact that the organization of BR changed after 1987, divided into the production side and the business side. Production was concerned with running the railways; business with making them pay. Unfortunately, as a result, there were bound to be conflicts between the two and consequential uncertainties among staff.

The organization of the railway industry in the UK recognizes the difficulties in getting management to accept the need for, and act on the requirements of safety. The Railway Inspectorate exists as an independent body whose duty is to keep a watch on the railways. Often, the inspectorate has been criticized for being too cosily linked to the railways; nevertheless, it had asked for investment in various safety devices, mainly radios and automatic train protection, a system that automatically stops a train if it passes a red signal. But these had not been implemented. The inspectorate, moreover, failed to demand action after the Oxted incidents.

The Clapham crash had no single cause but rather a series of causes. The authoritative *Railway Gazette International* spoke in an editorial of 'a shocking and deep-rooted deficiency in installation and testing standards throughout British Rail

Southern Region' (December 1989, p.851). From a psychological point of view, what remains telling is the number of people who must have been uneasy about or worried by various factors: too much overtime worked, lack of clear planning, lack of good organization of weekend work, failure to carry out the reforms of SL53. Yet no action was taken. Interestingly, only the overtime issue was in any sense an economic one; the other issues were far more to do with what has come to be known as 'management culture', the climate in which people worked.

I have said little so far about the effect of Clapham either on the families of the bereaved or on the survivors. In one respect, they did benefit from the bad publicity that London Transport got after King's Cross. London Transport had tried very hard to deny guilt, initially alleging that the fire was the result of arson, a story that never stood up. As a result, London Transport did not immediately accept responsibility or offer large payments to the victims; it took them some weeks to accept liability. British Rail learned from that experience and immediately announced that they accepted liability, a move which helped to placate some critics.

The inquiries into the Clapham disaster were much more incisive than at King's Cross. They focused clearly on how easy it is for management to be complacent and to ignore repeated warnings. Neither the formal inquiry report nor any of the newspaper accounts, however, offered anything constructive by way of help. One irony of all the British disasters in 1987 and 1988 is that they took place against a background in which transport companies were marketing themselves as never before, yet few of those marketing skills have been used to impress the needs of safety either on staff or on passengers.

Lockerbie

Airlines, ever since the hijackings of the 1970s, have learned to be worried about security. Yet all their painfully accumulated knowledge about safety did not help prevent the Lockerbie bomb. The subsequent police investigations have been dogged by internecine squabbling between the German, Scottish and

American police forces, but what is clear, through a succession of leaks and counter-leaks, is that the tragedy might have been prevented if security lessons from past incidents had been learned. By focusing solely on this one aspect of Lockerbie, I do not mean in any way to belittle the tragedy; it just seems an excellent example of the ways in which it is hard to implement the lessons of past disasters.

Pan Am Flight 103 crashed on 16 December 1988, outside the small Scottish town of Lockerbie. Sections of the plane fell into the streets, making a huge crater. Wreckage was found up to fifty miles away. The scatter of the debris convinced police from the start that they were dealing with a bomb. There had been a breach of security, and a number of American investigations into this breach are still proceeding.

Security experts always maintain that perfect security is unattainable. But it now seems well established that the American Embassy in Helsinki was phoned with a warning that terrorists might strike at a Pan Am flight, a warning convincing enough for many American diplomats to change their travel plans and rebook themselves on carriers other than Pan Am. Remarkably, these warnings specified that a bomb might be concealed in a Toshiba cassette recorder. A diagram accompanied the telex which Interpol sent to all European airports and airlines. The diagram showed how the explosive Semtex would be buried in the machine. Clues would be that the cassette recorder would not work and that it would weigh some 400 grams more than it should, all details which were surprisingly accurate.

The inquiries set up after Lockerbie showed how poor safety procedures were when it came to dealing both with hand-luggage and baggage in transit. Security at Frankfurt failed to pick up any explosive or metal device either in hand-luggage or in the hold. Most of Flight 103's luggage was boarded in London, where it was x-rayed, but the passengers and the bags loaded at Frankfurt were not subjected to any further search; they were simply moved automatically from the plane which had brought them from Frankfurt to the plane which would fly out of Heathrow. A passenger could, therefore, have got off at London while his other luggage stayed on board. Indeed, two weeks after the Lockerbie crash, to the embarrassment of British Airways, this happened to an Indian passenger, who complained bitterly that his suitcase had flown without him. Security procedures should have made this quite impossible.

The attitudes of airlines and of transport authorities to safety are, in fact, deeply compromised. Only airlines which are under considerable threat, like El Al, seem to make a commitment to safety above all else – even if it costs passengers time and trouble. It is therefore worth examining in detail the very different attitudes that El Al bring to security. Its security personnel are trained to assume that all passengers might be terrorists, that they are guilty till proven innocent. In most airlines inspections of security procedures are usually announced. As a result even 'on the spot' checks are a little artificial. El Al's inspectors behave differently. They try to act rather as they imagine terrorists would, and the security team fail if they do not spot them. Many of the security personnel have to travel on the plane that they have just checked. This results in their having a completely different degree of motivation: at Heathrow, the security staff know that if they make a mistake, it will not affect them fatally; El Al's staff have no such assurance.

The attitudes of experts in security to El Al's measures are ambivalent. While everyone admires the airline's record, no one actually imitates it. Michael Yardley, a security expert, like the Department of Transport in a number of reviews, points out that air traffic would grind to a halt if every carrier acted like El Al. The evidence for this, however, is dubious. There would certainly be some congestion at check-in desks and passengers would have to report between an hour to ninety minutes earlier. Security staff would also have to be trained far more rigorously. These improvements would be costly and would require a different expectation of the delays passengers have to accept for security, but they are hardly Utopian fancies.

I discovered soon after Lockerbie how unsatisfactory safety procedures remain in Britain. I was travelling with 16mm film which I did not want x-rayed. At Gatwick I was searched and made to open the cans in a dark room. The search was thorough, if a little clumsy. I then needed to fly from Edinburgh to Birmingham after we finished shooting, and I was told that if the film went in the hold rather than as hand-luggage it would not be x-rayed, since domestic air flights luggage did not go through that procedure. In other words, if a terrorist had given me a present which concealed an explosive, and I had packed it in my suitcase, there would have been virtually no chance of it being picked up. It is precisely that eventuality that El Al guard against.

The Lockerbie families have campaigned for improvements in safety. As they say openly enough, such improvements would offer them some consolation. An interesting example of the lack of urgency that prevails, however, is the Department of Transport's attitude. After Lockerbie it decided that it had to study the question of screening luggage, both at the airport of origin and at any transfers. The decision to set up a working party was taken on 2 February, but this working party did not meet until mid-June.

The House of Commons Transport Committee also studied ways of improving security after Lockerbie. They offered a number of radical suggestions, which included checking passengers' tickets before they leave the airside of an airport to make sure they are not cutting short a trip and leaving luggage on board. A second suggestion was searching every passenger. Third, they recommended not allowing passengers to collect duty-free goods till they are on the plane, since it is all too easy to switch them. Like El Al, they suggested, too, that inspectors should pose as terrorists. Security experts like Michael Yardley, however, responded as if the committee were composed of rather naïve idealists. The Department of Transport itself has not responded, shielding itself under the cover of 'security', good security apparently involving not revealing what improvements have been made. The facts outlined suggest that there may have been few of these.

Certainly, the families of those killed at Lockerbie remain astonished by official inertia. They noted in a letter to the *Guardian*: 'Lockerbie was uniquely preventable. It is unlikely that ever again will the security services be presented with warnings as to the grouping of terrorists, the precise description of the x-ray identifiable bomb to be used, the airport of origin, the identity of the airline to be hit, the destination of the flight and the approximate date.' Yet they assert no special precautions were taken. The families offered some suggestions on how to improve security, based on their study. Pessimistically, though, they note: 'Security remains essentially unchanged and those in charge of it fail to see even that they could have done better.' If those in charge are unable to admit shortcomings, they say, 'what chance is there of those in the same administration organizing disaster management?'

If procedures change for the better, the bereaved and survivors will at least feel that their sacrifices were not wasted, but it is rare for them to have that luxury.

In September 1989, there were two developments. The American Federal Aviation Authority fined Pan Am over $600,000 for lapses of security relating to Lockerbie. The families of victims in the UK also met the new Secretary of Transport, Cecil Parkinson. He promised that there would be some inquiry into both the causes of Lockerbie and what could be learned from it. It had taken nearly a year to wring this concession from his department. The official reason for the delay was that an inquiry would hamper police work, yet it was always clear that there was not much chance of arresting anyone for the Lockerbie outrage. There was, however, realistic hope of learning from it to improve security.

The US Presidential Commission into the Lockerbie disaster reported in May 1990. It found that there had been grievous lapses in security both at Frankfurt and at Heathrow. It made a number of recommendations concerning baggage handling. More controversially, it urged that the US government should be willing to attack terrorists in return. There was some sign that the British government reacted. In May 1990, not wholly by coincidence, security procedures at airports were stepped up. As a frequent traveller, I did notice that there was a tendency to search more pieces of hand luggage. Not much else was evident.

For Dr Jim Swire, of the Flight 103 Families Association in Britain and the other relatives of survivors, the reaction in Britain to the American report wasn't satisfactory. Despite Cecil Parkinson's assurance, there is no sign of any major inquiry into Lockerbie. After the publication of the Presidential Report, Dr Swire again called for one. He has consistently complained that the British government is unwilling to investigate what went wrong. No one is really sure why there should be such a refusal. For the families that feels like an additional rebuff which just causes more stress. It's a sign of the way in which real investigation is often avoided.

I have tried to show here both how various the experiences of survivors have been, and how complicated the psychological factors – both of the causes and effects of disasters. It is this complexity which makes it especially important to have some systematic co-ordination of relief. The psychiatric services worked well at King's Cross, but although they have tried to disseminate the experience they gained there, there are no structures to facilitate this process. And learning from their experience is important, particularly if disaster planning is to be effective. It needs tremendous flexibility, and social and psychiatric services have to shed a number of traditional attitudes, particularly reaching out to 'patients' when 'patients' want care.

The Lockerbie crash did not just reveal how avoidable mistakes were made in ignoring warnings; after the crash, there were also many mistakes made, as pointed out by relatives. The police and aid agencies were confused and unhelpful. Social workers went there in large numbers from many parts of Scotland, but nevertheless, many of the bereaved felt angry and confused that they did not get the help they needed when they wanted it. Learning from recent disasters, despite the very evident need for it, remains astonishingly hard. At present, British politicians, for all their pious words in debates like that after Clapham, refuse to will the means to do it. Some form of national disaster agency would not be a panacea but it should avoid some of the haphazard muddles that made life more difficult after King's Cross, Clapham and Lockerbie.

4

Radiation

Three Mile Island

In all the chapters so far, I have relied heavily on individuals'
accounts of what happened to them before, during and after a
disaster. The first part of this chapter is very different. It
reports research results largely because the incident at Three
Mile Island was in some ways a disaster that never happened.
Radiation did leak in dangerous amounts and a plume of
radioactive cloud drifted over Harrisburg, Pennsylvania. Yet
very little measurable damage followed: no one was killed; no
one was burned; two technicians received mildly high doses of
radiation; there has been no convincing proof of damage to
babies. Yet Three Mile Island has become part of history.

It seems likely that this non-disaster has achieved this distinc-
tion for two reasons. First, it was a warning of what might
happen and later did, disastrously, at Chernobyl. Secondly,
Three Mile Island reflected our complex fears of radiation.
Many dangers plunge people back into primitive fears: children, for instance, dream quite normally of fire or drowning,
accidents all too easy to imagine. Radiation is different: few of
us understand what it is or can visualize it, yet we live in a
world that constantly warns that it could kill us. The shadow of
the Bomb still darkens all our lives.

Apprehension concerning radiation has increased as green
issues have become central to the political agenda. In a recent
TV debate, David Montgomery of the *Today* newspaper highlighted these as the concerns that ordinary people cared about.
The highbrows (he was debating with the editors of the
Independent and the *Daily Telegraph*) might be obsessed with
the tittle-tattle of politics but the man from the tabloid,

reflecting grass-roots opinion, was desperately worried about the environment. Radiation is widely perceived as a major threat. That perception helps in understanding the reactions to the radiation leaks at Three Mile Island and Chernobyl. The green prognosis is terrifying, claiming that we are clinging perilously on to life on a planet in mortal danger. There is a hole in the ozone layer; acid rain is falling on the planet; nuclear power stations are leaking invisible rays of radioactive death.

Three months before the incident at Three Mile Island, a surprise cinematic success was *The China Syndrome*. The film told the story of a wicked and negligent power company whose lust for profit led to the ultimate nightmare, a meltdown in a nuclear reactor. In a meltdown, the core of the reactor glows so hot and radioactive that it melts into the earth and contaminates it. A vast area is left 'dirty'. The nuclear lobby rubbished *The China Syndrome* as alarmist Hollywood hype, but within a relatively short time, real life had imitated art. Three Mile Island showed that *The China Syndrome* was not the clumsy propaganda the nuclear lobby had stigmatized it as. The Three Mile Island accident almost perfectly confirmed the film's worst fears, but had the added bonus of not producing any casualties. I shall argue that these underlying, half-spoken fears affected the West's view of Chernobyl.

For all its dangers, radiation does not immediately put workers on the alert. Both at Three Mile Island and Chernobyl control room operators did not realize for some time that they were dealing with critical situations. At Chernobyl, indeed, human actions, or lack of them, were largely responsible for the incident.

It is worth comparing the situation of nuclear power station workers with that of personnel on oil rigs in the North Sea, or with astronauts, who know full well that they are in an extremely dangerous environment, and that therefore they have to be alert. They sense their risk. For this reason, it would never have occurred to oil riggers to attempt the experiments that the Chernobyl staff undertook. In nuclear power stations, the risk is less palpable, the atmosphere cold and clinical enough to enable staff to describe what they do as essentially routine. They are, of course, aware of the risks of radiation, but the work atmosphere does little to dramatize them.

Nuclear power stations in the West are, nevertheless, usually sited far from large centres of population. The majority of those who live near them either work there or are otherwise connected with them. As a result, more than most other groups, they have intensely ambivalent feelings towards radiation and its associated risks. They both need, and fear, the power station.

Three Mile Island is situated near Harrisburg, Pennsylvania. The local town has very much grown up around Metropolitain Edison, the electricity supply company. The residents often expressed concern about the safety of the power station, but there seemed little hope that any action would be taken. In addition, many of those who lived at Three Mile Island worked for Metropolitain Edison and so were unwilling to press objections. (A similar situation exists at Sellafield in Britain, where workers often feel the environment lobby overplays the risks associated with their plant.)

The design of the plant at Three Mile Island was complicated: the main reactor, which generated electricity, was housed in a supposedly impregnable building, literally wrapped for safety in a containment dome. The near accident took place in this building, and it was caused by a problem with the cooling system. The fuel rods inside a nuclear reactor can reach temperatures of 3,500 degrees Centigrade. Keeping them cool is therefore a critical part of the nuclear energy process; if the rods get too hot then the plant can go critical. The rods are cooled by a constant supply of water which, as it loops around the system, becomes radioactive and has to be disposed of. This system provided the background for *The China Syndrome* and it was crucially involved with what happened both at Three Mile Island and Chernobyl.

At 4 A.M. on 28 March the sirens wailed in the control room of Unit 2 at Three Mile Island. A pump feeding water into the secondary cooling system of Unit X had failed. Its failure activated the plant's turbine to provide an alternative source of coolant. Electricity production stopped but, inside the containment building, the reactor continued to generate heat.

Three Mile Island's primary coolant system was meant to work at 300 degrees Centigrade. With the secondary cooling system inoperational, the temperature rose. Operators did not panic, though. They had seen such crises before and they assumed the turbine would cope. The turbine, however, did not cope: it failed. Almost as soon as the alarms stopped ringing, the warning lights flashed again. Fifteen seconds later, the temperature in the primary loop had risen to 611 degrees and the pressure fallen to 2,147 pounds per square inch. The pressure continued to fall. Automatically, auxiliary pumps should have started a new supply of water flowing to make up for the absence of the normal coolant. No water came. At this point, it was vital that operators in the control room should stay calm and controlled. Instead, there was confusion. The instrument panels were displaying two conflicting sets of information: one set showed they were still losing coolant and pressure – the recipe for a blowdown or a meltdown – a second set indicated that pressure was rising. This was a hopeful sign, since it should provide an automatic solution: as pressure rose, it automatically opened other relief valves. These would in turn release the first amounts of radioactive vapour from the pressurizer into the containment dome.

The design of the reactor had, in theory, allowed for such emergencies. When pressure in the primary loop fell to 1,600 pounds per square inch, the emergency core cooling system was activated automatically. It was meant to flood the primary system with 350,000 gallons of reserve water. But before this happened, bemused operators watched as the pressure level indicators went off the scale at the high end. This was the very opposite of what should have been happening; the computer delivered a series of printouts full of question marks, as no one had anticipated this situation.

Luck, however, was with the power station. Either out of panic or because he had misread a printout, one operator shut down one of the high pressure pumps meant to inject the emergency 350,000 gallons. Ninety seconds later, the reactor coolant system was spewing steam, and pressure bottomed out at 1,350 pounds per square inch. The temperature in the core rose sharply, perhaps as high as 2,700 degrees Centigrade. Cladding structures which were designed to protect the core of the reactor fell apart and the water could no longer flow in some of the structures.

It was at this point, at about 4.08, that the operators finally realized that the automatic pumps were not doing their job; water was not getting through to the core. The mistake was spotted. The valves attached to these pumps had been closed during a maintenance drill and were still closed. When the operators at last grasped that this vital equipment was malfunctioning, they opened these valves by throwing a manual switch.

For three seconds, they did not know if their tactic was working, if, finally, water was getting through. President Carter's later inquiry concluded that during those seconds the fuel rods could have been exposed and the events depicted in *The China Syndrome* might have happened in real life.

Three minutes after the water had flooded into the reactor core, the situation improved. Steam bubbles formed in the containment dome. At 5.40 the auxiliary feedwater pipes were shut down to prevent a burnout. The reactor core temperature soared off the scale and may have reached 3,600 degrees Centigrade. Large volumes of radioactive gas were released. The damaged primary loop system could not belch them out and so they gathered at the top of the reactor.

Radioactive material began to seep out into the air earlier at 4.07 A.M. Two hours later came the first and only injuries. Two technicians absorbed 3.7 and 3.2 rads, more radioactivity than it was safe to absorb in twenty years, as the waste tanks blew out radioactive steam. Vapour clung to the walls and primary coolant dripped to the floor. Extractor fans vented the radioactive steam into the atmosphere and the hot plume drifted over Harrisburg.

The radiation alarm sounded at 6.50 A.M. The Nuclear Regulatory Commission was told of the crisis but the Mayor of Middletown, across the river, heard nothing until 9 A.M., and there was no public announcement till 11 A.M. when there was immediate panic. Probably, this delay was due to a muddle, but the public saw it as sinister. When the Nuclear Regulatory

Commission arrived, it did so in a style that suggested a doomsday scenario, with state police and US Army troops. The Signals Corps drove in, as the telephone system could not cope. Metropolitain Edison offered glib, unconvincing reassurances to worried locals. Its vice president, Jack Herbine, said: 'When we say general emergency, it does not mean that an emergency exists. There was nothing catastrophic or unplanned for.'

Local residents did not stop to quibble about definitions of emergency; thousands simply left the island, jamming the roads out of Harrisburg. In the first twenty-four hours, 10,000 people left. The fact that it was a radiation accident profoundly influenced public reaction. Studies had shown that people believed the government would never tell them the truth about nuclear problems. If the local river had flooded, a proper emergency would have been declared and evacuation organized, but the nuclear danger was too politically sensitive. Herbine also continued to irritate everybody with his anodyne assertions. He said, 'We didn't injure anyone, we didn't overexpose anyone, we certainly didn't kill a single solitary soul.' He did not seem to grasp the fact that the nuclear component made the incident different, more terrifying.

By 9 A.M. the extent of the crisis became apparent. The Pennsylvania Emergency Management Agency reported a release of xenon 133 gas into the atmosphere. Twelve hundred mrems readings were taken, a worrying amount. To make room in the waste tanks for the highly radioactive coolant, 40,000 gallons of less dangerous waste had to be dumped into the Susquehanna River. The Republican Governor of the State, Dick Thornburgh, ordered schools to be closed. Pregnant women and children under school age were advised to leave. The Pennsylvania civil defence staff were told to draw up evacuation plans for 165,000 residents within a ten-mile radius.

Washington declared Three Mile Island a national emergency area. President Carter, once a nuclear engineer, went down to Harrisburg. He emphasized that safety would be paramount and ordered an immediate Presidential Commission to find out what had gone wrong.

Local people had good reason for anxiety. No one was

certain just what the situation inside the reactor was; there might have been a partial meltdown or an explosion. There was indeed immediate cause for concern. On Friday, a gas bubble was discovered inside the reactor building. It was composed of 2.6 per cent hydrogen and appeared to be rising. It might explode and blow off the top of the reactor. Eventually, a way was found to increase the water flow through the primary loop system. The bubble subsided, but that still left 400,000 gallons of radioactive, contaminated water on the floor of the reactor building, along with the krypton gas inside the containment building. No one knew how these elements would combine or even just how radioactive they might be. The local population feared the water and the gas might well explode.

The uncertainty of this period made residents of Three Mile Island extremely nervous, and those who had gone did not know if they would have homes to return to. The emergency was formally declared over two weeks after the end of the incident. It was also shown that there had been no significant leak of radiation. The Nuclear Regulatory Commission and Governor Thornburgh both declared the power station safe, but it was not easy for people to be reassured. First, many suspected the authorities might just want them to think it was safe. Then, gas was still leaking occasionally from the containment building. Returning home, many said they felt that they were living next to a crippled plant that was still 'hot', 'hotness' being a concept derived from our experience of fires, and easily adopted to describe fears, unspecifiable, of radiation.

America is very psychologically-oriented. The magazine *Psychology Today* sold over a million copies a month in 1979; the American Psychological Association had nearly 100,000 members. Lawyers knew about the Buffalo Creek case. Not surprisingly, therefore, teams of psychologists began to investigate in Harrisburg. There were academic psychologists who saw the disaster as a splendid opportunity for research; there were company psychologists hired to cope with the stress in Three Mile Island staff; there were government psychologists. And, of course, there were psychologists hired by lawyers who would later want to prove how damaged their clients had been.

Three questions dominated: first, had human error contributed to the accident? Second, what kind of stress did the two-week emergency cause? Third, what were the long-term effects likely to be?

The question of error was tackled by the Presidential Commission on Three Mile Island, which found workers had failed to monitor all the necessary information but had not been helped by the delays in the printouts. At times, information lagged ninety minutes behind real time.

The first studies were reported to the 1979 convention of the American Psychological Association that same August. Dohrenwend suggested that people who lived near the plant suffered considerable mental health problems: they felt afraid; they said they were demoralized; they reported an abnormally high number of physical symptoms, including headaches, stomach problems and fears of cancer.

The situation was different from Buffalo Creek, where hundreds had died, but Buffalo Creek did offer a model. Despite the fact that few people were directly affected, the evidence of psychological damage at Three Mile Island accumulated. People who lived nearby had an above average risk of suffering from depression and anxiety; their sleep was disturbed. Their dreams, however, were very different from those of actual disaster victims: they did not dream they were being burned, like the victims of King's Cross. As a result, many suffered from a looser, more nebulous anxiety.

Despite official assurances that Three Mile Island had not been exposed to any radiation at all, many did not feel safe. This was partly because they tended not to believe official assurances, but it was partly to do with the invisible nature of radiation itself. Flynn and Chalmers (1980) found that many residents continued to perceive threats as a result of the plant's very presence. The paradox was clear: despite no real disaster having taken place, people were behaving as if there had been a major catastrophe. Few psychologists traced this behaviour to the awe with which we, rightly, regard radiation. Rather, they pursued what might seem to be slightly esoteric lines of inquiry. They compared the anxieties people felt with the distance of their homes from the plant. They retained some scepticism, and asked whether the anxiety they were picking up was simply a general one. Might the actual accident be irrelevant? Did anyone who lived near a nuclear installation suffer considerable stress? Was whether or not that installation was damaged not the issue?

Baum and his associates at the University of Uniformed Health Services in Maryland compared four groups: Three Mile Island residents, people living near an undamaged power plant, people living near a more traditional coal-fired power plant, and people living more than twenty miles away from any power installations. Methods of testing for such anxieties are not models of scientific precision. The psychologists collected a number of self-report measures, basically questionnaires. Questionnaires ask subjects to rate on a scale of 1 to 5 or 1 to 7 how worried or elated, for example, they feel. These tests are inevitably subjective. Worse for objectivity, subjects knew what these studies were about and, in all likelihood, could guess what the desired result would be. In an attempt to be more objective they also used physiological tests. One of the substances that is secreted under stress is an enzyme called catechlamone; a high amount in the urine suggests that the sympathetic nervous system is aroused. Baum and his colleagues therefore studied how much catechlamone Harrisburg residents secreted.

The findings were intriguing. Seventeen months after the accident, Harrisburg people still reported significantly higher levels of depression and anxiety than any other group. Three Mile Island residents did not just outscore people who lived far from power stations or near coal-fired ones, they had far higher levels of depression and anxiety than people who lived near an undamaged power station. Being close to a power station, the study suggested, was not enough by itself to trigger these feelings.

Yet seventeen months after the accident it was clear that there were no gross health problems. There had been no upsurge in deaths. Deformed babies were not being born. In one sense nothing had happened. That is a very different scenario from Sellafield, where there is alleged to be a cluster of leukaemia cases. Yet, doctors on Three Mile Island knew they were dealing with a very real effect: their practice records showed that they were being consulted far more; their patients had more somatic problems and needed more medication than before.

Baum understood the nature of the puzzle. He wanted more objective proof of whether or not subjects had been changed. He therefore asked them to carry out two performance tests. The first required them to spot the number of figures embedded in pictures, a test a little like one of those cartoon quizzes which ask newspaper readers to ferret out of one picture ten objects beginning with S. The second test was a simple proof-reading test where subjects had to spot mistakes in a printed text. These may seem curious tests of depression and anxiety, but both require total concentration, and victims from other disasters often reported that they felt they had lost both motivation and concentration. Three Mile Island subjects did far less well than the others at both tests.

Baum also tested their urine, in samples taken over fifteen hours. The aim was to find whether the levels of contrisol, epinephrine and norepinephrine excreted were above average. These substances are associated with stress and the adrenal system. Again, the results were positive: the levels were significantly higher. Baum and his colleagues nevertheless are careful not to claim that residents of Three Mile Island are suffering from massive adrenal problems; the levels of stress are relatively mild, but the tests still showed unmistakable signs of stress.

These studies were done fairly soon after the disaster. They provided the basis for some legal actions and they encouraged Baum and others to speculate on whether the fact that there was someone to blame affected the way the victims perceived the disaster. Indeed, Baum went on to claim that the fact that there was an organization, Metropolitain Edison, with which residents could be angry, materially affected their reaction – a point to which I will return later.

Even though the results were not conclusive, psychologists did not abandon studying Three Mile Island residents. Scientif-ically, they formed too useful a sample to abandon. Second, there was the continuing question of whether or not Three Mile

Island was to be reopened. Metropolitain Edison constantly pressed for this to happen once the technical problems at the plant had been solved. The prospect alarmed local residents, who protested vigorously.

Finally, in 1986, there was discussion that the plant might be recommissioned, which led to a new series of studies. They showed that during the period preceding the recommissioning, local residents who had been in Harrisburg during the initial accident did suffer relapses of symptoms, rating themselves as more anxious and more depressed than before. Local doctors again reported a rise in the number of patients who wanted to see them. By now, as some of Baum's evidence showed, what mattered was not so much whether or not people had suffered in the original incident but how they viewed what had happened. The results often highlighted the fact that those who were more sceptical of government and official assurances felt more under stress.

Chernobyl

Ironically, in the midst of discussions on the reopening of Three Mile Island, a far worse radiation accident occurred. On 26 April 1986, the nuclear power station at Chernobyl came much closer to a meltdown than Three Mile Island ever had. It seemed that engineers had not just ignored basic safety procedures but that they had been experimenting with the system. A commission of inquiry eventually censured the chief engineer for running a series of experiments on the reactor and many of his senior staff for not putting a stop to his irresponsible behaviour.

In its official report to the International Atomic Energy Agency in Vienna, the Soviet Union did not specify what the purpose of the experiment was, merely reporting that operators were trying to work out how much electricity could be generated by a freewheeling turbine generator. With this in mind, they cut off the normal supply of steam to the turbine from the reactor as a deliberate act. As at Three Mile Island, Chernobyl had an emergency core cooling system. During the experiment, the operators tried to increase the flow of coolant through the reactor by using an extra pump. The additional water decreased the amount of steam generated. Pressure fell in the steam drum in which the water/stream mixture is collected before being led off to the turbine. The pressure in this drum controls the pressure in the coolant circuit, so the coolant pressure fell, a drop in pressure which should have triggered the emergency shut-down systems. At Three Mile Island, the pressure failed to do this because key valves had been closed during mainten-ance and no one had remembered the fact. At Chernobyl, the situation was different because it was intentional.

The build-up to the disaster was slow. At 01.00 on 25 April, operators decreased the output of reactor number four. At 13.05, when the reactor was producing 1,600 megawatts, elec-tricity generation was switched from turbine seven to turbine eight. The emergency core cooling system was shut down. For the rest of the day, the reactor's output of electricity went lower, going down to a mere thirty megawatts.

By 01.00 on 26 April, the control room managed to stabilize the amount of electricity produced at 200 megawatts. The reactor could not churn out more because the nuclear reaction inside was too low. From 01.03 to 01.07, more water was pumped into the coolant system round the reactor so that less steam was produced. Pressure in the steam drum decreased.

It was at 01.22 and thirty seconds that the experiment began to go badly wrong. The reaction level reached the point at which an emergency shut-down should have been started, but the control room, instead, continued with their experiment. Thirty-four seconds later, the stop control valve of turbine number eight was closed. The reactor now had absolutely no protection, a situation that was risky to the point of insanity.

At this point, in fact, Chernobyl's number four nuclear reactor and the number eight generator were working without any emergency core cooling system. In the next thirty-six seconds, it finally became clear to the control room that something had gone badly wrong. The control room chief ordered that all the emergency control rods should be slammed back into the reactor core. That should have stopped the nuclear reaction. It did not.

Instead, several seconds later, there was a bang. This was followed by an explosion, and a fireball and sparks blew out of the reactor. Part of this fireball landed in the machine room and started a fire. Radiation's effects had suddenly become visible.

Japanese nuclear engineers told *New Scientist* that they guessed the Chernobyl staff might have been trying out a way of compensating for problems in the emergency power supply that was used to start the core cooling system. In an old reactor like Chernobyl, commissioned in 1961, it was extremely risky to carry out these procedures without shutting down the reactor. The safety regulations, the Soviet report pointed out, were clear. The staff were, however, under orders from their chief to try this experimental procedure. The reason the staff had switched off the emergency shut-down system was that it might have interfered with their unauthorized experiment; it might have triggered a shut-down and stopped their technological games.

As at Three Mile Island, there was some delay in making public what had happened. By 21.00 on 26 April, the doses of gamma radiation in the nearby town of Pripyat were high, between 14 and 140 microrontgens an hour, and getting worse. By 7 A.M. the next day, the level was up to between 180 and 600 microrontgens an hour, as radioactive material which had blown out of the reactor landed back in the town. Yet the authorities did nothing for another seven hours. Leonid A. Ilyin, of the Soviet Academy of Medical Sciences, told the world's press that the evacuation delay was the result of the local authorities underestimating the radioactivity.

The evacuation procedure followed at Chernobyl was very different from that at Harrisburg largely because so few Russians have cars. Those who could packed on to trains for Moscow. Many made for Kiev. But the majority had to wait for a caravan of 1,100 buses to be assembled. In the end, 100,000 people were moved from an area thirty kilometres around the power station. Pripyat became a ghost town. Cars that had been near Chernobyl at the time received new licence plates and are banned, for ever, from going outside its contaminated territory.

In much of this book, I have argued that one of the major factors in disasters is that safety conflicts with profit. In a Communist society, in theory, profit is not a motive. Indeed, the formal instructions at Chernobyl emphasized the needs of safety: there was no question of skimping in order to satisfy shareholders. Yet this did not prevent the foolhardy experiments with radiation. No one has succeeded in explaining satisfactorily just why the Chernobyl workers took the risks they did. Official explanations were not so much anodyne as vague. One Soviet expert noted rather unsatisfactorily that the sequence of events leads to 'deep questions of interpretation about the man–machine interface'.

The casualties were very different from those at Three Mile Island. A number of the reckless technicians paid with their lives. Twenty-eight people died either from burns or from exposure to massive doses of radiation, estimated to be over 500 rads. (A safe year's exposure is to 0.025 rads, for people living near a power station – 5 rads for workers – according to the International Atomic Energy Commission.) Many of the dead were either workers at Chernobyl or the firemen who tried to bring the situation under control. All the dead had received doses of over 600 rads in their bone marrow. Two hundred and thirty-seven people developed radiation burns. It was estimated that fifty patients received more than 500 rads; 100 received between 300 to 500 rads and a large number received between 100 and 300 rads.

The Soviet authorities responded well to the emergency, according to an account in the *Journal of the American Medical Association* by Jack Geiger. Within twenty-four hours, 299 patients had been flown to Moscow's number six hospital. There doctors began the heartrending process of identifying those who might recover; these were the only ones lucky enough to get bone marrow transplants. The others were, as after battles, simply and unavoidably, left to die.

The impact of the disaster across Europe was enormous. It was reported that clouds of radiation were drifting across the continent; it was alleged that the Soviets were not telling the whole truth about the incident. *New Scientist* noted, however, that the reaction of much of the press was ill-informed and exaggerated; scare stories predominated. The public in the

West had suspected, since Three Mile Island, that nuclear authorities were not honest about the risks of nuclear energy, and the Soviets were known to hide their own disasters as shameful. The combination of these two pieces of justifiable scepticism provided fertile ground for panic. There were many signs of this immediately after Chernobyl. For example, it was suggested that milk would not be safe; stories claimed that Welsh hills were being inundated with radioactive fallout; lambs might not be safe to eat. In Princeton, two American doctors announced that there would be perhaps 40,000 cases of thyroid and 400,000 cases of cancer as a direct result of the accident.

Soviet health services set up a screening service for those who survived. Five thousand doctors and nurses went to the Chernobyl area or to help the evacuees. Eighteen thousand evacuees were sent for intensive tests. Psychological tests were also arranged for the Chernobyl engineers.

The studies of Hiroshima and Nagasaki had proved that high doses of radiation could produce a lifetime's suffering. But there has been considerable controversy as to the effects of lower doses. Did they have a proportionately lower effect? Or, beyond a certain point, did the radiation somehow wash out of the system? A US cancer specialist, Professor Robert Gale, flew to the Ukraine to help and said the accident would result in thousands of extra cancer cases. The Soviets reacted angrily to this, Leonid A. Ilyin riposting that Gale was an expert in a narrow field, that of bone marrow transplants, and was not an expert in the long-term effects of radiation exposure. Ilyin said – a little glibly, perhaps – that there was no risk of a rise in cancers.

Concerns about health were understandable, but the data did not unequivocally back them up. There were within a few months, indications that genetic damage would not be found: the Ukraine's Minister of Public Health, A. Romanenko, said that research showed that the abnormalities of pregnancy remained stable; they had not risen. The Ukraine Ministry of Health backed research to study women who lived in a thirty-kilometre radius round Chernobyl. The delivery statistics, the Russians claimed, were much as before. Ilyin suggested that it was only people directly exposed to the radiation, or those who were pregnant at the time, who ran risks of genetic abnormalities. Studies of the plant and animal life in the area also failed to come up with any major genetic changes. One reason for this was the fact that the main contamination agent was iodine 131, which has a short half-life: about two and a half months. It then fades away.

In the year after the explosion, there were considerable numbers of people who came from Kiev, worked for twelve hours and then rested for twelve hours at special rehabilitation centres where they underwent medical check-ups. According to Professor Alexandrovsky of the Serbsky Institute, the survivors also needed considerable psychological help, counselling much like that provided after the King's Cross fire. As a result, those who have returned to work stay in the area for only a few days. Usually, they are on duty for five days, after which they return to Kiev to rest for seven days before facing Chernobyl again.

Chernobyl was the worst radiation disaster in peacetime. It triggered, just as the incident at Three Mile Island had done, our underlying fears of radiation. The death figures were relatively small, the casualties equally so. The most visible effect was on the surrounding countryside, which was completely devastated and declared unsafe for habitation. Within a year, however, many of the evacuees returned – some much sooner. Yet Chernobyl received far more attention in the long run than the earthquake disaster in Armenia – an illustration of the power of radiation in our imagination.

The West praised the Soviet Union for being open about Chernobyl. To local people, however, this openness was not so evident three years on. First, it took almost a year before Soviet officials admitted that the bulk of the radiation had fallen to the north of Chernobyl on the Republic of Byelorussia, and that, as a result, nearly a fifth of the republic's land was contaminated.

The Soviet authorities have, nevertheless, undeniably been energetic. The thirty-six-acre site round Chernobyl was paved to prevent radioactive dust blowing across the countryside. One million cubic metres of topsoil, which had been contaminated, was taken away and buried. Vegetation has been planted to help bind new soil in place. Twenty-one thousand new houses and fifteen thousand new flats have been built, largely in a new town. Five million people receive medical check-ups regularly and 600,000 have been entered into a special databank which monitors chromosome abnormalities. Despite this, there continues to be evidence that local residents have no faith in these official actions. Their scepticism both is, and is not, unjust. Official smooth talk may be glib, but radiation itself provokes many fears. As at Three Mile Island, there is a tendency to think that governments will never reveal the full truth of a nuclear accident. Second, the invisible nature of radiation and the fact that its effects continue to destroy over the long term make it especially worrying. People never feel safe in their bodies and such anxiety is not irrational.

In July 1989, a semi-official British visit revealed the extent of local anxieties. Michael Barnes QC, the inspector in charge of an inquiry into whether or not to build a pressurized water reactor at Hinckley Point, wished to assess the case both for and against. He therefore visited Chernobyl, together with representatives of the main parties to the inquiry. These visitors found that there was still a great deal of local disquiet. Despite the five billion roubles spent (five billion pounds at official exchange rates) on clean-up operations, local people were irritated. They disliked the dismissive attitude of officials. In February 1989, for example, the fairly radical paper *Moscow News* carried an article which described congenital abnormalities in farm animals in Narodichi in Ukraine, some 100 kilometres from Chernobyl. Increasing health problems were also appearing. In April and May, there were reassuring official noises. Konstanin Gordyev, of the USSR Ministry of Public Health, accused *Moscow News* of being 'sensationalist', a dreadful sin in the USSR. There was, he said, no reason to be afraid because the evidence that radiation caused these deformities was poor. Increases in lip and mouth cancers were within normal fluctuations. Acidly, *Moscow News* pointed out that while this letter was being prepared, three villages were being evacuated, an unaccountable precaution if there was really nothing to worry about. The paper also carried a letter from

135 people in the Narodichi district who complained that their children's health had deteriorated, that they felt 'low and indisposed' and that headaches were a virtual epidemic. Doctors at far-off and grand Kiev, the capital of the Ukraine, made soothing noises to the effect that nothing was wrong. Physicians on the spot, however, knew better.

At the end of 1988, the authorities also decided to change the criteria for the amount of radiation that a person could absorb safely in a cumulative dose. The lifetime limit was reduced to 0.35 sieverts. This new limit was cautious and in line with new international standards. But it meant that twenty-five more villages had to be evacuated. In others, residents could hope to stay within this limit only if all the food they ate came from outside the Chernobyl area. They were given an extra 25 per cent in their wages plus an additional thirty roubles a month (large sums in the USSR) to pay for this more expensive food. Again, local people felt worried because they felt they had not been told the whole truth.

Four years after Chernobyl, new evidence collected by the Byelorussian Academy of Sciences suggests that the medical effects have turned out far worse than predicted. Doctors report that the number of chromosome abnormalities is increasing. They have risen by about 70 per cent since the accident. Major abnormalities, which have to be notified, have risen by about 50 per cent. In Mogilyov, an area which has had a high level of pollution, nine-year-olds are developing very slowly. On most measures of physical and intellectual growth, they are three years behind their physical age. This is a truly staggering finding.

Doctors are recording a rise in cancers of between a third and a quarter. Thyroid cancers especially are rising. Animal studies show a severe depression of the immune system. The Byelorussian Academy of Sciences notes that hypertension has increased. They claim this is partly due to radiophobia, fear of radiation, but there is also evidence of kidney damage. The Byelorussian Academy of Sciences issued an appeal for help to the international community. It made it clear that no one could yet know the final toll of the disaster.

* * *

The continuing anxieties at Three Mile Island and at Chernobyl reveal how hard it is to recover when people feel that they have been hit by a disaster which does not end neatly and visibly. Radiation has seeped into their bodies. It is embedded there for ever. Flames, floods, the jolts of air crashes can produce long-term psychiatric damage, but people involved in these soon know just how bad their physical injuries are. This knowledge enables them to fix a baseline from which to rebuild their lives. The victims of radiation, however, feel that they never know what the toll is; there is no point at which their disaster ends. Psychology here has a clear role to play, in offering not so much therapy as advice on how to cope.

It slowly became clear that the residents of Three Mile Island felt rather more helpless than average about their environment. As the stress problems persisted, psychologists began to wonder if different ways of coping influenced the level of stress. Baum and his colleagues therefore compared two different reactions. Some residents at Three Mile Island had tried to cope by adjusting their emotions. They did not expect to be able to do anything either about the continuing leaks or about plans to recommission the station, so instead they concentrated on letting their feelings out. They were determined not to be emotionally intimidated. They said what they felt. Baum and his colleagues labelled this emotional regulation, and compared it with problem-solving coping. The problem-solver is a tough-talking optimist. He, or she, is not content to fulminate against Metropolitain Edison and the authorities, and instead makes plans of action. He, or she, organizes and joins campaigns, becomes political, in short. In a situation like that at Three Mile Island, however, these demonstrations were unlikely to succeed.

The results of Baum's comparative study were clear-cut and perhaps unexpected. Those who used emotional strategies had far fewer stress-related symptoms. They reported far less depression and their urine analyses also suggested that they were less stressed. In a way this is sad, since clearly this strategy is unlikely to force any changes, but paradoxically, Baum and his colleagues believe the emotional strategy worked at Three Mile Island simply because it was the more realistic one. People felt they knew what was happening. They did not gear themselves up for actions that turned out always to be disappointing. They maintained, Baum suggested, a sense that they ran their lives. In the Three Mile Island case that meant they were politically apathetic and complained. Inaction worked best, Baum claimed, for psychological health. This is a curious finding and in other disasters, the issue of control over one's environment is totally different. After the *Piper Alpha* disaster, for instance, workers' attitudes to oil safety changed drastically. Interestingly, few people seemed to have exerted their right to a simple option: moving off Three Mile Island.

Another question that Baum and his colleagues examined concerned blame. Again, their findings appear paradoxical. Much of the literature on emotional loss emphasizes that victims have a right to be angry, they need to flare up at those who hurt them. In general, psychological research favours people who take responsibility for themselves; in the running of their lives, they take credit for success and blame for failure. One psychological theory divides people into those who feel that the 'locus of control' for their lives depends on their actions, and those who believe it depends on what outside forces and other people do to them. Individuals with an 'inner' locus of control expect to determine their fate and control their own lives. One would expect a disaster, therefore, to be all the more shattering for them.

Baum found that there were few residents who blamed themselves for the actual incident, but he used his ways of coping test to study the degree of self-blame people felt. In industrial injuries, those who blame themselves often take longer to recover. At Three Mile Island, however, the results were different: people who tended to blame themselves in general suffered less stress about the situation. Baum's method did not, however, allow him to know what people were blaming themselves for. It seems merely to have been a general personality characteristic. He argues, though, that it also highlights the fact that people need to feel in control of their environment; you blame yourself for things going wrong only if you believe your actions can affect events. These findings are not conclusive, but they do show how much we struggle to feel in control of our lives and our environments. Natural disasters are so huge that these rules cease to apply. They are events beyond our ken, acts of God. In technological disasters, the situation is more accessible. We therefore try to reassert control, either through talking about our feelings or blaming ourselves even if it is hard to see how any of our actions could have prevented the disaster.

Both Three Mile Island and Chernobyl were disasters that were to have a huge political impact, largely because they illustrated the nuclear fears we all share. The continued stress at Three Mile Island, even though there were relatively few 'real' reasons for it once the emergency was declared over, reveals how deep those fears are. The Chernobyl story is far from over and will not be for another quarter-century at least. That is when, according to official estimates, it will be safe for people to live in Pripyat again – the optimistic ones, that is!

5
Piper Alpha

'I was telephoned by one of my son's friends. He said there was a fire on *Piper Alpha* and he advised me to watch television,' Eric Woodcock said. His only son, John, was one of the 167 men to die in the worst ever oil industry disaster, a disaster that made both survivors and the bereaved furious because they felt it was needless. Eric Woodcock added: 'There is a big difference between man-made and natural disasters. Natural disasters lead to much greater loss of life. But in some ways, natural disasters are different because the victims themselves say, "These things happen." In the case of a man-made disaster, it isn't one of these things. This disaster should never have happened.'

Risk is part of the routine in some industries. In *The Right Stuff*, Tom Wolfe's essay on how the Americans got men to the moon, he showed how cool the astronauts were about the dangers they ran. Wolfe invented the concept of righteousness: the righteous flyer took risks with grace; he never complained. To remain silent in the face of such hardships was the mark of the true man. Supreme macho never showed off. The test pilot, Chuck Yaeger, was the most righteous of all the early test pilots. He was the first man to break the sound barrier and did it with a dislocated shoulder. The day of the crucial flight, he could not tell anyone he had a dislocated shoulder because it would have resulted in his being taken off the flight. Righteousness meant never admitting that the risks were so high that your next flight might be your last. Disasters like when Gus Grissom's Mercury flight blew up on the pad at Cape Canaveral in 1965 were handled with constant grace under constant pressure, Wolfe noted. Wolfe argued that the Apollo astronauts radiated the right stuff more than any other group. In his glorification of American razzamataz, Wolfe played down the extent to which similar attitudes prevailed in other air forces. The RAF, for instance had its heroes during the 1940 Battle of Britain, when most pilots knew that their life expectancy was extremely short. Few survived more than thirty missions and yet many volunteered to do more than that number.

The right stuff, Wolfe suggested, could be found only where men were tested to the limits. This is an elitist view. Miners are much less glamorous and well paid than test pilots, but working-class tradition, at least, has long pictured them as heroes. They might be forced to work down the pits because there was no other way of making a living open to them, but they could transcend their situation. They had the nerve to do what weaker men quaked at. There was right stuff in the seams as well as in the stars.

The industrial revolution created a whole class of such dangerous jobs. When disasters occur in such industries, they are terrible but not totally unexpected. Experience taught the wives of miners and sailors, for instance, to fret because their loved ones were never wholly safe. The battle between the needs of safety and the needs of profit is an ancient one.

I have argued so far that we need to be aware of the differences between different types of disaster. No one expects an earthquake to happen to them and, despite the fact that people have been aware of the obvious dangers since 1906, the year of the great San Francisco earthquake, people subsequently flocked to live there. After the 1989 quake, few left. On trains and aeroplanes, especially since the travel industries constantly tell us how safe they are, we are encouraged not to think of safety when we step on them. In many technological sites like Chernobyl and Three Mile Island, workers may know, rationally, that they are in a risky environment but they do not seem to feel it. Indeed workers in power stations, nuclear and otherwise, often speak of them as rather boring places to work.

This perception of tedium sets them apart from other environments, perceived as being high-risk. Duckhams' *Great Pit Disasters* has spelt out just how dangerous the conditions were in the nineteenth century and how after an 1812 disaster, in which ninety-two colliers were killed, pit owners refused any

inquiry. Even today, miners are unable to forget how dangerous coal-mining is. The literature of mining portrays the miner
both as hero and as a victim of the poverty that drives him
underground but, here too, he is celebrated as brave enough to
do his job.

Arthur Scargill, President of the National Union of Mine-
workers, made his early reputation through the effective pres-
entation of the NUM's case at the inquiry that followed the
Lofthouse Colliery disaster of 1969. The pit collapsed and
seventy-two people died. Scargill discovered old pit plans which
had revealed that the particular seam at Lofthouse was peril-
ous: Coal Board engineers knew the risks. The Coal Board,
however, either forgot these warnings or simply ignored them.
Scargill argued that miners accepted the dangers underground,
but only if everything possible was done to ensure their safety;
they did not want to take more risks than absolutely necessary.
It was hardly a contentious point.

Increasingly, in some pit areas, mining is no longer the only
work available. Those who work in them have skills that could
be marketable elsewhere. Why, then, do they choose high-risk
businesses?

Psychologists have identified certain personalities as being
interested in taking risks. These 'characters' like the edge of
danger. Typically, they are extroverts, seeking new stimula-
tions. It has even been argued that these people's brain biology
is different: the extrovert brain easily habituates; it gets used
quickly to incoming stimuli sensations. Extroverts therefore
need a flow of novel stimuli in order to keep their brain biology
at a high state of arousal or, to put it more picturesquely, to
keep the cells bubbling. Risky environments offer that stimulus.
This is a highly speculative area, but there are also certain
theories, like Michael Apter's Reversal Theory, which claim
that certain individuals crave 'arousal jogs'. They tend to go in
for high-risk sports, certainly, and for some risky occupations.
The oil industry, with its macho image, is seen as rather more
glamorous than most. It is not on a par with being an astronaut
but, as Tom Wolfe might have put it, 'semi-righteous'.

Originally the oil industry involved little of this glamour of
braving the elements. Petroleum was a matter of wells and

dollars, money not macho. Writing about the foundation of British Petroleum, Henry Longhurst explained how William Knox D'Arcy created the Middle East oil industry. Legend had it that D'Arcy wandered the deserts in search of oil. The truth was more pedestrian: 'D'Arcy, a plump figure with a walrus moustache and avuncular expression, never in all his life set foot in Persia.' His greatest daring was to send off, at his expense, Alfred Marriott, a cousin of his secretary, to Persia early in 1901, 'to negotiate for a concession, one of his more explicit instructions being that he was in no circumstances to dispense any cash'.

There were plenty of political intrigues involved in obtaining these concessions, but few physical risks. Oil production became far more dangerous when it moved out to sea – especially the North Sea. By the 1960s, it seemed worthwhile to try to extract gas and oil from depths greater than 300 feet, depths that had once seemed beyond reach.

As soon as oil exploration in the North Sea was mooted, governments both in Britain and Scandinavia tried to lay down reasonable safety standards for rigs and platforms. The oil companies played a clever political hand from the start. They were naturally all in favour of safety, but in practice, they lobbied for the safety standards imposed on them not to be too stringent. It was a question, they argued, of being realistic. Total safety would be a total disincentive, meaning no exploration, no oil, no profits, no jobs and no taxes. Investigations into all the disasters in the North Sea have suggested that they occurred as a result of this conflict between safety and profit.

There were a number of disasters in the North Sea from the start of drilling. In 1974 the *Ecofisk* disaster led to some tightening of standards of safety. In 1980 the Norwegian drilling platform, the *Alexander Kielland*, twisted off one of its legs and buckled into the sea, killing 126 people. Positioning the accommodation block on top of the actual working area of the platform had vastly increased the number of deaths, a Norwegian inquiry found in 1981. After that, Norwegian platforms had to have separate accommodation and production areas. The British government accepted the conclusions of the *Kielland* inquiry in theory but did nothing about introducing

comparable standards for UK platforms and rigs. The unions
did try to make an issue of that failure but met with little
success.

The arrangements for supervising health and safety sparked
anxieties in the unions from the start of the exploration of the
North Sea. Under British law, there are two kinds of installations in the North Sea: drilling rigs and platforms. A rig is used
for exploration and can move under its own steam. It is
therefore considered a vessel. Its master has the sweeping
powers that a captain traditionally has. Safety on ships comes
under the Department of Transport, whom the unions accept
as impartial. A very different situation, however, exists with
platforms: they are not mobile, but are fixed structures bolted
down on the sea bed. Consequently the Department of Transport has no jurisdiction over them. They are licensed and
inspected by the Department of Energy.

After the disaster on *Piper* had happened, the Scottish Trade
Unions Council emphasized an old argument: that giving
supervision to the Department of Energy made it much less
rigorous. Duncan Henderson, the Scottish TUC industrial
officer, told me that many people who work in the oil industry
spend part of their careers working in the Department of
Energy. The oil companies, he alleged, like to get their men in
the department so that they can learn how the corridors of
power function. As a result, the links between the companies
and the department which is supposed to supervise them are
very close, too close, in Henderson's view.

In theory, each installation has to be inspected every six
months, but it is traditional for inspectors to arrange visits in
advance. The manager of a platform therefore has the time to
make everything look good so that when an inspector calls, he
will see nothing irregular. Dangerous practices may be suspended for the period of the inspection. To obviate this
possibility, safety inspections clearly need to be unexpected,
deliberately designed to catch things as they are ordinarily.
Henderson alleges that this is precisely what does not happen.

The Department of Energy does not accept these criticisms,
although the dangers of the North Sea were evident week in
and week out to those who travelled and worked it. Initially,

however, it was assumed that the most risky part of the job was going to the rigs and platforms by helicopter. Eric Woodcock remembers his son ringing, like many men, to say that he had arrived safely. Such an attitude made sense, as there have been many helicopter crashes, including the occasion when a Chinook helicopter ditched into the sea causing the deaths of forty-seven people.

Over the years, as the North Sea businesses settled down, some safety rules were established. Anyone going to work on a rig or platform had to have taken a course in survival in the sea; all rigs and platforms had to have specially designed survivor suits which increased survival time in the sea to perhaps forty-five minutes. Information about the risks run on the rigs, however, was certainly not publicized. There were, for instance, two incidents on *Piper Alpha* itself before the fire. In 1982 one man died and in 1984 there was a blaze which caused the platform to be shut down. The Department of Energy investigations into both incidents were never published. In the first week of July 1988, there were two incidents in the North Sea: there was a blast in some storage tanks in the Shetlands and on 5 July, there was a fire on another platform, the *Brent Alpha*.

Survivors said later that in the two days before the fire on *Piper Alpha* they had smelt something strange. It seemed to them eventually that there were problems in the equipment separating high value and low value gases. In the days before *Piper Alpha* exploded, the pattern of production was changed. On 3 July, the *Piper* platform switched over to burning off the gas. Oil production continued normally. The workers did not get written instructions on how to operate under this method, despite the fact that it had been used for only sixty days in the whole history of *Piper*, after the explosion in 1984.

On 6 July, much maintenance work was going on round the gas condensate pumps. These pumped a mix of natural gas liquids either back into the main oil line or into the reservoir. The events that followed were curiously similar to those at Bhopal. A technician removed the pressure safety valve (psv) on pump A, stuffing the open pipe ends shut with special flanges. After the valve had been serviced, however, it could not be put back immediately because the crane required for this was in use on another operation. A new shift came on at 18.00. They were not told that the psv was not in the pump, so they thought everything was in normal working order. For the next five and three-quarter hours nothing peculiar happened. Then, at 21.45, the gas processing system began to react oddly: the gas flare on the south west of the rig began to roar, the flames much bigger than usual. At 21.50, the condensate pump B tripped.

At 21.58 there was a huge leak of gas and a violent explosion in module C. The psv that should have shut down oil production was blown away in that explosion. Occidental's operatives at Flotta noticed that there was a drop in the flow of oil production, but not an absolute cessation. This led them to conclude that there had been a production hitch – not a catastrophe. In fact, oil continued to flow into the area of the broken valve and so kept on fuelling the explosion. This led to the many subsequent explosions which shook, and broke, *Piper Alpha*.

On the platform itself, it was almost at once clear that there was a major incident. The control room filled with smoke and dust. Two of the men inside were injured. Alarmingly, all the platform's communications systems were devastated. The many back-up systems did not survive the first explosion. There was therefore no way to give warnings or orders. Astonishingly, fire-fighting equipment was not really available. As there was diving going on, the controls for the containment systems which would isolate a fire – and that included the fire pumps – were not on automatic, a routine precaution with divers in the water. But the manual controls in the control room had been destroyed, *Piper Alpha* faced a fire with virtually no usable fire-fighting equipment. There was a tiny amount of water in the system but, ironically, no means, in the middle of the sea, of getting any more water to douse the fire.

Men poured out of the cinema, where they had been watching *Carrie*. People ran to put on their survival suits; they improvised while sticking, initially, to the safety drill. Most made for the muster point at the gallery. The heat was already intense.

Mark Reid, a survivor, poured juice from the drinks machine

over his head to stave off the heat. He was badly affected by the confusion and shouting, later telling the inquiry that he had panicked: 'I shouted, "Is there anyone here from Bawden drillings?" I thought I was going to die and I wanted to be with somebody I knew.' Men were squashing tomatoes over themselves in a desperate attempt to keep cool.

At 22.22, there was the largest explosion of the disaster: the other gas pipelines connected to *Piper* blew up. It was this massive fireball that later dominated the TV pictures. It billowed out, a bizarrely beautiful crimson, across the sea. It looked, and according to survivors, was, a veritable inferno.

The support ship near the rig, the *Tharos*, had to move further away to avoid being set on fire. The jib of the crane on *Piper* melted in the intense heat. One of the small boats from the *Sandhaven*, which was picking up survivors underneath the platform, was destroyed. Only one of the men aboard, Ian Letham, survived. The sea itself was aflame.

Only sixty men had been on duty when the fire started; the rest of the crew were either in the cinema or on their way to bed. Dave Lambert, from Thornaby in Cleveland, was dropping off to sleep when he heard a bang. 'I thought it was metal dropping against metal. The operator came in and said there was a fire.' Lambert looked around the cabin. It had four doors and each of them was spouting flames. 'I was trapped for about half an hour. I thought I was dead. I thought I had had it.'

Men clambered out on to various parts of the rig. About seven of them, wearing survival suits, made for the helicopter pad, where they screamed for help. John Maxwell, from Belfast, who was on the *Tharos*, guessed they thought they stood a better chance of being saved if they stayed put on the pad: help could surely come. Then, the whole rig was rocked by a further explosion. Maxwell remembered: 'A fireball shot across the helicopter pad and the men disappeared.' He supposed they must have been rocketed 200 feet down into the sea. No survivors were found from the pad.

In the accommodation module, windows and emergency doors were cracking in the flames. Men shouted into radios that they needed breathing apparatus. Those who could grab towels dipped them in anything wet to make breathing easier.

The situation was chaotic. Reeling under the storm of secondary explosions, the rig began to tilt. It was hard to see the sea.

On the *Tharos*, Maxwell then saw a group of young men clambering first on to a derrick and then down again. It looked to him as if they were trying to get to a point where they could leap safely into the sea. But the intense heat beat them back and he felt agonized and helpless, watching them. For many men, like Roger Carey, there was no choice: 'It was a case of fry and die or jump and die. There was no time to ask.' Carey acted on his instincts, leapt over seventy feet into a sea he could not really see – and lived.

In theory, North Sea workers are trained to cope with such an emergency. No one can work on an oil rig or platform if they do not have a survival training certificate. Mr Sheridan, a square-jawed man in a blue blazer, is a deputy director of the Offshore Survival School at Aberdeen. He knew how frightened many of the men would have been. Fifteen per cent of those who work in the North Sea cannot swim, and he told me, 'They aren't the roughie-toughie tigers that the image is.' The training the survival school provides is fairly brief. A course consists of three days' training in basic survival. There are class differences even here: executives have a longer course, four days on actual survival, and then five days fire-fighting at Montrose. Sheridan explained that executives used the extra time 'learning how to lead a fire-fighting team'.

Sheridan took me to the large pool which is the centre of the teaching. Here, men are taught how to jump into the sea in the proper way, holding their noses and curling themselves into something of a ball. Sheridan pointed out there were a number of men who lose their bottle even in the safety of the pool. They shy away even from the tall three-metre board. He believes that many of those who survived *Piper Alpha* did so because they remembered to jump in the correct fashion. He added that there was proof of the efficacy of the training in previous disasters like the Chinook helicopter ditch. There, the crew all had on their survival suits and 'subconsciously they used their training because they were zipping them up'.

Once people jumped, however, they found themselves in a hostile sea. It is calculated that, without a survival suit, the average person is likely to survive five minutes in the North Sea. Many on *Piper* did get into their suits, but some did not: there turned out to be a shortage of suits. There were, in theory, enough lifeboats but there was not time to launch a single one.

Those who survived the jump into the sea often found themselves confronting harrowing sights. Edward Amaria of Alnwick saw a rescue boat with at least nine people on board go up in flames. 'There was nothing we could do except gasp in horror. As we looked back at the rig from the dinghy that had picked us up, all we could see were bodies silhouetted against the flames.' Maxwell on the *Tharos* described the scene as appalling.

The rescue mission was slow to get started – partly because it was not immediately clear ashore how serious the disaster was. The Cullen Inquiry paid tribute to the emergency services but did note that there were delays.

For those who had managed to get off the *Piper* there was now a long ordeal in the water. Many lasted longer than normal largely because they had survivor suits, but the inquiry heard that there were many men in the sea without suits. Survivors tried desperately to make for the Z ships, the little boats attached to the support ship, but many were left in the sea and some had been injured as they jumped.

For over an hour, no helicopter appeared on the scene as a result of some confusion about the Mayday signals. When the first helicopter arrived, it did not provide an overly sympathetic service. There were seven badly injured people on one Z boat, and the helicopter winched down an airman to take off those who needed emergency medical care. Ed Punchard recalls, in his book *Piper Alpha*, that the winchman said: 'We're already topped up with dead bodies so I hope you haven't got too many.'

The oil business has changed much of Aberdeen, though the city, full of buildings made of grey granite, retains its ancient, rather dour, character. It is a very old port: lorries carry slogans that proclaim they belong to the Shore Porters Society, founded in 1498 and still in business. Archie Robb, the deputy director

of social work for Grampian and the man who tried to co-
ordinate some of the disaster after-care, explained that Aberdeen was a city used to maritime disasters, 'and the people here
feel it's a problem for them to take care of'. They therefore
resented the suggestion that the city could not cope on its own.

There were some curious similarities to other rescue operations. When Punchard finally got ashore, he learned that they
had not been getting a stream of survivors. He wanted to
telephone his wife, because he was desperately worried about
how she would feel, yet when he asked to use a telephone, he
was not allowed to do so. First, he had to see a doctor, and
only when the doctor declared him fit could he tell his wife that
he was not dead. It was a repeat of what had happened to Prinz
and the others in the Dutch hijackings.

In Scotland, the work of a coroner is done by the Procurator
Fiscal, who uses the police as his inquiry agency. *Piper Alpha*
might have been 100 miles from the British mainland, but it
nevertheless came under the jurisdiction of the police of its
home port. The first two tasks were to log the bodies and
inform the relatives. Grampian has a small police force of not
more than 1,000 men and has a policy that all deaths are dealt
with by the CID. Superintendent Ritchie of this force explained
how they started to handle the job the Procurator Fiscal gave
them. To cope with the bodies, Ritchie explained, they took
over a hangar at the airport: 'We have contingency plans but,
at the beginning, a nice way of putting it is that everything is
very confusing. But hours into it, certainly days into it, it isn't.'
They brought all the remains to the hangar, a grisly business,
Ritchie noted: 'Many of the first batch of bodies that came to
us, about ten to twenty, were self-identifying. They all had ID
cards or they had survival suit numbers. You could tell from
documentation who they were. We had colleagues identify
them where possible, in order to prevent relations from going
to a hangar that was none too savoury a place.' The bodies that
were recovered later, however, could not be identified visually.

The police found that their instincts clashed with social work
theory. The police wanted to protect relatives from seeing the
bodies but social workers said families wanted to see the
corpses. The police recommended that they do so only 'under

very controlled circumstances with a doctor or social worker there'. The condition of the bodies would be a great shock to the relatives. Dealing with the emergency was a shock for police officers themselves. Ritchie said, 'We were very conscious of our own stress from the start. As a way of minimizing it, we decided to rotate staff who were doing the physical body handling. They did it for a maximum of five days.'

Most of the bodies were not recovered. That was to make difficulties for some of the survivors but it also meant that the police could not finish their task. Later, Occidental decided to transport the accommodation module (in which there were 122 bodies) to Flotta in the Orkneys. Ritchie had just asked for volunteers to cope with handling these bodies, and he had found that many of the men who had been on the initial details said that they would do it again. When I first talked to Ritchie, he was making detailed plans for this operation, as the module was just about to be lifted off the sea bed by a giant crane.

The police and hospitals are geared for emergencies, but in one way *Piper Alpha* was odd: few of those who survived were badly injured. Only two of the sixty-three survivors had major burns, and some survivors walked back home still in something of a state of shock but physically fit.

On the night of 6–7 July there was a great deal of confusion. Relief agencies did not properly co-ordinate their activities. The Red Cross were heavily present in the lobbies of the hostels and, according to some social workers, claimed the right to treat survivors even though few had injuries that required much first aid. Disputes broke out about which agency had the prior right to offer care.

Good liaison between agencies at the site of a disaster seems very hard to achieve, perhaps because there is no clear structure of command, everyone simply piling in. Allegations of disputes between agencies were also made after Lockerbie. There, with so many dead and remains scattered, relatives who visited the site needed help with the harrowing process of identifying bodies. In a letter to the *Guardian*, the Committee of the Lockerbie families noted: 'We were left feeling that the handling of the relatives of those killed at Lockerbie was for the most part callous, inept and cruel. Such preparations as were made to care for the relatives were largely in the hands of Pan Am.' Many relatives felt extremely uncomfortable with that. They were angry at Pan Am and a few suspected that what they said could conceivably be noted and later used by Pan Am in any litigation.

The lack of any national co-ordinated plan for dealing with disasters can muddle the way emergency services co-operate. Part of the problem is that usually the most powerful welfare agency present at any disaster, social services, is not geared to handling large-scale emergencies. It is essentially an individual service. It also takes a certain period of time for most social services departments to respond. Grampian Social Services were typical. At first there was considerable confusion and resentment about the way the Red Cross behaved. Within twenty-four hours, the social services department set up round-the-clock helplines, and contacted social work departments in Bradford – who had dealt with the football ground's fire – and Kent (who had dealt with the Zeebrugge disaster). Grampian also realized that they were dealing with victims whose families lived in different areas of the country, from Somerset in the south to the highlands of the north. They contacted them. As a result of the experiences in Zeebrugge and Bradford, Grampian decided on an assertive policy: they would not wait for the families to contact them with problems; rather, they would offer their services. In the first week, this meant that it was all hands to the pump: everyone worked on *Piper Alpha* victims. After a week, four workers were assigned to what came to be known as the outreach team, and an additional eight workers were assigned part-time to it.

Anne Bone, who led the outreach team, claimed later that the basic philosophy succeeded. Bereaved families and survivors did often specify the help they wanted when they were asked. About 70 per cent of families responded. Often, the help that was required was information rather than counselling. What would be the procedures for compensation, for instance? Bone noted, almost with pride, that many of the families they helped had never before called in any social workers. That would affect their response. Many of the survivors did not perceive themselves as helpless. The literature tends to emphasize psychological problems, but some of the emotions survivors felt were constructive, a source of energy.

Ed Punchard resolved that the anger he felt would be put to positive use: he would campaign for better safety precautions. Punchard and a number of other survivors lobbied Members of Parliament. He talked to unions. He joined a delegation that went to see Cecil Parkinson, then the Secretary of State for Energy, to argue for better safety conditions. Despite this commitment, Punchard found he could not escape the psychological symptoms: he found that he was often frightened. A week after the explosion, he heard a loud bang and dived under the bedclothes in a state of panic. Weeks later, he would find himself remembering things that had happened on *Piper Alpha* and 'at times an awful feeling of dread would sweep over me'. Despite his commitment to seeking reform, he found himself becoming listless and decided to seek the help of a psychiatrist. Other survivors also found themselves in something close to despair. Many found loud noises triggered flashbacks of the night of the explosion. The explosion kept recurring in their heads.

After *Piper Alpha*, there was a particular reason for anger among the bereaved families and survivors. In a great glow of publicity, Armand Hammer, the chairman of Occidental, arrived in Aberdeen. Hammer is an historic figure: he met Lenin, and helped organize early contacts between America and the Soviet Union after the 1917 Revolution. In his autobiography, Hammer cuts the figure of an international statesman of the oil industry. He was not a little man and, in the aftermath, he did not behave as a little man: he promised that all Occidental workers affected would get £100,000. Everyone assumed this meant that all those on the platform would get £100,000. But it did not: only those who were directly employed by Occidental would automatically receive that sum. Only thirty-one of those killed on the rig had been direct employees, and they had been insured for that sum by the company. The contract workers would not necessarily get that. The claims are still being settled and, certainly, in the first months, there was no sign of contract workers getting any such grand sums; they had, in effect, become second-class citizens – something they bitterly resented.

The variety of legal and psychological problems in the wake of *Piper Alpha* had practical consequences because it was an accident at work. This made it different from both King's Cross and Clapham. Many survivors felt that they could never contemplate working on rigs again; the dangers seemed too extreme. Often, families of survivors were unhappy about the prospect of the men returning. There was also a knock-on effect on workers who had not been on *Piper Alpha*. Recruiting for North Sea jobs became difficult. Deciding not to go back on to the rigs meant that a number of survivors faced unemployment. Anne Bone found some wanted to retrain. This had echoes of Zeebrugge, after which nearly all the seamen involved who worked for P&O abandoned seafaring as a career. A year after *Piper Alpha*, of the sixty-three survivors, very few were still working at sea in the oil industry.

According to Ed Punchard, the oil companies, despite all their publicized concern to improve safety, did not exactly approve of criticism being made. Punchard himself was contacted by many diving companies anxious to get him to state that their gear had not malfunctioned. Unions have also suggested that some of those who spoke out about safety conditions were subsequently victimized by potential employers.

After Occidental announced their 'generous' offer of £100,000, there was considerable effort to get families to settle. Scottish lawyers argued that they should not do so, because compensation claims in America would be significantly larger than in the UK. (The same problem emerged at the Bhopal disaster.) The Scottish lawyers' co-ordinating group found, however, that many families simply did not want to face a long process of litigation. Social workers discovered that it was the slightly less central relatives who were most at risk: girlfriends, co-habitees and ex-wives, because often, they had been dependent on the men who had died but had no official status. As a result, it was much harder for them to establish claims – especially if their men had been working for sub-contractors.

The nature of the disaster left one particularly nasty problem unresolved for months: the unrecovered bodies. At first, the accommodation module sank to the bottom of the sea. It was then lifted from the foot of the sea bed in a well-publicized operation. Then it was towed to the Orkney Islands at Flotta. Ritchie sent policemen to supervise and to identify the bodies. From the planning stage, he asked for counselling help for the police who would be involved.

Experts on bereavement often stress the need to find the body of someone who has died. When the accommodation module was towed to the Orkneys and lifted, the authorities wanted that to mark the end of the tragedy. Nevertheless, thirty-one bodies of the *Piper* victims remained unaccounted for. John Woodcock is one of those who are missing. It hurts his family deeply that the search for the bodies has been abandoned. Eric Woodcock explained that the families travelled to Westminster to lobby Parliament, and argues that, even there, concern for profit overrode safety factors. The families wanted Occidental to carry out extensive searching at the *Piper* site, but both the company and the Department of Energy argued that to do so would put divers at risk. 'Divers have disagreed with that,' Woodcock pointed out. The search was not continued, however, and the families remain extremely bitter.

The experiences of the *Piper* families were well publicized within the tight-knit group that comprises Scottish welfare agencies. Yet, in the matter of how to handle bodies, this experience did not help the relatives of the dead at Lockerbie. When relatives heard that the flight had crashed, they rushed to Lockerbie. The UK families of Flight 103 said in a statement: 'Every conceivable obstacle was put in the way of allowing us to see the bodies. Some of us had to turn up with solicitors to gain access. The police tell us [in June] that they had been advised by a hospital [unnamed by note] that they should not allow the dead to be seen by their relatives; if this is true the advice was wholly mistaken.' In addition, the families of UK Flight 103 noted that the death certificates were mysteriously and upsettingly timed a day or two after the disaster. One man reached the crash scene to find that wreckage was being collected while bodies were 'apparently ignored'. All this added to their distress.

In all the disasters covered, there have been varying degrees of psychological trauma and anger. Many of the survivors continue to bear psychological scars. Many, like Brian Barron from the *Piper Alpha* disaster, describe themselves as changed men. They are much more irritable than they were. They have lost their old willingness to go out and socialize. Brian Barron said that all kinds of things had started to go wrong, even in his marriage. Mrs Barron agreed her husband was not the man he was before the disaster. Ed Punchard claimed that the main effect on him was to have become obsessed with establishing the cause of the accident. He had also suffered psychologically, but he was mainly concerned to fight for better safety standards so that there would be no more *Piper Alpha*s – a hard job.

Oil companies were confident enough politically to be frank about the equation between profit and safety. Basil Butler, chairman of British Petroleum, made a speech to the Institute of Petroleum in Glasgow on 13 October 1988. He said: 'Everything has an economic cost. And if safety measures were to rule out entirely the risks which are inherent in extracting oil from a province like the North Sea – which is in any case impossible – then operations would have to cease. We have to draw a balance between our expenditure and the levels of safety we achieve. It is as simple, and as complex, as that.'

Butler's comments were made as work started on raising the accommodation module from the sea bed at Flotta. The speech caused a row, since it appeared insensitive. To many of the *Piper Alpha* survivors, it was more than that: they saw it as a warning from the oil companies to the government to the effect that drastic safety measures would lead to the end of production. If too much were required, the companies would shut down the oil field. The oil companies denied that this was a fair interpretation but, after *Piper*, the survivors were understandably suspicious.

Other business organizations, like the Association of Diving Contractors, seemed to recognize that safety arrangements were not adequate. The traditional manner of inspection, for example, was not good enough. Jim Morrison, their chairman, told a conference in Aberdeen that 'top management strategy seems aimed at reducing cost without regard to medium-term implications or even to short-term cost-effectiveness'. Morrison argued that paying a diving company a lump sum for an inspection was 'fundamentally flawed', commenting sardonically that one would not pay a doctor a lump sum.

The determination to effect change is perhaps the most interesting aspect of *Piper*. In many ways it is rather unexpected: the campaign has continued for well over eighteen months with considerable sophistication. There was a stoppage of work for a number of hours on all Scottish rigs and platforms on the anniversary of the disaster in July 1989. It was made clear that the stoppage was not just a question of respect for the dead: it was supposed to bring pressure for safety reforms.

This emphasis on pressuring the oil industry to effect reforms has led, at least, to a public debate on oil safety. The Department of Energy has finally been forced to publish its internal document on the 1984 *Piper* explosion, although it was embarrassed by the revelation that the department had actually asked Occidental itself to compile the report. The company at fault was, in effect, judging itself. The *Piper* families and the Scottish TUC both point to this as an example of the over-close relationship that exists between oil companies and the government. There is now a review of safety arrangements in progress from the Department of Energy.

It seems to me that the survivors of *Piper*, like Punchard, could contribute to that review, because they are both highly trained and highly motivated. It is not surprising they are keen to do so: it is a means by which they could take control over their lives again. They could use the disaster and try to make sense of what had happened to them to help others. This impulse is not just commendably altruistic, but useful.

In other disasters, like that at King's Cross, this has not been possible, largely because those affected were not experts. In aviation disasters, it might be possible but it is hard: pilots who work for particular airlines are unlikely to blow the whistle on their employers. The Institute of Aviation Medicine at Farnborough, however, does operate a scheme whereby pilots can give anonymous details of near misses and accidents, a scheme which has led to many near disasters being logged and studied. But confidentiality prevails; no one is asked, usually, to give names or flight numbers. With *Piper*, the survivors have made practical recommendations about how to improve inspection techniques, about the design of platforms and about survival training. They have named names. The problem has been to translate their commitment and knowledge into action.

Eric Woodcock noted that the group of *Piper* families was determined that there should be justice done. He wants to see the company prosecuted. I spoke to him soon after the decision to prosecute P&O for corporate manslaughter at Zeebrugge. He was not encouraged, however. 'We haven't got anywhere. That's partly due to the difference in judicial procedures here in Scotland. There is no inquest. There's no forum by which the next of kin can make a representation to the coroner. There is a fatal accident inquiry.' By justice, Woodcock does not just mean reasonable compensation for victims and their dependants, but action to improve safety.

There were problems concerning the anniversary of *Piper*. Families of the thirty-one men whose bodies had not been recovered were invited by Occidental to travel out to the *Piper* site to pay their respects. Many families felt that Occidental should make it possible for all families to travel out there, and asked why some were especially privileged. Woodcock was concerned that there might not be room for everyone at the Kirk of St Nicholas for the memorial service. It was another sign of the tension and insensitivity that many felt Occidental had shown that a row should also develop about a municipal memorial to the dead. Aberdeen Town Council decided to provide a rose garden, but a garden which would not be dedicated exclusively to the dead of *Piper*; other victims would also be remembered. In the rose garden there would be a sculpted monument. Woodcock explained that they had received contributions to the memorial fund from about two-thirds of the sub-contractors. The one company that declined to contribute, by July 1989, was Occidental itself. It justified its curious decision, Eric Woodcock said, by claiming there should not be a proliferation of memorials. Occidental have countered such criticisms by saying that they have paid for a memorial book, in which a page is devoted to each of the men who died.

As in other disasters, the legal battles have been complicated. In Chapter Nine on the law, I look at the growth of so-called 'mid-Atlantic settlements' of which *Piper* is so far the prime example. For the survivors, however, the battle to improve conditions in the North Sea remains the one positive thing to come out of that appalling fireball. It demonstrates perhaps more clearly than anything else how, after a disaster, people need to avoid lapsing into feeling helpless. In the disaster at Bhopal (studied in Chapter Seven), people had very different expectations. Nothing in their culture or their circumstances would lead them to expect to have much of a say in their fate.

6

Hillsborough

In most disasters, from the Lisbon earthquake onwards, the dead and the survivors have been seen as innocent victims; disasters where victims appear to contribute to the tragedy are rare, and in very few disasters are either all or some of the victims portrayed as evil or guilty.

It is one of the grim ironies of Britain between 1985 and 1989 that in three major disasters the victims have been football supporters, a group who are widely perceived as being out of control. The Popplewell Inquiry found that the Bradford City fire was initially caused by a fan tossing a cigarette under the stand. Worse, the Heysel Stadium tragedy in which fifty-six died was due largely to fans fighting and rioting, bringing a wall down on themselves and others. The press claimed some fans then urinated on the dead, on police and on ambulancemen who were trying to bring aid to the injured. The British tabloid press was torn between patriotism and moralizing: fans were labelled as animals and yet it was also claimed that the Italians should share the blame.

There was no British inquiry into the Heysel disaster, since it took place abroad, but English clubs were banned from European soccer competitions as a result. Mrs Thatcher argued that its football fans were letting England down. The Heysel tragedy, moreover, took place during a season marred by many incidents on the terraces, confirming the image of fans as an uncontrolled mob. This image would affect both what happened at Hillsborough and how the incident was perceived.

The club involved at Heysel was Liverpool, representing a city with a highly ambiguous reputation. On the one hand, it is a very religious city: its bishops, both Anglican and Catholic, have great authority, probably more than most local bishops.

But the city of God, football and the Beatles also has a darker
side: a massive drugs problem, endemic unemployment and a
resultant capacity for mass disorder, as demonstrated in the
Toxteth street disturbances.

Historians suggest that Liverpool has been in decline since
the 1920s; it has lost its place as a major port, partly because of
the decline of the industries in the north west of England which
it served. Footballing success, however, has restored the city's
pride. No one would claim, though, that Liverpool supporters
are perfect gentlemen: they have the reputation of being loud,
arrogant and sometimes drunk. After the Heysel tragedy, many
went on television and showed not a shred of remorse. Violence
was glorious; the Italians got thumped and deserved it; the
Belgians were now persecuting poor Liverpool lads by keeping
them in a gaol which dared serve foreign food. The image of
Mersey *über Alles* was an ugly one.

When Sheffield was chosen as the venue for the FA Cup
semi-final between Liverpool and Nottingham Forest in 1989,
South Yorkshire police insisted on several safeguards, reflecting
the ferocious reputation of the fans. Police accepted, however,
that Hillsborough had hosted the identical match in 1988, and
that it had passed off without too much trouble.

Built in 1899, Hillsborough is one of the oldest football
grounds in England, but boasts new stands, built for the 1966
World Cup. It accommodates a total of 44,056. The ground
had witnessed some previous, and worrying, incidents. In 1981,
there was a semi-final held there between Tottenham Hotspur
and Wolverhampton Wanderers. During the match there was
crushing because a large number of people arrived late and
surged into the pens on the terraces. The police report on that
incident noted that 'the flashpoint occurred when Tottenham
scored at the Kop end after only three minutes. The spectators
who had just come in pushed forward to see what was happening and caused a crush.'

In that year, Hillsborough already had perimeter gates,
designed to stop fans running out on the pitch. These were
opened after a police inspector gave the order, but despite his
action, many fans were injured. Some had broken arms and
legs. Thirty-eight people were treated in hospital, but no one

was killed. As a result, perhaps, there was little pressure to change existing arrangements.

When the police came to look at the records of people admitted through the turnstiles at this 1981 match, they found that more than the licensed limit of 10,100 had been let into the Leppings Lane terraces. Later, the police suggested that the safety certificate for 10,100 spectators was too generous for that part of the ground; fewer spectators would be safer. Sheffield Wednesday knew of these concerns, but did nothing. The Taylor Inquiry into the disaster claimed that no one really took responsibility for making sure ground safety was maintained after 1981. This legal confusion meant that the club felt it was not ultimately responsible for safety.

The 1988 semi-final went well. It was supervised by Chief Superintendent Brian Mole, commander of F division. He was due to retire in 1989, and his successor was Chief Superintendent David Duckenfield. Both men went to a meeting on 22 March 1989 to make initial arrangements for the forthcoming match, but on 27 March Chief Superintendent Mole bowed out, leaving Duckenfield in sole charge.

Duckenfield had spent ten years in the CID. He had been a skilful officer in the division, albeit doing a completely different job from that required at Hillsborough. Hunting bank robbers demands stealth, patience, good relations with informers and the ability to make sense of forensic evidence. None of these skills is strictly relevant to controlling a large event and making sure that angry or excited fans do not get out of hand.

The scale of the operation that day was huge. Duckenfield had 1,122 men under his command, 38 per cent of the South Yorkshire force. In addition, thirty-four mounted officers from Liverpool and Nottingham were meant to keep fans calm, employing their local insights. The last time Duckenfield had been in Hillsborough as a policeman had been in 1979. The Taylor Inquiry noted that he did not fully grasp the size of the challenge confronting him, concluding that Duckenfield did not try to find out as much as he might have done, either about the 1981 incident or even about the details of how the 1988 semi-final had been policed.

The perception of fans as potentially violent had intensified since Heysel. Editorials during the 1988/89 season mused on whether lager-lout violence was the new British disease. Psychologists like Peter Marsh of Oxford University compared football clubs to primitive tribes: chants, emblems, scarves and drunken fury against outsiders were all hallmarks, apparently, of Neanderthal man.

Such views made police determined to keep rival fans well apart. Nottingham and Liverpool fans would not be allowed to meet in the ground or, if possible, outside it. Nottingham fans would be steered to the east, or Kop side, which took 29,800, while the Liverpool fans would be sent to the west, or Leppings Lane end. Liverpool's fans' reputation worked against them here: the police insisted fewer tickets be allocated to them: only 24,256. Of these 10,100, the same number that had been reckoned too high in 1981, were for the cheaper standing places on the terraces. Nottingham had 21,000 standing places and 8,000 seats. Liverpool thus had fewer tickets, and far fewer cheap ones, a fact that made for bad feeling even before the match began. The police's insistence on this, despite knowing the allocation seemed unfair to Liverpool fans, made the former even more nervous about potential trouble.

One of the insights gained from research is that fans on the terraces include a number of middle-class, even professional, people. The Nottingham terraces' fans included a number of psychologists, who were not there to observe scientifically but simply for the football. One was Phil Banyard, a teacher of psychology in his thirties. Banyard was looking forward to the match: 'This was going to be an epic.' He recalled that the 1988 match, won by Liverpool, had 'ended with a pitch invasion by the victorious Liverpool fans, who had come to the Forest end to taunt us'. This image of aggressive Liverpool fans would influence 1989's events.

The geography of Hillsborough is complex, but important to understand in order to grasp fully what went wrong at the semifinal. The ground itself was built on what were then green fields on the banks of the River Don. As fans walk down Leppings Lane they reach a large entrance where there are six gates, allowing people into the ground. Three of these gates lead to sixteen turnstiles which lead, in turn, to the expensive stands where everyone is seated. Fans for standing on the terraces also pass through three gates at the entrance. They are then squashed into a much smaller area in front of just seven turnstiles marked A to G. By the side of these turnstiles is gate C. Normally, this gate remains firmly shut.

Fans bound for the terraces pass through turnstiles A to G and down into a tunnel. This tunnel leads down underneath the expensive west stand and out into a set of seven pens. It is, incidentally, not surprising that they are called pens because they look rather like cattle pens, apart from the fact that they are set on terraces. In each pen there is a crush barrier which looks just like a set of railings. At Hillsborough, the barriers are painted blue to match Sheffield Wednesday's colours.

The terraces are part of the mystique of football. Peter Marsh, like a number of academics, finds the energy they unleash attractive. Strangely, this slightly romantic view is echoed both in the interim and final Taylor Report, which notes that there are often exciting surges of emotion. Body contact promotes camaraderie; it adds to the exciting atmosphere – and to the risk.

In 1947 and in 1971 there were fatal accidents at Burnden Park (Bolton Wanderers' ground) and at Ibrox. Both led to a review of safety at football grounds. The 1975 Safety of Sports Grounds Act allowed the Home Secretary to require any stadium with a capacity of more than 10,000 to hold a safety certificate. The local authority is supposed to inspect and issue this certificate; no safety certificate means no crowd can be let in. A handbook, the *Green Guide*, sets out the basic criteria for the certification of grounds.

Hillsborough had been granted a safety certificate on 21 December 1979 by the South Yorkshire County Council. This certificate was granted 'for an indefinite period', a curious state of affairs which meant that no one felt under any pressure to review or amend safety arrangements. Even when the police warned in 1981 that 10,100 was too high a limit for the section of the ground at Leppings Lane, no one took any action.

The Hillsborough certificate, however, had conditions attached to it. Schedule three gave the maximum capacity for various areas of the ground. The west terrace was to hold 7,200 and the north-west terrace 7,200. The *Green Guide* advised that the maximum safe density for spectators was fifty-four in ten square metres, and conditions on a terrace had to be excellent to allow even that. Sticking to fifty-four persons per ten square metres would have resulted in no more than 8,000 fans being allowed on the Leppings Lane terrace, according to calculations made by Dr Wilfred Eastwood, the engineer employed by Sheffield Wednesday. Yet the certificate for the Leppings Lane terrace was not amended; it enshrined a capacity of 10,100.

After the 1981 incident the police suggested the terrace be divided into three sections, believing that reducing sideways movement of the crowd would improve safety. The club agreed and installed three fences. There were now, in effect, three pens. Dr Eastwood calculated that this newly created centre pen could hold 2,200 with safety, but the safety certificate was not altered. Even if it had been, there was in any case no means of checking how many people went into this or any other pen.

In 1985, when Sheffield Wednesday were promoted to the First Division, the club tried to improve the ground. The three Leppings Lane pens were divided again to yield seven pens. Two more radial fences were built to prevent the crowd toppling sideways in a surge. The turnstiles got computerized equipment to count fans in. There was still no way, however, of checking that the fans who were admitted were going into one particular pen.

The Taylor Inquiry found that the pens did not conform to the *Green Guide*. The basic trouble was that the safety certificate was too generous. Dr Nicholson of the Health and Safety Executive calculated that on *Green Guide* criteria the two central pens (three and four) should have accommodated 1,015 and 1,036 respectively – fewer than the permitted 2,200. Nicholson stressed that even his figure assumed that everything inside the pens was in perfect condition. This was not the case: most of the crush barriers did not conform to the *Green Guide* standards. Four out of five of the barriers in pen three and six out of nine in pen four were not high enough. They were old barriers which had been repaired, and were unlikely to withstand the weight of any large surge. The *Green Guide* also recommended that spectators should not be more than twelve metres from an exit. In fact, about 40 per cent of the fans were further away. The Health and Safety Executive argued that, given these lapses, the real maximum capacity should have been 822 for pen three and 871 for pen four. In other words, the safety certificate allowed 507 too many spectators to be in that part of the ground, some 23 per cent of overcrowding.

These calculations were almost academic issues, of course, since there was no certificate issued specifically related to the pens. The only safety certificate that Sheffield Wednesday had to comply with was the 1979 one. Though this had been granted for an indefinite period, it would clearly have been prudent for it to be updated, and the local authority was not wholly unaware of this, nor was Dr Eastwood. There were, however, bureaucratic complications.

When, in 1981, South Yorkshire County Council stopped running Sheffield, responsibility for licensing the ground was handed over from South Yorkshire to the new Sheffield City Council. The city's licensing office then had the role of inspecting the safety arrangements at sports grounds and other venues. Mr Bownes was responsible for licensing thirty-two different kinds of facilities, with an available staff of five inspectors. There was a safety of sports grounds advisory panel but it worked 'in a very informal manner', the Taylor Inquiry noted. For example, it did not have properly convened meetings with a designated chairman and agenda. The inquiry asked Mr Bownes who chaired it. He replied that no one seemed to chair it, adding that they were not so much meetings as inspections and that formality was not their forte. Counsel for the inquiry put it to Mr Bownes that: 'There is no point in having inspections unless you form conclusions as a result of that inspection?'

'That is correct,' Bownes replied.

'There must presumably have been some form of meeting following the inspection, at which you got together and decided what, if anything, needed to be done,' said Mr Andrew Collines QC.

'There was not, to my recollection.'

No written record was kept of decisions to change safety arrangements. The committee did visit Hillsborough to discuss one particular crush barrier, which was eventually removed, but it did not grasp the basic point that the increased number of pens meant that the safety certificate itself should be reviewed.

Dr Eastwood knew that the alterations affected capacity but, the Taylor Report noted, he 'took no active steps to see appropriate amendments were made'. His assistant sent him a memo which stated that the capacity 'needs to be adjusted; better do it sooner than later'. Despite this prompting, Dr Eastwood took no action and was never put under any pressure from the local authority to do so.

The day of the semi-final, 15 April 1989, was a fine spring one, much warmer than the year before. Many fans lingered in pubs and on the street, enjoying the sunshine. They did not see any reason to rush to the ground and stand for forty-five or thirty minutes before kick-off. As a result, when they did try to get in, too many people tried to enter in too short a time. The tragedy of Hillsborough was that no one in charge recognized in time that this was happening.

Stephen Hendry was nineteen years old and in a party of ninety-three Liverpool supporters. He had arrived at the ground between 2.15 and 2.30, after they had been given 'nonsense directions' by the police. Like a number of fans, once there he found complete confusion reigning. Another Liverpool fan, Keith Hay, said: 'It was absolute bedlam outside the turnstiles. There was no crowd control at all. Fans were getting very anxious they might miss the kick-off.'

Outside the turnstiles people could hardly move. The seven turnstiles serving the Leppings Lane terrace were supposed to admit 10,100 people and, to achieve this, they each had to move roughly 1,450 persons in the hour before kick-off. At the other Penistone end, sixty turnstiles dealt with 29,800 people each, roughly 500 an hour. The *Green Guide* suggests that under good conditions turnstiles can push through no more than 750 bodies an hour. The Leppings Lane turnstiles could not, on a good day, cope easily with the demand placed on them.

In many disasters, the perception of where the risk comes from affects people's reactions in the crucial, usually short, interval when the accident might have been avoided. At Hillsborough, the police saw their main problem as preventing a pitch invasion; there had been, as already noted, some problems with the crowd running on the pitch the previous year. But, nevertheless, the police were extremely slow to recognize a crisis in the making. The Taylor Inquiry concluded that this slowness was partly due to the fact that they were convinced that public disorder was the main threat. Afraid that fans might riot, the officers in charge did not see that they had a major safety crisis unfolding in front of them.

According to witnesses, the mood of the crowd up to 2.30 was good-humoured. Phil Banyard said, 'The Forest fans were in good voice and, as usual, were outsinging Liverpool.'

Many Liverpool fans arrived between 2.30 and 2.40. This was not unreasonable for a three o'clock kick-off, but as people tried to get in to the ground, they were perplexed because the Leppings Lane turnstiles were marked in a confusing way. Tickets marked A did not admit you through turnstile A. Police complained that they were being pestered by fans who did not know where to go. The overworked turnstiles slowed down even more. Later, South Yorkshire police were to claim that many Liverpool fans deliberately turned up late in order to buck the system, reasoning that if they caused enough trouble the police would have to admit them late and maybe even let in fans without tickets in the general confusion. This had indeed happened at three matches in 1988 – at Watford and twice in Southampton. The police would also later accuse many fans of being drunk.

By 2.40, it was evident that the crowd was not entering the Leppings Lane end in an orderly manner. Fans were pushing through the perimeter gates which 'guarded' the way to the turnstiles. Queues were forming at the perimeter gates and even on the road outside. Superintendent Roger Marshall, who was in charge there, told Duckenfield in the control room that there was a dangerous pressure of people building up.

At turnstiles A to G, there were an estimated 5,000 people piled up, shoving and pushing. Stephen Hendry later wrote a letter in which he detailed what had happened. He noted, 'The worst crushing was at the front of the turnstiles, not because of impatience but because of fans trying to get away from police horses.' One police horse was actually lifted off its legs by the pressure of the crowd.

The police undoubtedly had to deal with some real threats to order: one man tried to climb over gate C. He was ejected by the police, but they had to open another gate to pursue him, and in the chase, some fans slipped in. Both the exits at A and B were rattled; the police lost control and the horses could not operate in the crush.

There was apparently no contingency plan for dealing with the crush, though it was a predictable problem. Superintendent Marshall became increasingly worried. At 2.47 he asked for permission to open gate C, saying that there was serious danger here.

One Liverpool supporter, Anthony Barnbrock, said that, on going through the tunnel, he wanted to turn back when he saw how crowded the pens were. He was unable to, however; with his father and his thirteen-year-old brother he was pushed to the front of pen four.

In the control room, Chief Superintendent Duckenfield was getting many messages demanding urgent action. Both Marshall and Police Constable Michael Buxton saw that it was going to be hard to kick off on time and suggested a postponement so that people could get in. Duckenfield turned their requests down. Outside the turnstiles, by 2.50, Marshall described the conditions as atrocious, and asked for permission to open gate C to help the flow. He did not know of the chaotic situation at the front of the standing area, ironically just under the police box. At first Duckenfield refused permission to open the gates, and Marshall and Duckenfield spoke tensely to each other, Marshall finally shouting that 'people are going to be killed'. It was at that point that gate C was opened.

The fans saw things differently from the police. Stephen Hendry said: 'Inside the actual stadium it was much worse. There was lots of pushing and jostling.' When gate C was opened, the police, unaware of the overcrowding inside, had not anticipated the consequences. As people streamed in through the gate, Stephen Hendry said, 'The crushing got worse. People were screaming to push back the crowd.' He felt himself being shoved and some people were already beginning to scream with pain.

A stream of some 2,000 fans poured through gate C. There were five minutes when orders could have been given, by Duckenfield, to ground stewards or to Superintendent Roger Greenwood, the ground commander, to make sure that the fans were allowed in in manageable groups. After the gate was opened, Duckenfield could see the rush on his TV monitors. Yet he took no steps either to manage the flow of spectators or to direct them to the emptier pens. Taylor compared this to the situation when gate A was opened at the Penistone end, where Duckenfield had ordered officers to monitor the situation, since fans could get on to the pitch that way. Those coming in through gate C, on the other hand, could not get on to the pitch. 'The possibility of overcrowding was not considered,' Taylor noted.

As this was happening, the teams came on to the pitch.

Anthony Barnbrock said the situation at the front of pen four remained reasonable until just before three o'clock. Then the pressure increased tremendously. He became separated from his father. His feet came off the ground. He shouted to the police through the fence to get help but the police did not react. Other fans also shouted for help. It was beginning to be clear, even to Banyard at the Nottingham side of the ground, that something strange was going on. A number of people there, however, thought the trouble stemmed from Liverpool fans being provocative.

The fans showed considerable distress, yet the police did nothing. From the back of the pen came even more pressure as the gate C flow made itself felt. The match began. Some fans shouted to the Liverpool keeper Bruce Grobbelaar that they were being hurt. In a statement to the Taylor Inquiry, Grobbelaar said, 'Kick-off happened and we got into our stride pretty quickly. We forced a corner pretty early on and the ball came down my end.' Then, Peter Beardsley hit the Nottingham crossbar. 'I remember,' Grobbelaar said, 'just after that there were shouts and screams from the crowd just behind me. It was different, not the ordinary crowd noise, and I turned back to look. What amazed me was the concentration and squash of fans in the centre section. The end areas still had plenty of space.' Then Grobbelaar noticed that the crowd could not spread sideways because they were being held in by the side fencing.

The police commander should have realized that there was a massive overcrowding problem when fans started to climb out over these side fences. Grobbelaar added, 'I saw fans climbing out over the front of the pitch, which was particularly difficult because of the spikes on the top of the fencing. But they were getting out.'

To a police commander worried by the risk of crowd violence, these movements would look like the first signs of a pitch invasion. The orders for the day focused entirely on that as the sole risk; they did not mention overcrowding. Opening the gates on to the pitch was ruled out unless someone needed urgent medical attention. Given such orders, when some policemen began to realize fans were in distress, they were worried about how to react. One constable told the Taylor Inquiry that he 'debated' about whether or not to open the gates, but he was afraid he would receive 'a right bollocking'. So he did nothing.

The Hickses had gone to the match as a family, with tickets for different parts of the stand. Victoria and Sarah Hicks, the daughters, went into pen three. From 2.15 onwards, Mr Hicks kept an eye on the pens as he could see they were filling up. He told the inquiry that from 2.50 on, he could see people in trouble there. At about 2.55 he called to a police officer, trying to draw his attention to the fact that people in the crowd were showing clear signs of distress. The policeman did not pay any attention to him. Finally, Hicks shouted: 'Can't you see what's going on?' Hicks could not identify the policeman who replied, but did remember precisely what he shouted back: 'Shut your fucking prattle.'

The Taylor Inquiry judged that Hicks was an impressive witness and was inclined to believe that he had been abused as he claimed.

Bruce Grobbelaar also saw that it was not going to be easy to get the police to react to the situation: 'Play was going on still and I was in a terrible position, trying to concentrate on play and having my attention taken by what was happening behind me.' Then, he heard a fan scream, 'Bruce, please help.' Grobbelaar turned round to see fans squashed against the railings at the Leppings Lane end. One fan was yelling, 'Please get the fucking gate open.'

A crucial factor was the collapse of one of the barriers in pen three so that now nothing restrained the push of people coming into the back of the pen. Inspector David Bullas, who was in the west stand, said, 'I saw from the direction of the tunnel a kind of movement down the terracing, the type of thing that you see on the nature programmes: the molten lava flowing down the mountainside, but the molten lava was a river of people.'

The barrier that collapsed had been tested and had passed the *Green Guide* criteria, but these criteria were themselves confused. In the crisis, the barrier simply could not take the pressure.

As the lava-like mass of people flowed down the pens, it would have been sensible to open the perimeter gates and to make some announcement on the Tannoy system. Under the orders of the day, however, both these courses of action required the express consent of an inspector. Inspector Colin Darling, who was in charge of the men on the perimeter track, said he would take such actions only if fans were in danger. Now something strange occurred. Some officers did realize how dangerous the situation was and they therefore opened a few of the perimeter gates, without having formal permission to do so. The moment they did this, some fans poured out and others climbed sideways to try and get out. Seeing what they took to be the beginnings of a pitch invasion, the police shut the perimeter gates again.

At 3.04, as mentioned by Grobbelaar, Beardsley nearly scored. This led to a final surge on the terraces, even at the crowded Leppings Lane end. It was at this point, according to Bruce Grobbelaar's statement to the inquiry, that he turned round to the police and asked them to help the fans. Whether it was because he was a football star or because the situation was clearly critical, the police then, finally, did start to open the gates.

Phil Banyard watched it all from the other end. He did not realize fully what was going on. The events of that day, even though he was not hurt himself, have stayed with him for months. They have led him to study the psychology of crowds, and he suggests that in a crowd people behave recklessly, more dangerously than they would on their own. One particular reason for football crowds taking risks is, he says, 'the male culture of the popular end. Being careful is discouraged in all male company. If you are playing a game whose unspoken rules state that no one is a coward, that "real" men never run scared, it's very easy to misread a situation and to ignore the extent to which it can be dangerous.' Banyard believes this was happening in the pens. He also argues that 'another factor that contributes to this incorrect evaluation is the myth of invulnerability that develops in a crowd. Each member tends to think that nothing can happen to them.' The crowd is all-powerful.

Myths are important in football. The late Bill Shankly, Liverpool's famous manager, quipped that: 'Football is not a matter of life and death. It's more important than that.' Banyard notes that both Liverpool supporters and their critics often refer to this quote. It illustrates and even reinforces the fanaticism of the club and its supporters. Liverpool cultivates an air of invincibility, never admitting, for instance, to being beaten. The pitch was bad. The referee was blind. The goal was off-side. Banyard wonders if this cult of invincibility might not contribute to the sense of invulnerability and so lead to more reckless behaviour. Usually the reckless behaviour manifests itself in aggression; at Hillsborough, it consisted of ignoring signs of danger.

It is just possible that if the crowd had been warned that there was serious overcrowding and advised to stay still, the tragedy might have been avoided. They did not get any such information, however. When Beardsley hit the crossbar, therefore, there was the familiar surge, and as it swept forward, fans struggled to reach the gates in the perimeter fence. There was, as the Taylor Report put it, 'a horrendous blockage of bodies'.

One of the other people in pen three, Stephen Hendry, realized that the situation had become worse after the near-goal: 'Now people had been put on the floor underneath the barrier and were getting trampled by fans who were helpless as the big surge happened. It was now obvious how desperate the situation was. People couldn't breathe.' Hendry alleged that the police saw what was happening and did nothing. In the crush and confusion that followed, Hendry managed to clamber out over a rail. Once he got on to the pitch, he passed out for a few moments. When he woke he saw at least eight dead, and commented: 'What followed was absolute mayhem.' The dead, the dying and the desperate were pressed together at the front of the gates, and those at the very front crushed against the wire netting. Those who had any strength left tried to clamber out over other people who were submerged in a human heap.

The BBC football commentator, John Motson, realized just after the kick-off that there was an overcrowding problem. So did Banyard, who recalls that: 'Very slowly it began to dawn on people that something serious was going on but there was an array of signs to tell us the opposite.' The Liverpool fans looked to be in distress, 'but, on the other hand, a platoon of police had now come into the ground'. These police were not helping, however, but 'were lined up, watching the fans'.

The police began to realize only at 3.06 that they were dealing with a safety incident. They then radioed for a fleet of ambulances. But the police messages also continued to treat the incident as a threat to the pitch, calling for extra officers and dog handlers. No one ordered police officers to enter the tunnel and relieve pressure by stopping fans coming through, but a few officers did this on their own initiative.

The perimeter gates, allowing access to the pitch, were so narrow that only two or three police could do anything to help the fans who were now crushed against the wire, many being trampled. Each body had to be prised from the pile by the police. Officers began to run to the pitch from the gymnasium, and many started to help fans clamber out over the fencing or to comfort the distressed. But no officer took charge; policemen stood around the perimeter gates not knowing what to do. They had come running thinking they were going to deal with a pitch invasion; instead they found carnage. Young officers were shocked into impotence by what they saw, according to the Taylor Report.

Taylor described the scene as 'truly gruesome'. Victims were blue, incontinent and cyanotic. Many were vomiting. Many had their eyes open in death. People were bringing more and more fans out on to the pitch and laying them out on the grass. There was still, however, no effective command being taken from the police control room.

Fans were angry at the police. The ones who were coming out of the pens were often bitter, and they spat on some officers and abused others. A few officers were even assaulted.

The first aid arrangements worked only fitfully. There were thirty St John Ambulance men posted at the ground, and they got on to the field quickly when the first casualties appeared. The man in charge, Mr Peter Wells, tried to feed oxygen through the wire of the fences to those in distress.

From the other end of the ground, however, all that could be seen was chaos and the players leaving the pitch. Banyard noticed: 'An ambulance appeared and drove to the far end of the ground.' It was at the Penistone end because it was impossible to get the ambulance to the Leppings Lane end because there was no access there. There was not enough first aid equipment: the whole ground had only nine stretchers. As the scale of the disaster became clear, and as some fans were obviously only just alive, fans improvised makeshift stretchers out of advertising hoardings, and ran with these to the other end of the ground, to the ambulance. Again, Banyard noted that the lack of information meant that fans were getting very mixed messages: 'Liverpool fans were running, but several of them were holding the hoarding with one hand while making gestures at the Forest crowd with the other. Hostility and compassion were mixed.'

There was still no public announcement that there was a problem. The Tannoy asked for the pitch to be cleared, but spectators remained in the dark concerning the scale of the tragedy. Until 3.30 there was not even an appeal for any doctors in the crowd to come forward. Inside the police control room, Chief Superintendent Duckenfield was still not being decisive, according to the Taylor Inquiry. He froze, the inquiry concluded. Duckenfield made no attempt to follow up his order to open gate C. 'When he was unsure of the problem he sent others down to assess the situation rather than descend for himself to see.' As a result, police officers were not ordered to go and stop fans coming through the tunnel. A few policemen did do that, but many of the fans who were still trying to pour in would not do as the police asked. As a result of this police indecision, the situation out on the pitch remained chaotic.

There was no attempt made to cordon off an area where first aid could be given. It was not till 3.12 that Chief Superintendent John Nesbit of the traffic police arrived on the pitch, and took effective charge at gate three. The first priority was giving first aid, but facilities were meagre because ambulances had not been called in time.

At 2.59, Police Constable Brian Waugh at central police control had radioed Hillsborough to ask if ambulances were needed. He did so because his chief inspector was worried by snatches of conversation he had overheard. For eight minutes, however, nothing more was heard. Finally, at 3.07, after getting a call from Mr Murray, the police did ask for ambulances, and in the end forty-two turned up. But they had been called out far too late and they faced difficulties gaining access to the ground, hence the makeshift stretchers. In addition, once fans had been brought out, there were more problems, because injured people were being laid out in the tunnel itself.

After the call to the ambulance brigade, a further seven minutes passed before anyone called the fire brigade, who possessed the equipment needed to cut the perimeter fence. Police Constable Trevor Bichard called police HQ, requesting hydraulic equipment for this purpose. The following conversation then took place between the police and fire control.

Police: 'Can we have cutting gear for Hillsborough, please, straight away?'

Fire control: 'Just a minute. Right – what's the address?'

Police: 'Cutting equipment for Hillsborough football ground – straight away?'

Fire control: 'Hillsborough football ground.'

Police: 'Yes, Hillsborough football ground.'

Fire control: 'What road is it on? Do you know?'

Police: 'There's been a major accident. All the ambulances are up there.'

Fire control: 'What road is it on?'

Police: 'I have no idea. Hillsborough football ground.'

Hillsborough is one of the major landmarks of Sheffield, yet this conversation still took place. The fire control then asked why they were wanted, since they had heard there had been a road traffic accident. This whole conversation took one minute thirteen seconds. The Taylor Inquiry concluded that, on the face of it, fire control seemed pedantic, but that they were right to be specific. The police constable had given the information requested but police HQ did not convey all the information he gave. The inquiry therefore concluded that the blame for this delay lay with the police.

The fire brigade was not summoned until 3.13, and when appliances first arrived at 3.22, the police outside the ground told them that they were not wanted. This was not surprising, since the police control room had not explained the nature of the crisis. At the Kop end, two engines arrived. The emergency tender was too tall to go further, so it backed out and went to the Leppings Lane end. This took it a further eight minutes. By the time the fire crew got out on to the pitch with their wire-cutting equipment, the last of the dead and injured were being removed. They had arrived too late, through no fault of their own.

For most of the crowd, the situation was mystifying. Obviously something was happening, but they could not see what it was. The mood of the Nottingham fans, who believed that Liverpool supporters were causing trouble, was getting nasty. All that was necessary was for someone to explain on the Tannoy that there was an emergency and to appeal for calm and help. This did not happen, but Chief Superintendent Nesbit, who had taken charge at gate three, threw a cordon of police officers across the ground to stop Nottingham fans getting near Liverpool ones. This action seemed provocative to some fans, though the inquiry vindicated Nesbit, saying that it would have been obscene to have had fans fighting while people were dying.

It was only, Banyard said, 'as a relentless procession of stretchers shuddered by that the crowd became still and quiet. The Forest fans were prisoners in the stand, fenced in and sentenced to watch this gruesome spectacle unfold. By now we had guessed that a barrier had collapsed or something. Guessed, mind: nobody told us anything. I was standing next to an experienced casualty nurse. Why didn't anyone ask for help from medics in the crowd?'

On the press benches, reporters and photographers were slow to realize the horrific nature of what was happening. Rather like the police, the press expected that if there was trouble, it would be due to crowd violence. Then photographers started to take pictures of fans trying desperately to get out. The police alleged that these photographers got in the way of the rescue efforts and that they infuriated fans as they tried to photograph the dead and the dying.

In the control room, Duckenfield was beginning to receive visits from people with questions to ask. The first was Assistant Chief Constable Walter L. Jackson, in civilian clothes, and at the match as a guest of the club. Duckenfield could not tell him what was happening on the field. Significantly, Duckenfield did not say that the exit gates had been opened on his authority. He was afraid, perhaps, that it might look as if his action had created a pitch invasion. Jackson then went down to the pitch to see for himself what was happening.

Some minutes later, at about 3.15, Graham Kelly, the Chief executive of the FA, accompanied by Graham Mackrell of the host club, went to the control room. It was by now obvious how grave the position was. Duckenfield said that there did seem to be some deaths and that the game was likely to be abandoned. He also said that a gate had been forced and there had been a resultant inrush of Liverpool supporters. To confirm the point, Duckenfield pointed to one of the television screens. When Graham Kelly appeared on television, therefore, he gave both that story and the story some fans were beginning to tell: that the police had opened gate C because of the overcrowding.

Out on the field, the situation continued to be chaotic. One hundred and seventy-two fans were taken to hospital. It was not until 3.56, however, that Kenny Dalglish, the Liverpool manager, was asked to go to the control room and address the crowd. He appealed for calm. For his part, Banyard noted that Dalglish 'asked us to co-operate with the police. That was the most information we received from the authorities. The rest of the news was passed along from people with radios in the stand. The makeshift stretchers were still making their way from one end of the pitch to the other.' Banyard was beginning to feel something that Gerhard Vaders had experienced in the Moluccan train siege, a desperate desire for information: 'After an hour people were still being carried out on advertising hoardings, the police were still watching and the Forest fans were just wanting to go home.' As the radio news made clear what was happening, fans in the terraces engaged in 'gruesome speculations that the FA would order the match to be played still', following the Heysel precedent.

At 4.20 fans were finally told that the match had been abandoned and advised to go home. It was not easy to do so: the streets were blocked all around the ground. The final irony for Banyard came when he found himself on a bus, marooned in the traffic jams surrounding Hillsborough; he wanted to get off to walk, but he was not allowed to. The police would not let him and his friends get off. This small detail left a very sour taste in his mouth after a particularly bad day.

By 4.30 it was clear that a large number of people were dead and many injured had been taken to hospital. When the final statistics were taken, ninety-five were dead and 730 people complained of having been injured inside the ground, thirty-six outside. Most of the injuries were bruising, especially to the ribs and chest.

The immediate reporting of the disaster reflected the perception that football fans were not innocent victims. Sections of the press blamed the fans for much of what had happened. This angle on the story was fuelled by some South Yorkshire police officers, who leaked the story that many Liverpool fans were drunk. All the corpses were actually tested for blood alcohol levels. None of the dead women's blood contained any alcohol, fifty-one of the males had no more than ten milligrams per cent, which is negligible, and fifteen had over eighty milligrams. Six had over 120 milligrams per cent, which would make them unfit to drive.

At the Inquiry, these allegations of drunkenness surfaced again, causing bitter anger and resentment in Liverpool. The then Chief Constable of South Yorkshire, Peter Wright, said that it had been wrong of his officers to spread that rumour, if indeed they had spread it. John Ashton, a Liverpool doctor, said the rumour showed how unfairly the city was treated. But the idea persisted that the Liverpool supporters were violent – and therefore not innocent. Perhaps because of this, the city put on more than a dignified display of civic grief. At Anfield, Liverpool's ground, many flowers were received. Some were thrown on the pitch. Three days after the disaster, the whole pitch was covered in flowers, an extraordinary sight. Kenny Dalglish said that this spontaneous display was moving and showed how much the dead were honoured. He also used the fact of this remarkable tribute to rebut the accusations that fans had been badly behaved. The Taylor Inquiry report bore out what Dalglish and other Liverpool dignitaries said, concluding that it was one of the tragedies of Hillsborough that the police had become so obsessed with the risk of the fans going on the rampage that they did not see the obvious disaster occurring before their eyes. Taylor was also extremely critical of the standard of competence and leadership the police provided. Duckenfield was suspended. Chief Constable Peter Wright offered his resignation to the Police Authority, but it was rejected. He had, after all, been nowhere near Hillsborough on the day.

In the press reports there were two long-running sagas. The FA could not decide whether to abandon the match or to reschedule it. It might have been, many felt, a fine tribute actually to suspend the FA Cup altogether and not award it, but no one seemed to consider this a real possibility. After much agonizing, it was conveniently decided that the dead fans would have wanted the match played; nothing need change.

More surprisingly perhaps, the government itself showed ambivalence towards the recommendations of the inquiry it set up. After the Bradford City fire, Mr Justice Popplewell in his report made twenty-six recommendations, only some of which have been put into effect. Academics at Bradford University, who have set up a Disaster Prevention Unit, claim that the complete implementation of the Popplewell Report would have prevented the Hillsborough tragedy because Popplewell stressed the need for proper evacuation procedures and better exits through perimeter fences.

The Home Secretary called for the initial recommendations of the Taylor Inquiry to be made before the start of the new football season. Taylor made forty-three recommendations and stressed that twenty-six should be implemented before the start of the 1989/90 season. Many points raised were basic and sensible. He recommended that there should be specific seating limits for each part of the ground and that clubs should make arrangements to close off each pen or area when it got near its limits. Given the many confusions that there had been about who was responsible for what, Taylor said there should be a written agreement between the police and every club concerned, setting out who was responsible for which aspects of safety arrangements. The chief constable for each force should nominate a liaison officer to deal with each club and the local authority. Taylor also called for much better co-ordination of emergency services. Like the writers of all post-disaster reports, he was fulsome about the emergency services, yet found a great deal wrong in the way they had operated. Specific recommendations included having liaison meetings between the police, ambulance and fire brigade. At these police should give the fire and ambulance services full details of any large event. Football clubs should have, on site, a doctor and one person trained in advanced first aid. The fire brigade should store wire-cutting equipment at every ground. Perhaps the most imaginative proposal was that, overseeing every pen, there should be one police officer designated, whose sole duty it would be to look for signs of overcrowding or distress. Taylor did not recommend the tearing down of perimeter fences. In addition to the officer watching for overcrowding, however, he said there should be an officer in charge of each fence, authorized to open the gates without getting permission from the control room.

The Home Secretary did not make any formal announcement before the start of the 1989/90 season specifying how many of Taylor's recommendations would now be legally required of clubs. In August 1989, just before the football season started, as if to remind the government of the risk of disaster, the *Marchioness* sank in the Thames, prompting swift action from

Cecil Parkinson, the new Transport Minister. He announced a series of measures, which would be treated as if they were law, by noon the day after the disaster. Such decisive action, however, has been rare, and was possible here because the pleasure boats plying the Thames are relatively small fry, easy to regulate. Even then there have been doubts expressed as to whether they have all been put into effect.

The first days of the 1989/90 season showed little progress: there was dangerous overcrowding at a number of football matches, including one at Hull. England fans travelling to Sweden got into fights. In December, players got involved in brawls. In May 1990, fans from Leeds rioted at Bournemouth. The police had repeatedly asked for the match not to be played on a Bank Holiday but the League refused to shift. The image of football remained poor.

If the reaction to the *Piper Alpha* disaster revealed the conflict between profit and safety, the football disaster revealed the conflict between safety requirements, the need to make a profit and the fear of disappointing fans. In the wake of Hillsborough people seemed reluctant to suggest that a proper tribute to the dead might be to suspend the FA Cup competition for a year. It will have been clear throughout this book that I do not support Thatcherite policies, but it must be acknowledged that every time Mrs Thatcher has suggested that perhaps England ought to drop out of a football competition because fans cannot be controlled, she is unthinkingly and somewhat unfairly criticized as a killjoy unsympathetic to and ignorant of the ethics of football. The carpet of flowers at Anfield was partly a reaction to the unfair press coverage Liverpool felt it had received, but it also served, consciously or not, to prepare people for the inevitable announcement that the dead would have wanted the match to go on. It was only after the Home Secretary had very publicly criticized the Football League for failing to cancel a Bournemouth v. Leeds match at the request of the Dorset Police that the League finally agreed to concede to the police the right to insist that a match should not be played on a particular date.

The Hillsborough disaster was very much the result of

inadequate policing, unable to see beyond a particular stereotype branding fans as violent, but, for once, there was some
truth in this police stereotype. The aftermath of the disaster
shows how hard it remains for the sport to take seriously what
happened, and in that sense, Hillsborough is very different
from all the other disasters reported in this book. In the wake
of Three Mile Island, *Piper Alpha*, King's Cross and every
other tragedy, there were many attempts on the part of relevant
authorities to wriggle out of responsibility, but in none of them
did anyone dare suggest that we owed it to the dead to carry on
pretty much as before – as if nothing had happened. Phil
Banyard has suggested that machismo pervades the terraces. It
seems also to pervade society's reaction to football disasters.

7

Bhopal: Disaster in the Third World

In the Third World, disasters are more common than in the developed world. In many ways, this is not surprising. In 1988, for example, the authoritative magazine *Flight* reported that an Indian regional airline, Vanuyut, was not only so short of money that it could not pay its phone bill, but that it did not actually fly to any known schedule. In such confusion, it was perhaps a bit much to expect its safety record to be good. The airline did in fact have three spectacular crashes in 1988 but none was reported outside India except in the trade press.

When a Third World disaster hits the headlines, therefore, it is either because a great many are dead or because there are implications for the West. The Bhopal disaster was much reported both because of the staggering number of victims and because it highlighted something that many Westerners worried about anyway: the arrogance of multinational companies.

The Bhopal disaster of 2 December 1984 exemplifies many of the ways in which victims in less developed nations are much more vulnerable than those in the West. Initial reports suggested that 1,750 people had died and an estimated 200,000 people had been badly injured by the cloud of toxic gas that drifted over the town; days after, American lawyers arrived. Some of them offered victims 100 rupees (£7) as an inducement to hire them. These lawyers knew that they stood a chance of making millions of dollars out of the damages that Union Carbide might be forced to pay. Their contingency fees would be massive.

In 1980, the American company Union Carbide had opened a plant at Bhopal to produce a pesticide called Carbaryl. The plant started producing in 1981, providing hundreds of local jobs. It was owned by Union Carbide's Indian subsidiary, whose chairman, Mr Mahendra, is head of one of India's major industrial families. The plant was set up to capitalize on India's enormous need for pesticides.

When it was built, the local town did not unreservedly welcome the plant, and it soon came under severe criticism: people were worried that it was built actually within the town. India has a healthy tradition of trade union activity, and unions protested at the lack of safety precautions at the plant. The first of a series of accidents did indeed occur in 1983, when a local boy died. The unions printed a series of posters which proclaimed: 'Warning – save yourselves from death. The lives of hundreds of thousands of people are in danger. The factory is making gas and doesn't use safety measures.' A local journalist, Rajkumar Keswani, wrote three articles for the Bhopal press and one for a national Delhi newspaper in which he called the plant a volcano that was likely to erupt with devastating consequences. There was no genuine response to these warnings, because, the unions claim, Union Carbide had bribed local politicians. The company, for example, ran the official state guesthouse at which important visitors were lodged. The only action Union Carbide undertook was to stage a Safety Week in which residents were informed about safety procedures. In Bhopal, after the Safety Week, sirens were often set off as a practice drill. As a result, when there was a true emergency and the sirens blared, at first nobody realized it signalled real danger.

Union Carbide is a multinational company. It is normal for its foreign plants to be inspected from Head Office, so in 1982 a team of safety inspectors from America visited Bhopal. Their report noted that the plant did not meet the standard required of American installations. Indeed Mr Tyson, one of the members of the inspection group, pointed to serious flaws in the design of the plant and warned that it would be unacceptable in the USA to have such an 'unsafe' plant in a highly populated area.

There was little chance that Indian experts would have reached the same conclusions, even if they had been equally zealous. The state government has only twenty-four industrial safety inspectors for the whole of Madhya Pradesh. *India*

Today, a magazine modelled on *Newsweek*, was told that it was rare for these safety inspectors to check procedures or equipment seriously, merely casually signing the paperwork to pass the equipment. *India Today* also repeated allegations that there were close links between Union Carbide and the state government, which, it claimed, had turned a blind eye despite knowing of the dangers at Bhopal. These general problems were to erupt on 2 December 1984.

At midnight on this day, there were forty-two tonnes of liquid methyl isocyanate (MIC) stored in an underground tank at the Union Carbide plant. A volatile substance, MIC reacts violently to a number of chemical combinations. Union Carbide recommended that it should be stored cold, preferably at nought degrees Centigrade and certainly under fifteen degrees. In Bhopal, where the temperature is often forty degrees, arranging cold storage is not easy. The MIC was in a series of tanks housed in a tower known as the MIC structure. The MIC in tank 610 had been there since October. There were difficulties in maintaining the correct pressure in the tank; nitrogen pressure helps prevent volatility. The absence of nitrogen pressure made it easier for water, alkali and even bits of metal to slip into the tank, which had not been cleaned or inspected, dry, since 1982. Operatives were unhappy about all these problems but were unable to do anything about them. The design of the plant accentuated difficulties. In many facilities, MIC is stored not in bulk tanks but in far smaller batch tanks that hold up to five tonnes. These smaller tanks can be inspected and cleaned on a regular basis. Union Carbide did not have such facilities in Bhopal.

The day before the explosion, engineers flushed water through the pipes above the storage tanks, pipes that were in theory quite isolated from tank 610. Between these pipes and the tank there was movement; a new pipe had been installed, running downwards to facilitate it. As the operators tried to flush water through the system, they realized that the valves they opened to allow this water to flow out were not working properly: the water should have drained off into a waste area but it did not do so. Two valves were blocked and two others partially blocked. The operators pointed this out to the engineer in charge of the MIC system, but he told them just to flush the water through again. In theory, this procedure should have been safe; water should still not have entered tank 610, which was meant to be protected by a valve closing it off. There was, however, a fault. The protecting valve was either leaking or open. About 2,000 tonnes of water therefore began slowly to leak into tank 610.

The leak of any water into an MIC tank is potentially very dangerous. 'The pressure in the MIC tank increases rapidly if MIC is contaminated with water,' noted a report by the Indian Council on Science. There was, however, no alarm built into the system to warn the control room of a rise in pressure. The measurement of temperature was also inadequate, only reading from minus twenty-five degrees Centigrade to plus twenty-five degrees. There was a high alarm setting at eleven degrees, but the contents of the tank were being stored at an ambient temperature around the storage tanks that was far higher than the alarm setting of eleven degrees. Further, as the temperature transmitter went off scale at twenty-five degrees, no one actually knew the temperature at which MIC was in fact being kept. There was no device to monitor, and warn of rapid rises in temperature which might increase pressure. With such poor design, the control room indicators did not provide adequate warning if something was going wrong. It is highly unlikely that in a developed country the industry inspectors would have allowed such a potentially dangerous chemical plant to operate in the middle of a residential area with such poor warning devices.

Not surprisingly, the first signs of trouble were seen by eye rather than on any control panel. The MIC tanks were contained in a structure that looked like a house on stilts. It was here that the first leak of dirty water was noticed near the vent gas scrubber, a device that looked like a gas flare tower, meant to scrub clean any gas emitted. This vent gas scrubber was to fail lamentably on the night of 2 December.

In the late evening of that day, the operators on the ground area found some dirty water spilling from higher up in the MIC structure. Their eyes also felt irritated. They therefore went up the stairs of the MIC structure and noticed that dirty water and MIC itself were leaking from it. They also saw that the pressure safety valve was missing, and they guessed that it had been blown off. Worried, at midnight, they told the plant supervisor that there was an MIC leak; they were told to spray water around the area of it.

By 00.15, the control room operators had confirmed the leak. Pressure in tank 610 was shooting up: it was between twenty-five and thirty psig. By 00.30, the operator saw that it had shot off the entirely inadequate scale. The volatile chemistry of the materials being stored made this very dangerous. Methyl iso-cyanate reacts extremely violently with water, coming to the boil to produce a runaway reaction. Alarmed by the readings, the control room operator went to the storage area. He heard hissing from the safety relief valve, which implied that the valve had popped off. Local temperature and pressure readings were also off the scale, at over twenty-five degrees – and fifty-five psig respectively. The operator rushed back to the control room and started the vent gas scrubber circulation pump. The design of the plant had envisaged that there might be an escape of MIC and had incorporated some routine precautions. The vent gas scrubber was a device supposed to dump a caustic soda solution on to the escaping, or venting, MIC to render it chemically inert. But the vent gas scrubber itself had been constructed on the assumption that only small amounts of MIC would leak; it was entirely inadequate to deal with huge leaks, containing an insufficient quantity of alkali. The flow indicator in the control room, however, revealed that the caustic soda was not even circulating to the limited extent it should have been.

There was, though, a second line of defence: a flare tower, built over the MIC structure, was meant to burn any escaping gas. But this flare tower was closed for maintenance. The response of the operators in the control room in trying to control the chain of events was sensible, but they were fighting poor safety design.

The first ominous sign to the inhabitants of Bhopal was a gas cloud coming out from the stack of the MIC structure. A field operator saw it. The plant personnel were warned. From around 01.00 they sprayed water on to the MIC structure but it did not reach the top of the stack from which gas was escaping. Thus, gas was emitted from around midnight to 03.00. As the gas escaped, so it got condensed on contact with cold air in the atmosphere. It then began to settle slowly on to the ground, rather as smog settles on Los Angeles. This cloud of gas looked yellow and virtually 'sat' in the air.

Mrs Madhur Mishra, Professor of Home Economics at Bhopal University, remembers, 'My eyes started watering and I could hardly breathe. I was choking.' She drove towards a hill and described the scenes she witnessed on the road as 'gruesome'. There were about eight or nine thousand people in the road in the dead of night all making for the hill. Behind them they left houses in which people died from breathing in the gas. Brigadier M. L. Garg, a retired officer who managed a paper plant, said, 'The gas was in the house like a yellow haze.' His chest felt constricted; his eyes ran. His wife could not see. With his army contacts, Garg persuaded the local military to evacuate the nightshift from his factory. Even so, fourteen of his workers died. Most people, however, did not have the privilege of his connections.

Survivors described the scene initially as strange, but not frightening. Bizarrely, the first sensation resembled the smell of chillies; many people woke up thinking someone was cooking or that there was a fire in their kitchen. It took a few moments before they suffered breathing difficulties. According to the police, anyone who could, then ran away from the fatal cloud. Ironically, this natural reaction added to the toll of injuries, because running made the victims breathe more quickly and more deeply; they were therefore likely to inhale more gas, as their bodies needed oxygen to run.

In any large disaster, people tend to remember both their feelings of terror and small incidents, the grotesque contrasting strangely with ordinary life. In Bhopal, one doctor described how, as he drove into town, people climbed on the roof, boot and bonnet of his car. Around him, people were fleeing, some carrying children, dying in their arms. All over Bhopal, there were grim signs of the pollution: vegetables like spinach were covered by a fine white film; the ponds were discoloured and lurid. Indian towns are usually alive with animals, but the methyl isocyanate had also killed them, leaving the roads of the city littered with dead donkeys, cows, chickens, dogs, monkeys. Vultures soon gathered. The few living dogs sniffed around the bodies. One father was seen desperately trying to chase dogs away from the body of his dead four-year-old son. The superintendent of the Hamidia Hospital said: 'This has been our Hiroshima.' It was a lurid description, perhaps, but not at all fanciful.

The handling of the dead and injured also demonstrated the disadvantages under which Third World countries labour. Bhopal's seven hospitals were overwhelmed, so medical facilities were set up in tents. It was not just a question of a lack of facilities, however, but also of a lack of information. One local doctor, Dr R. K. Jain, who ran one of the emergency clinics, said that they were seeing 1,200 people a day there. They came first with breathing problems, then many developed fever. After that, a number started to cough blood. Blindness was a particular problem. Doctors said that they did not know what symptoms to expect next, and the lack of information as to the nature of the poisoning made it likely that they were unable to provide the most suitable treatment. Jain saw twenty-five of his patients die in his makeshift clinic. The hospitals soon ran out of drugs. The provision of emergency services was poor. Many of those who died did so in the first two days after the disaster.

Indian medical facilities are variable at the best of times: outside big cities like Delhi and Bombay, there are far too few hospital beds. A number of Indian psychiatrists told me that they reckoned less than 10 per cent of the need for beds was met (Cohen, 1988). There were simply no resources to provide adequate care.

The employees at the plant soon grasped what had happened and took reasonable preventative action. As the Indian government report noted: 'Within the Union Carbide plant itself, everyone moved upwind, away from the emission and toxic gas direction. Only one person was affected to any extent and he recovered.' There were buses and other forms of transport in the factory car park which could have been used to evacuate people, but no one commandeered them; the vehicles stayed in the car park, useless. There was fury in the town, not just at Union Carbide, but at some of its Indian employees, who did nothing to warn or help neighbours. One of these employees, Shakeel Ahmed, was the only man at the plant to be seriously affected; he required a bodyguard for weeks afterwards.

The lack of information added to the death toll. Union Carbide executives knew that there were reasonably simple measures people could take to protect themselves in the event of an accident. The best advice was simply to stay indoors and cover one's face with a wet towel. But, despite its Safety Week, the company had never developed any sustained education programme telling local residents what to do in the event of a leak. This lack of information made the initial help provided less effective than it need have been. The Indian Ministry for Petroleum said that it expected Union Carbide to behave as it would have done had the disaster been happening in America. It must have known there was little hope of that.

In any chemical disaster, information is priceless; without knowing exactly what caused the injuries, doctors do not stand much hope of hitting on the right antidote. From the outset, the information provided by Union Carbide was confusing. Internal company reports warned that if MIC was heated under 'thermal conditions' it turned into hydrogen cyanide. Cyanide is, of course, a deadly poison. The Bhopal doctors were not told any of this. In addition, the company did not disclose at once what the chemical reaction in tank 610 had been. This may have been because there was far more MIC at the plant than had been admitted: forty-five tonnes as against the declared twenty-two. As a result, initially, no one was sure whether it was MIC or phosgene which had caused the runaway reaction and the resultant injuries. L. Loya, Union Carbide's medical officer, even insisted that the gas which had been emitted was non-poisonous. As much as fifteen days later, when the death toll exceeded 2,000, J. Nakund, the works manager, was also blithely reassuring. MIC was, he said, not lethal: 'In its effects, it is like tear gas. Your eyes start watering, you apply water and you get relief. What I say about fatalities is that we don't know of any fatalities either in our plant or in the other Carbide plants due to methyl isocyanate.' These tactics were similar to those attempted at Three Mile Island; the difference was that in India, thousands were dead.

As a result of these mistakes, local doctors were not sure what kind of poisoning they were treating. Disagreements and possibly rivalries among doctors did not help either. The local pathologist, Professor Heeresh Chandra, Director of the Medico-Legal Institute in Bhopal, did many of the post-mortems in the hours after the leak. He was puzzled by what he found. If the fluid in the lungs had caused the victims to die, their blood should have been bluish. It was not; it was cherry-red. It made him suspect that the victims had died of cyanide poisoning. Chandra, therefore, called for the immediate use of sodium thiosulphate, an antidote to cyanide. He was roundly ridiculed, even though this antidote is perfectly safe. The local district medical officer opposed sodium thiosulphate. A number of patients did indeed suffer adverse reactions to it, but there were only a few.

Union Carbide's American medical director, Bipin Avashiam, cabled the Bhopal authorities to tell them to use sodium thiosulphate if cyanide poisoning were suspected. That cable was subsequently withdrawn without any proper explanation. Avashiam defended himself by saying that he could not possibly know just what chemical each Union Carbide plant was producing. Avashiam never quoted the 1976 internal report in which Union Carbide had found that under 'thermal conditions' MIC broke down into hydrogen cyanide. The company did not then release news of that research, despite the fact that it was a finding which might have improved the treatment of victims and saved many lives.

It was only in February, some three months after the disaster, that the Indian Council on Medical Research changed its line. At the time, it pronounced itself mystified. Clearly, the victims had suffered cyanide poisoning, though the council could not begin to say how it had happened. Even after the Indian Council on Medical Research backed the use of sodium thiosulphate, it was available only in one thirty-bed hospital.

It is easy to be cynical about the reactions of multinationals. Aware of the risk of seeming a heartless corporation, Union Carbide at once put out a statement saying that it was shocked.

It offered to build an orphanage and to contribute a sum of one million dollars to the relief fund. Given the scale of the disaster, the sum was puny, and did nothing to appease the local residents.

Perhaps because there had been warnings that no one had heeded, the citizens of Bhopal were uncompromising. Brigadier Garg said, 'People are frightened and angry. They are frustrated and want justice. This is a devastated community. People have lost confidence. Our workers are reluctant to return. They don't believe the assurance of the authorities that the gas has gone.'

The state government may have been accused of having too close links to the company, but local anger was so great that it was forced to act. Arjung Singh, the Chief Minister of Madhya Pradesh, argued that the company had been criminally negligent. When Union Carbide's president, Warren Anderson, arrived in town, the state government had him arrested, together with the chairman and chief executive of the Indian subsidiary. They were under arrest for most of the day. But there were immediate interventions behind the scenes: the Indian government in Delhi had made accusing noises. Rajiv Gandhi, the new Prime Minister, said that he would expect Union Carbide to behave as it would in a Western disaster; nevertheless, he did not appear to relish a confrontation with a major multinational. The American Embassy also pressed for Anderson's release. After a day in the local courthouse, where he was 'very politely treated', Anderson was released on his own bond of the grand sum of $2,000. The Indian government then provided an aeroplane to fly him back to Delhi, the state government claiming that his presence in Bhopal was inflaming passions.

It was not only American executives, however, who descended on the town; soon American lawyers were also there, led by Melvin Belli, a flamboyant San Francisco lawyer who had often represented film stars in divorce cases. Belli warned from the start that American corporations routinely tried to wriggle out of their responsibility for disasters, and that the fact that this calamity was an Indian one would make it easier for them. He stated, accusingly: 'These people in India are nobodies. Some poor little bastard living in a railroad shack goes home to find his wife and child dead. Now Union Carbide have the effrontery to offer them an orphanage and a million dollars. It's a major goof.' Other lawyers descended who were not as flamboyant or as good at presenting themselves as champions of the underdog, some offering 100 rupees to local residents to encourage them to sign up as their clients. The Attorney General of Connecticut denounced them as jet-setting ambulance-chasers. More ominously, experts in chemical warfare also arrived in Bhopal to study the effects of mass poisoning.

One of the immediate problems facing the city was the fifteen million tonnes of MIC in tank 611, next to tank 610. This was a major hazard. The Indian government decided that it had to dispose of this, but knew that the process would arouse panic. The investigating committee therefore insisted that the public be given proper information. People were terrified that there would be another leak. As a result, the disposal of the rest of the MIC was nicknamed 'Operation Faith'. The state government had to provide transport to all those who wanted to leave the city, and an estimated 150,000 people took buses and trains to what they saw as safety. The Indian government dramatized the situation skilfully. Helicopters hovered overhead, dousing the plant with water. From 16 to 22 December, forty-five tonnes of MIC were destroyed. (It seemed that the plant had been storing more MIC than was known or permitted.) With the successful conclusion of Operation Faith, the city was safe, but the medical complications and the long-drawn-out legal battles were just beginning.

There were some frightening developments in the immediate aftermath: a third of all the town's babies between December and February were born dead. Clearly it was due to the gas, but no one could explain why. The lack of medical facilities continued to be chronic. As well as the 1,750 dead, some 110,000 living souls were affected. Of these, 10,000 had serious, long-lasting lung conditions. Many needed special diets. All of them would benefit from injections, but these were being given at such a slow rate that it would take seven years for everyone to be dealt with. The only optimistic note concerned injuries to the eyes. Initially it had been rumoured that there would be many cases of blindness, but in the event very few victims had long-lasting eye problems.

The Psychological Dimension

Though India is an underdeveloped country in many ways, it does have a tradition of psychiatric care. The first mental hospital was established in Calcutta in 1787, though it dealt exclusively with white men who had gone berserk in the heat of the tropics. Since then, Indian psychiatry has grown and though its psychiatrists accept that they provide for only something approaching 10 per cent of the needs of the population, the care they do provide is often imaginative.

Leading psychiatrists realized quickly that they would need to intervene at Bhopal. At a meeting from 12 to 14 December of the Advisory Committee on Mental Health, it was decided to send down a team of doctors to investigate the emotional state of the population. The situation turned out to be complex and shot through with contradictions.

Clinics that were faced with thousands of patients felt overwhelmed. Few doctors had much sympathy with psychiatry; most of Bhopal's doctors had no training at all in mental health. One of the team who went down was a psychiatrist from Bangalore, Dr Srinivas Murthy. Murthy had once driven me into a tiny Indian village to introduce me to a long-term schizophrenic whom he had started to treat twenty-five years into her illness. Her family had been locking her up because there was no other way of coping with her outbursts. Murthy is not the kind of man to register shock at the oddities of India, but even he was not quite prepared for the attitudes of his medical colleagues. Their lack of psychiatric training, he said, was 'reflected in their poor perception of the emotional needs of the disaster victims'. Most of the doctors expressed the view that 'distribution of monetary compensation would solve the physical complaints of a large number of patients'. They were clearly of the opinion that Bhopal inhabitants were malingering if they said they were depressed.

The doctors argued as follows, Murthy and his colleague, Isaac Mohan, explained: the Indian government was providing free rations. This, the local doctors believed, 'was the reason for the weakness and inability to work complained of by most patients'. It was their expert medical opinion that lethargy and associated ills would disappear 'not by doctor or by the free use of drugs but by stopping the free rations and distribution of compensation money'.

Faced with this reaction, Murthy and Mohan set up a training programme to explain to their colleagues the well-established effects disasters were likely to have. The irony was that, in both academic and practical terms, Indian psychiatrists were well aware of the traumas that follow disasters. In 1981, fire broke out at a circus in the city of Karnataka in Bangalore state. An electric cable fell on to the big top and set the ring alight. Seventy people died. Karnataka was in a panic for a number of days. As the flames could be seen from many points in the town, people who thought their relatives had gone to the circus went to try and help, many besieging the local hospitals and police stations for information. In psychiatric terms, the victims of the circus fire were well cared for. Bangalore houses the National Institute of Mental Health, a leading national centre of Indian psychiatry, set in a large airy hospital in the middle of Bangalore City. It runs a series of walk-in clinics where the local population can get immediate help.

The Bangalore psychiatrists were in a position to monitor thoroughly the grim consequences of that disaster. Some of their findings were gruesome. The fire had been very intense. In 39 per cent of cases it had been impossible for bodies to be identified because they were too damaged by burns. Relatives had to rely on tatters of clothing, jewellery and shoes, a process which was extremely harrowing. Many of the bereaved relatives told the psychiatrists that 'it was impossible for them to remove from their mind the image of the disfigured body of the deceased due to burns'. There was a paradox here: the bereaved had not usually seen the body, because there was not a body that was 'theirs' for them to view, but the relics of things associated with the dead were both precious and unbearably sad. In one case, a couple never knew for sure if the body that was handed over to them was really that of their child. In 30 per cent of cases, the victims had not died instantly but had regained consciousness and been able to talk a little to their relatives. This did not seem to make any difference to the bereaved's eventual reactions. The psychiatrists interviewed 137 surviving relatives, some of whom had been at the circus themselves and just escaped. Initially, these relatives had been distraught and shocked, as might be expected.

In Indian culture, funeral rites offer an important means of adjusting to death, but 9 per cent of those interviewed were themselves too injured to attend the funerals. Like nearly all of those who lived through Bhopal, many of the circus fire people were both bereaved and survivors. Many had attended the doomed circus that night and got out alive. As a result, their feelings of guilt were high. The interviews revealed that many people did not just feel guilty because a loved one was dead, but because they felt they had failed them at the moment of death. In two cases, guilt was felt because the survivor had not been able to save the dead person even though the survivor had been close by and had taken the dead person to that show. In many cases, parents had allowed their children to nag them into going. They had stood out, at first, against letting them go to the circus, but had finally yielded to pressure. In some families, the wife had allowed the children to go to the circus without telling the husband. Now they were alive and their loved one was dead.

In Indian culture, fate or karma is supremely important. It is used to explain many tragedies, such as becoming schizophrenic, Dr Murthy told me. Here, in the wake of the circus fire, many survivors did blame karma. In Indian philosophy, a person's past incarnations and how he, or she, acted in them determine their next life. This belief left relatives with a problem: to die in a fire suggested that, perhaps, the deceased had behaved badly in previous lives. However, there was no sign that the dead were blamed for their fate, rather the opposite. In 91 per cent of cases, the interviewers found they were idealized as incredibly beautiful and clever. There were many descriptions of the personalities of the dead that were simply too good to be true. This is not an uncommon reaction to sudden death, though it is a particularly interesting one in the Indian context given belief in karma and in reincarnation. Did the fire literally purify their sins?

A number of relatives had hallucinatory dreams in which the dead appeared to them and were burning. Talking to the bereaved and survivors six months after the tragedy, the researchers found that many were still suffering despite the fact that six months is often cited as a normal grieving period and that after it, one should begin to recover. The circus fire victims, however, were still showing many acute signs of distress: the percentage of those exhibiting psychiatric symptoms was high and is worth listing, as this was a thorough study. The number after each 'symptom' denotes the percentage of the 137 interviewed who showed it:

chronic grief: 74 per cent
sleep disturbance: 66 per cent
eating problems: 57 per cent
excessive guilt: 51 per cent
general health problems: 46 per cent
change in pattern of social and recreational activities: 44 per cent
dreams: 38 per cent (These dreams were often of the fire)
excessive anger: 36 per cent
change in attitude towards God: 30 per cent
misidentification: 19 per cent
death wish: 18 per cent
inhibited grief: 13 per cent
suicidal ideas: 7 per cent

This is a massive tally of distress. The psychiatrists found families instinctively tried to cope. Mourning rites continued longer than usual. Some families clung to them as a way of comfort and of remembering their dead. In 57 per cent of families, photographs of the dead were kept separately, or with those of gods and goddesses. Only in 8 per cent of cases did the families remove photographs because they brought back too many sad and dreadful memories.

The psychiatrists found that forty-nine of the 137 would actually benefit from psychiatric treatment. Eleven men, for example, had started to drink heavily. Patients were usually offered a mixture of counselling and anti-depressants. The forty-nine were followed up for two years, and the psychiatrists argued that all but two had recovered relatively well; it gave them confidence in their procedures.

When Bhopal happened, the Indian psychiatrists knew they would be dealing with a much worse situation. First, much of a city had been devastated. Second, many of the survivors also had to cope with long-term physical problems. Despite good intentions and an awareness of the problems, however, no psychiatric service was set up for over three months. It was not until 1985, on 23 February, that a team of psychiatrists and nurses established a base at Chhola Road Policlinic in Bhopal. From there, they toured ten other clinics providing treatment. The psychiatrists in Bhopal did not use exactly the same tests as those in Karnataka, so it is hard to compare the results precisely, nevertheless they found that 45 per cent of survivors were suffering from a neurotic depression. Thirty-five per cent were in a state of anxiety. Not everyone who was anxious or depressed after Bhopal was sick: the more serious cases were fewer, though still considerable; 22.6 per cent were found to be suffering from a definite form of psychiatric disorder.

Two problems stood out. Many patients at Bhopal were in constant fear of having sustained damage to various organs of the body, due to the toxic effects of the gas. Then they had terrible flashbacks and dreams. There were recurrent and intrusive recollections, dreams and nightmares and the threat of the disaster happening again. Pictures of corpses, clouds of gas and vultures would not leave their minds.

The clinics did their best to offer a service, but it was estimated that perhaps 40,000 people would need psychiatric treatment. Few countries could have coped with an emergency of that size; India just did not have the resources to meet the need. Overstretched international agencies did not see it as a priority, either, reckoning that the main task was to feed the population and provide medical attention for the cyanide poisoning. The emotional and social help victims did need – and it was a real need – was, as a result, somewhat neglected; there was simply too much else to do. In this way, Bhopal was very different from a Western disaster.

On the political front, the handling of the rights of the victims also showed the differences between the First and Third World. In law, everyone who had been affected by Bhopal had the right to sue. The American lawyers may indeed have acted as 'jet-setting ambulance-chasers' but their very greed could profit the victims. As in the *Piper Alpha* disaster, establishing the right for compensation cases to be heard in the States could have been an important bargaining counter for getting better compensation.

The Indian government, however, did not appear to like this idea, declaring itself shocked by the antics of American lawyers. As a result, the government decided that it would act on behalf of all its citizens; Indians would no longer have the right to carry on their own legal cases. The government justified this interference on the grounds that many of those who had been worst affected by the disaster were poor and ill-educated: they could not hope to cope with American lawyers themselves. There was a germ of truth in this, but nevertheless victims were thus deprived of choice. Moreover, the contingency-fee-driven American lawyers were not doing at all badly. Within a month of the disaster, they had managed to persuade American courts that the cases had to be heard in the States. In theory at least, the victims of Bhopal would be treated as if they had rights equal to those enjoyed by Americans in similar situations. But all this work proved wasted when New Delhi took over the cases.

The action of the Indian government might have seemed less cynical if it had shown itself able to distribute relief properly. Operation Faith had been a success. Getting medical and social aid to Bhopal proved to be a very different matter. In theory, everyone who had been affected by Bhopal was entitled to a payment of 2,000 rupees. Food and medical treatment were also meant to be provided. But within four weeks of the disaster, citizens were complaining that they were not getting enough food and that none of the money promised by the government was forthcoming. A year after the gas leak, there were demonstrations, as people complained that they had still got nothing from the 'concerned' government.

Union Carbide protested its regrets but acted defensively, warning the citizens of Bhopal against suing. It also attempted to negotiate with the state government to have the factory reopened. For a period of time this appeared to be a real possibility, but in the end, the public outcry was so violent that it proved impossible.

In all Western disasters, the pressures of publicity and the threat of legal action oblige the responsible parties to begin legal negotiations quickly. The victims of the King's Cross disaster feel they have been treated badly, but they have received sums on account which have allowed them to start living their own lives again. I have repeatedly argued in this book that after a disaster people strive hard to re-establish control over their own lives and that this is a healthy thing to do. In Bhopal, victims were not allowed to do that; their right to act was taken away from them.

What was also startling was that although Bhopal was identi-fied as the largest environmental disaster ever pre-Chernobyl, after it, very little of a constructive nature happened for a long time. The government did provide some food and free medical services and it did make sure, in the end, that the factory did not reopen. But that was all. Neither Union Carbide nor the Indian government felt under huge pressure to act and help the people who had been so badly hurt. The effect of the delay on Bhopal's residents was demoralizing. There were, throughout 1985, a number of demonstrations but these always petered out. By 1989, it was reckoned that the majority of relatives of the dead had received only total compensation of 2,000 rupees, a sum not much in excess of £100. There was, as a result, a great deal of impotent anger among victims. A number of children's groups lobbied New Delhi, but to little avail.

The Indian government did eventually settle their claims with Union Carbide at $470 million. Lawyers denounced the settle-ment as paltry. For the local population, these legal manoeuvres were meaningless. Most had lost any faith in the system. As Melvin Belli had warned, it had been much easier for the authorities to get away with paltry compensation because the dead and injured had been 'Indian nobodies'. If *Piper Alpha* showed a group determined to change things by using the authority the accident gave them, Bhopal showed how easily people can be rendered powerless.

Psychiatrists who have studied Bhopal's aftermath tend, sadly, to be part of the Indian establishment. They continue to study the effects of the disaster, but perhaps since they are funded by the Indian government, they have not raised these political issues. Did the government's taking over the legal process and its willingness to settle 'low' actually add to people's distress by taking more control out of their lives? It would be embarrassing to show, after all, that the Indian government's actions had actually made life even more difficult for the victims of Bhopal.

8

Counselling

Even in America, Mecca of therapy, the idea that survivors of disasters need psychological help was slow to develop. After the dam disaster at Buffalo Creek, for instance, there was no plan to provide counselling services: family doctors and social workers were simply left to muddle through. It was only as the psychologists investigating the after-effects began to report their results that it became clear help was needed. In the United Kingdom, a similar situation obtained until after the horrendous fire in the football stand at Bradford in 1985.

The initial impetus for developing disaster counselling services came from Holland and Scandinavia. After both the Dutch train hijacks of 1975 and 1977 and the North Sea *Ecofisk* disaster, there was a determined attempt to contact survivors and to offer them help. Since then, the issue of how to provide counselling after disasters has become important and controversial. In this chapter, I want to look at how counselling can be provided, at its uses and at the limits of what it can achieve, for to regard it as a panacea is misguided.

Texts on counselling usually suggest that people undertake it because they have come to the conclusion that they want to change, that their lives are no longer satisfactory to them. The motive comes from within them. Accounts of therapy such as Stephen Murgatroyd's (1986) start from that basis. Murgatroyd is a psychologist who argues that seeking help is a conscious, willed decision made by people who realize that they are in trouble.

In a disaster, the situation is radically different. As we have seen, in the immediate hours and days after a disaster, victims are in a state of shock. Even those who have not been seriously injured physically feel that they are not themselves. To cope with this phenomenon, social service departments in Britain have organized helplines within twenty-four hours of most of the disasters that have occurred since 1985. They also allocate staff to help: Grampian Social Services, for example, had twelve social workers making visits to both the bereaved and survivors after the *Piper Alpha* tragedy.

Victims of disasters do not have the choice of deciding that they want to change, the choice that Murgatroyd sees as being the basis of any 'good' decision to seek help. Partly, this is due to their having been plunged into a crisis, but it is also partly due to the fact that counselling is now sometimes virtually forced on people. After *Piper Alpha*, Grampian Social Services adopted what it called an 'assertive policy', contacting all the affected families and asking if they wanted help. Anne Bone, the social worker in charge of this operation, said that they had a response rate of 70 per cent.

Such an assertive policy is not necessarily ideal. In Holland, psychologists and social workers at Assen found that many of the ex-hostages resented being asked if they needed help. They would have preferred a number they could contact if they wished. In Britain, seeking help is still seen as a somewhat self-indulgent thing to do. Many people appear to think that they ought to be able to cope in a crisis with a little sympathy from family and friends, that only the psychologically inadequate have to seek professional help. Many psychiatrists report that survivors often resent, and even resist, offers of help. Freud would not have been surprised by this, since he argued that patients often put up resistance to therapy. Survivors sometimes admit that they feel conflicted when they are offered help, as Dick Bates did after King's Cross. It was not something he expected ever to have to accept. Going to a psychiatrist, in short, still carries stigma. It tells survivors that they are no longer fully themselves, no longer quite the people they were before.

Disaster counselling has to cope with sudden crisis, and it has drawn a good deal on the practices of a related discipline, bereavement counselling. There are, however, some fundamental differences. The bereaved do not want to change their personalities: nothing is fundamentally 'inadequate' about them. Rather, they have to accept what has happened and make sense of it so that they may be free to move back into their own lives. Survivors, on the other hand, need to deal with 'unfinished business' and then resume their lives.

Bereavement counsellors have identified a series of stages that individuals typically work through. These are, first, denial, during which it is hard for them to believe that the person concerned is actually dead. Next comes anger, usually at the dead: how could they go away and abandon the living? This response is clearly irrational, but that does not mean it is any less strong or sincere. Sudden deaths often tend to provoke the most anger. Both families of the bereaved and survivors find it easier to express anger at the railways, the airline or hijackers that caused the disaster. That anger makes sense, it is natural. Often, though, people find it more shameful and confusing to admit that they are angry with their loved ones who have died. Yet decades of work on bereavement has shown that it is normal to be angry with the dead, even more so, perhaps, when death is unexpected. Much counselling involves giving people information and, through that, making them see that the violent feelings they experience are not a sign of craziness. After disasters, this process is absolutely vital.

The Survivors

Survivors of physical disasters, like the King's Cross fire, are often in a state of shock. David Sturgeon, remembering the night that people from that fire came into University College Hospital, told me: 'They were deeply shocked when they first arrived in hospital and were in intense pain from their burns. Many needed immediate operations in order to try and, for example, save the use of their hands. And I think that they were very preoccupied with having come so close to death and yet survived that experience. But soon after, they would have flashback experiences when they would relive events of the disaster. For example, they would see flames round their beds, they would smell smoke, they would hear the screams of people who were trapped in the station, and these were hallucinatory experiences. They would occur in clear consciousness while people were awake, and they would also disrupt their sleep. They would have difficulty in staying asleep, they would awake from these nightmares. These experiences we know are quite common following disasters, and they can persist for quite some time. In fact many people experience intrusive, unwanted thoughts about the disaster which just come into their mind unasked. In the middle of people doing all kinds of other tasks, suddenly they'll find themselves reliving the experience again.'

In this case, the pain survivors faced was atrocious and, often in disaster studies, psychiatrists skim by such obvious physical symptoms. Sturgeon, however, realized that his patients found the pain very difficult indeed. In fact, many people required treatment with incredibly strong painkillers, heroin-type painkillers, in order to contain it. And of course pain fluctuates, and when it suddenly comes upon you and is very intense, that is also very trying from a psychological point of view.

The temptation is for counselling teams immediately to descend on individuals and, in effect, lecture them about the need to express their feelings. From the Dutch hijackings to Lockerbie, there have been sceptics who have criticized psychiatrists and social workers for being too eager and almost hustling victims to talk out their trauma.

Many survivors also find that, although families and friends try to be supportive, they are unable fully to comprehend what victims went through. Survivors are irritated by attempts to tell them to be thankful they are alive and to cheer them with platitudes. David Sturgeon pointed out that there was a paradox in the attitude of families: 'The first thing that was important to do was really just to be there for them. These people wanted to talk about their experience and to talk about, well, really reliving the experience. To go over it in their own minds, and it's very important that they should be allowed to do that. The trouble is that sometimes they get stuck in just going round and round and over and over these experiences. What we have to try and do is to help them get the feelings about the experience out. And that can be very difficult for relatives and for friends. For example, if someone you know and love suddenly bursts into tears, your immediate response is to try and console them and to comfort them and to try and stop them from crying. What we were trying to do was to help them to cry. To actually enable them to get these feelings out. This would sometimes apparently add to the distress they were in, but in fact, in the longer term, we know that it brings great relief.' This is not easy to prove, however, since scientific proof could be derived only from comparing victims who were helped with those who were not offered counselling. Now that psychiatrists believe that counselling helps, it would clearly be unethical to withhold it merely to provide a sample group of survivors for purposes of research. Irving Sarason and Barbara Sarason (1984) in their textbook, *Abnormal Psychology*, list many disasters, from Buffalo Creek to the volcanic eruption at Mount St Helens, where counselling is deemed to have helped survivors. But the evidence is anecdotal. David Sturgeon would not deny this, but he nevertheless feels convinced that it proves his point.

If families are nervous about raising the topic, it makes for collusion between them and the victim. Families avoid dragging survivors through harrowing tales 'which will only upset them'; the victim does not wish to be forced to remember. As a result, evasion becomes easy. Sturgeon added that, quite often, survivors 'might be talking about their experiences and their eyes might glaze over with tears and they might say: "I'm lucky to be alive," and start to cry'. For relatives, this could easily be extremely distressing, but Sturgeon would gently press victims further down this line. 'Then we would talk to them about how many times they thought about dying, what might have happened if they had died, how that might have affected their families, their friends.'

The need for counselling is therefore fairly well established. But psychiatrists, psychologists, social workers and therapists who offer it need to know when and how to start; they have to be available without being pushy. Many counsellors feel that it is important for individuals not to feel rushed, or pushed, into accepting help. The trouble is that there is no easily predictable time at which survivors want to start to speak about their experiences. For some, it can be as soon as a few hours after they are rescued; for others, days and even weeks pass before they want to say anything. Both Grampian (after *Piper Alpha*) and Camden Social Services (after King's Cross) found that some people made their first contact with helplines only weeks after the disaster. Mike Napier, a lawyer who specializes in disaster litigation, has come across cases in which symptoms of distress did not appear until well over a year after a tragedy.

Often, it is only when victims realize that the bad dreams and feelings of guilt are not going to go away that they become willing to confide in a counsellor. After the King's Cross fire, Sturgeon spent a good deal of time at University College in the wards making it clear that he was there if people wanted him. Not forcing the pace has its merits: it allows people to speak when they feel able to do so, which makes them feel, importantly, in control of their fate.

Dick Bates found that he needed help coping with the question of going back on to the tube. He did not want to feel that he could never do it again. Sturgeon said, 'I'll come with you. We'll take it one station at a time or we'll just go down the escalator, we won't actually get on the train. We'll take it stage by stage.' This was reassuring to Bates.

Good counsellors recognize that some people will take time to talk. Alan Simper was a parish priest in Dover the day that the Zeebrugge ferry sank, and he quickly became involved in providing some sort of comfort for the bereaved, spending a number of days at the harbour. He was, he confesses, initially suspicious of what counselling could achieve, but over a number of weeks, he realized how it often complemented what he could offer as a priest. He was used to offering some form of comfort to the dying and to families in bereavement, but most of his previous experience had been gained from cases where death had been expected. Then, tragically, Simper himself experienced a loss in a disaster. His only brother died in the Purley rail crash. Simper was utterly depressed at the loss of his only blood relative, and he admits to having very unChristian thoughts about the train driver who raced through the red signal at seventy miles an hour. For Simper, however, his Christian faith has proved a bedrock. He believes his brother is with God and he says, 'Every time I take a service, I pray for him.' Simper had seen some sceptics turn to God in such a crisis and, conversely, many turn away, believing that disasters were a proof of the random malice of life, showing there could not be a God. Despite having derived his own comfort mainly from his religious faith, however, Simper recognizes the value of secular counselling.

The explosion of new therapies in the last twenty years has led to the establishment of many different kinds of counselling. Murgatroyd suggests there are six different models, but only one of these, the cathartic, is really appropriate to counselling after a disaster. Catharsis is the ancient Greek word for purging the emotions; one of the functions of Greek tragedies like *Oedipus Rex*, according to Aristotle, was that witnessing his story allowed audiences to feel purged of their emotions. Cathartic counselling allows victims to talk about what happened to them, taking them through their stories step by step. It encourages them to tell the whole truth as they feel it, including moments about which they may feel guilty or regretful. Hans Prinz, for instance, one of the hostages on the Dutch train at Assen, still felt obscurely that Bert Bierling, the last passenger to die, could have been saved if he had managed to convince the Dutch authorities that the hijackers were not bluffing. Many of the King's Cross survivors had been travelling with someone whom they had lost in the panic. The counsellor offers not just the chance to retell the story but also to feel the powerful emotions that accompany it. The procedure calls for a mixture of relaxation, pressure and tact, especially in a country like Britain where there is considerable ambivalence about seeking help. Ron Lipsius said that it often seemed to him that the best thing to do was to put it out of his mind. Counsellors have to explain why there is a point in going through the experience again.

The experiences of psychiatrists during the 1939–45 war provide a useful comparison. Stephen MacKeith who was a senior army psychiatrist used to relax patients, and start by talking generally about what had happened in a particular military operation. He felt that it was important to have a good deal of specific knowledge about particular incidents in order to be able to prompt patients gently. The more they could feel that the process was like sharing a story with a comrade, the better. MacKeith would then lead them towards telling the story of a particularly difficult piece of action, the event that seemed to be causing their problem. In one case, he told me of taking a sailor through the journey on a ship from Bordeaux back to Britain, a fearful journey after weeks of battle. It required patience and tact to keep on pressing but MacKeith, like most of his colleagues, was influenced by psychoanalytic ideas, feeling that only by getting patients to say what had happened to them could they conquer it and get on with their lives. This technique was called abreaction. Often, at the end of a story, the man would be in tears and terribly upset. The evidence, however, was that it worked well. The British Army regularly used psychiatrists and had a large psychiatric section in the Sutton Emergency Hospital, where they specialized in such techniques. After some battles, especially in North Africa, battle-shocked soldiers were even taken back to the battlefields by doctors to talk about what had happened to them. After describing each incident, they were asked, 'What happened then?'

The war produced its own imperatives. Psychiatrists wanted not just to cure patients, but to make it possible to send them back to the front as quickly as possible, so if patients could not talk easily, they were given drugs like sodium amytal, to help them relax and open up. In a number of research papers, it was shown that it did help relax patients so that they talked more.

The personal style of the counsellor is important, in war or in peacetime: he or she needs to establish a warm and empathic relationship with the survivor. It is particularly important to give patients time; Ron Lipsius, as already noted, was impressed because Sturgeon would allow ten-minute silences to take place during their conversations. Dr James MacKeith, the son of Stephen MacKeith, is now one of Britain's leading forensic psychiatrists. He counselled some of the Zeebrugge victims, also found survivors needed plenty of time. As a priest, not a psychiatrist, Alan Simper said that what he often found himself doing was just sitting with people and holding their hands. He saw his function as a priest as being to wait for them to be able to speak, and often, they relied on him to express what they could not express themselves.

Counselling the Carers

It is not only survivors, however, who need help. On 28 November 1979, 257 passengers on an Air New Zealand non-stop tourist flight were killed in the Antarctic when their plane crashed into Mount Erebus. The rescue operation was rendered very tough because of the climate. Police and mountain climbers joined scientists already in the Antarctic in trying to recover the dead, but it took ten weeks to locate and bury all the bodies. Even then, 16 per cent of the passengers could not be identified and were buried in a communal grave in Auckland. The first part of the recovery took eighty hours on Mount Erebus at a time when the weather was extremely inclement. Packing and returning the remains took a further nine weeks.

In a follow-up study of the rescue workers, Professor I. Taylor of Wellington University found that the operation had taken its toll. He told the British Psychological Society in 1979 that, whereas next of kin are allowed extreme emotions after a disaster, professionals are meant to be cool, detached – professional. Policemen, for instance, should not burst into tears at the scene of a murder, however gruesome the corpse. Taylor assumed the rescue workers were reasonably well adjusted. They also knew what was being asked of them. He interviewed them nine months and twenty months after the rescue operation had taken place. He found that, despite their competence, many of the rescue workers had been profoundly affected by the experience, many having nightmares and intrusive thoughts. They could not forget what they had seen in the Antarctic: it reminded them all too clearly of their own mortality. The recovery workers, having found the bodies, passed them on to the repackers, who worked in short bursts. They packed the bodies into plastic bags and containers. They had to cope with the gruesome ooze caused by the bodies thawing, so they were forced to handle a great deal of decomposing flesh. Taylor found that they also had apparently insignificant problems, which loomed large in what was an extremely stressful situation: they could not take regular breaks because their schedule was determined by the timing of the helicopters.

Many rescue workers could not get out of their minds the

unpleasant sights they witnessed: gross disfigurements, fixed facial expressions, bodies rigid in contortions. Seven reported recurrent dreams in which they themselves were in aircraft collisions or trapped in mortuaries. A number dreamt that they were themselves dead and it was the corpses who were tending to them, rearranging their flesh.

The percentage of those who had significant symptoms for four weeks after the rescue operation was large. Taylor found that 81 per cent said they had experienced changes in their sleep patterns. Seventy-six per cent experienced loss of appetite; 49 per cent said they experienced changes in feelings, 33 per cent changes in social activities. At the final follow-up twenty months after the rescue operation, Taylor expected to find that most of these problems had been healed with time, yet 8 per cent of these professionals confessed that they still often felt the need to talk about what had happened, and its consequences for them, with friends or doctors. Fifteen still experienced occasional emotionally laden flashbacks; these burst into their minds unbidden. The best protection against distress, Taylor suggested, seemed to be to dehumanize the bodies, to see them not as dead people but as things. There was some evidence that older and experienced workers might have been better at doing this.

I have shown how in the wake of King's Cross, Lockerbie and *Piper Alpha* rescue workers were encouraged to seek counselling but often did not feel able to use what was available. In the light of Taylor's research, it does not seem illogical that members of the emergency services and others involved in disaster rescue operations should have a right to sue; for some, the experience did prove damaging. If such a right were to be established, however, it would create a paradox. Anyone who becomes a doctor, nurse, policeman or fireman must know that the job will require them to deal with emotionally charged situations like these, that they will have to deal with often gruesome deaths from which most of us are protected. The Police Federation has asked for policemen involved in dealing with disasters, especially in body handling, to have routine access to counselling. They have also asked, interestingly, for assurances that such requests would not count against those who made them in terms of promotion prospects.

Many policemen who dealt with the bodies from the *Piper Alpha* disaster and at Lockerbie were shocked both by the number and by the state of the bodies; these were not easy deaths. One undertaker who is experienced at recovering bodies from disaster sites explained to me that it was important to tell the police that it was quite acceptable to have to walk away from the body-handling routine. He is adamant that training helps because it prepares the recovery staff, letting them know what state bodies can be in. Sometimes, the 'remains' are literally bits of bone, of soft tissue, scraps of skin. Yet they can be valuable evidence as to the cause of the disaster. They need to be handled meticulously, which is not easy. After Lockerbie, the police asked for help from outside the area, from Scottish social workers, but only two policemen came forward, admitting that something was bothering them; the rest bottled up the stress. Even in less macho occupations, like nursing, this self-discipline is common.

At University College, psychiatrists were well aware of this risk, as David Sturgeon explained: 'Staff certainly were affected. After the disaster we put notices up about wanting to see people, members of staff who had been involved that night. And, of course, nobody came forward. I think one of the lessons we learnt from that is that it's no good putting up notices and inviting people to come; you have to go out to them. You have to go and find them, and offer a service. And so, this is what happened: people who were on duty in casualty that night were approached, and indeed many of them wanted to talk about that experience, many of them were deeply distressed by it. I remember talking to one anaesthetist whose job it had been, basically, to identify the bodies as being alive or dead as they were brought to casualty. And she could do that. She had seen very badly burnt bodies before. But when she went home, she burst into tears and cried and cried, for a long time, and was deeply upset and continued to be deeply upset by the experience and she thinks that it was just because of the number of bodies that had come. She was rather overwhelmed with the quantity of bodies that she was confronted with that night.'

Sturgeon accepts that the strain of those weeks affected him as a psychiatrist, too: 'I think there certainly is a toll. I was very fortunate in that I wasn't working alone. And other people who were seeing the victims, too, would have similar experiences and it was very important for us to share this. I mean, certainly as psychiatrists, we do see people who are distressed as part of our work, so that in a sense it isn't a new experience. But the sheer number, the sheer quality, if you will, of their disturbance I think does need help from other people.'

That carers themselves need care is hardly surprising, but is easily forgotten in the organization of services.

Rebuilding

The initial cathartic stage discussed above is not the end of the recuperation process. Some survivors have physical injuries. King's Cross left some twenty survivors with bad burns; Clapham left individuals with severe injuries, including a number who had to have amputations. Counselling here tries to get people to adjust to what their lives are now likely to be like. In a study of facial disfigurement, Ray Bull, a psychologist at North East London Polytechnic, found that people were shocked by the behaviour both of strangers and friends. Strangers stared rudely and muttered abuse. Walking down the street became a strain for the disfigured person. Bull also found that friends were not much more considerate: they tended to be embarrassed and evasive. Most disabilities can provoke that kind of response. One woman, Anne Kelly, was twenty-two years old when, almost overnight, she lost her sight. One day she had been driving; the next, she could hardly make out colours. She began, of course, to look different. Her brother did not take in what had happened to her till one day in hospital he saw her being led to the toilet. Anne told me she was 'all knotted up', but as she began to come to terms with what had happened to her she was amazed by the behaviour of some of her friends: they no longer wanted her in their lives. She embarrassed them because they felt they had to look after her. She tried at first to keep going to nightclubs, but kept bumping into people. Friends also felt awkward when they started to say things like 'Did you see?'. She commented: 'I didn't mind, because it's just a figure of conversation, but they apologized and didn't know what to say.' It took her a year to adjust, not just to her blindness, but to the often clumsy ways in which friends reacted, especially those who were young like her. The person who suddenly changes, or who has gone through a major trauma, is hard for others to deal with. As a result, the physical scars can easily lead to psychological ones.

In previous chapters I have argued that there is enormous variety found in people's reactions to disasters. Consequently, counsellors need to be acutely sensitive to this: they must not assume, for instance, that for everyone the disaster will have damaging long-term consequences. Even those whose dreams were shattered do not have to be themselves shattered. For Ron Lipsius, the most bitter blow was that the delicacy and sensitivity of his hands was gone, so he could no longer play music. He might learn to use a synthesizer, but part of his identity had disappeared for ever. In the two years after King's Cross, Ron had over twenty skin grafts and operations. He found the daily physiotherapy a chore. But the most positive change for him was becoming a father. He wonders if he would have been ready to do that if it hadn't been for King's Cross. Others' responses are more unspecific, though many still have particular fears: Sturgeon found that people who were involved in King's Cross, for example, 'are more disturbed by disasters that involve fire'. They then feel again that 'increased sense of vulnerability, an increased sense of human frailty. That it is possible that you could not survive the day. Because disasters are usually things that happen to other people. When they happen to you, you realize how fragile and how vulnerable human life is.' Dick Bates, the *Guardian* sub caught in the fire, recognizes this feeling: 'If I hear the word "disaster" on the television, then it's a triggerword: my mind immediately goes back to King's Cross.' Working on a newspaper, he has had to face the word many times since returning to work: 'It doesn't make me shake or anything,' he says, but it remains a trigger for memories he would rather not have.

Counselling here involves getting people to face up to where the disaster has left them. This process may provoke a re-evaluation of what they have done in their lives so far, and the counsellor should not shy away from this. Moving forward, deciding what they want to do now, often depends on this re-evaluation. Indeed one of the reasons psychiatrists like David Sturgeon insist on the need for people to express their feelings is that there is no chance for them to start to rebuild their lives until they own up to, and express, the strong feelings that go with the trauma.

Subsequently helping someone to move on requires a more conventional form of counselling. It involves identifying strengths and weaknesses; it involves looking at the relationships within families; it involves defining goals. In many of the stories in the previous chapters, I have suggested that families often find it hard to cope with members who have been through disasters, feeling that they are not quite the same people as before. Families are usually sympathetic but often themselves need counselling. Sturgeon says: 'Very often these families need support because they don't know what to do when someone who has been involved in a disaster suddenly becomes very upset at home. They do the best they can, but sometimes they're worried that maybe it's the wrong approach.' After the first few weeks, many families want normal life to resume and think that it would be for the best to act as if nothing had happened. Survivors often resent this. The families themselves often worry, according to Sturgeon, 'that maybe they shouldn't be telling somebody not to think about the disaster or to pull themselves together. I think a lot of the time it just involves not knowing.' But that uncertainty is itself a cause of tension.

At present all the counselling services in the UK are provided on a local basis; there is no national expertise. Every new disaster means that local teams have to devise their own ways of working. In some cases that has led to confusion. Often there have been desperate calls for social workers and counsellors who have had experience of recent disasters to help out. The trouble with such informal arrangements is that, at a time when people desperately need to know what they are doing, immediately after a disaster has happened there is no framework to provide this experience. It is, at this time, that there is considerable shock and surprise, as often people's decision-making abilities are impaired. It is at such times that a National Disaster Office would have the most valuable service to offer. Unfortunately, there is no sign that such a body will be set up; the Home Office has decided to appoint a peacetime emergency co-ordinator, but his or her role will be largely an academic one, it seems.

Eighteen months after the King's Cross disaster, Sturgeon was sceptical of how committed the government really was to providing the resources victims need. He said: 'I've learned really how little help there is available from the National Health Service and how much help these people need in the long term. I think probably the most difficult thing for all of them has been getting back to some kind of normal life.' Sturgeon also reiterated the view that all those who had been through King's Cross were now different people.

Alan Simper, as a vicar in Dover, offers a different perspective. He noted that the local social services unit, set up to deal with the Zeebrugge disaster, had plenty of work for two years, and he still regularly visits parishioners whose lives remain severely disrupted because of death or the after-effects of survival. In a town with a long seafaring history, he also noted that every seaman who had worked on the *Herald of Free Enterprise* had now given up the sea. They could no longer take the stress involved. Simper also noted something that is perhaps hard for psychiatrists to accept. For some people, the death of a husband appeared relatively untraumatic. Indeed he spoke of two cases where people had moved in with a new partner within a week. He was somewhat taken aback by what he saw as the cruelty of this, especially regretting the impact it had on children. One woman, who quickly remarried, had to brave the disapproval of her original parents-in-law; there had been bitter family rows, resulting in their being banned from seeing their only grandchild, a child who could have reminded them of their lost son. Simper was more acid than a psychiatrist would have been about the human capacity for survival, commenting that some survived all too selfishly, all too well.

For psychiatrists, the key question is why do some people manage well? David Sturgeon and James MacKeith argue that the reasons for these differences in reaction remain unclear. 'One possibility is that if you've reacted badly to stress of any kind in the past, you're likely to react badly to a disastrous event. But there have certainly been exceptions to that: some people who have reacted very badly before seem to react very well to disasters,' Sturgeon claims. He also suggests, on the basis of anecdotal evidence, that if people can be counselled early on, they have a better chance of coping. Certainly he feels they should have the choice of getting good counselling when they need it.

The provision of long-term services is essentially a political issue. It requires, as Sturgeon points out, a willingness to commit resources in a way that the National Health Service is unaccustomed to doing. It urgently needs to be done.

9
The Law

In 1985, Mrs Attia, wishing to improve her house, asked the Gas Board to install central heating. The Gas Board began the installation but, in the middle of it, hit problems. Mrs Attia was returning home one day when she saw that her house was on fire, and had to watch, helpless, as her home was reduced to ashes. She was, as a result, badly affected not just by the loss of her home but by the additional trauma of having to watch it happen. When, understandably, Mrs Attia decided to sue the Gas Board, she claimed additional damages for the distress caused by witnessing the actual fire.

This claim was not entirely novel, because plaintiffs had previously won damages for the 'nervous shock' of seeing a disaster that directly affected them. The Court of Appeal, in its decision in the Attia case, said: 'Her claim is accordingly one for what have in the authorities and the literature been called damages for nervous shock.' Lord Justice Bingham noted that judges had become rather 'restive at the use of this misleading and inaccurate expression'. Nervous shock seemed to denote any kind of psychiatric damage, including mental illness, neurosis and personality change. The judge added that a successful claim would have to depend on psychiatric damage, caused by seeing the tragedy. Key elements, he said, of a successful action included: 'careless action on the part of the defendant causing actual or apprehended injury to the plaintiff . . . acute mental and emotional injury by its witnessing or its aftermath; psychiatric damage suffered by the plaintiff'.

Lord Justice Bingham also pointed out that the Attia case expanded the law; 'no analogous claim' had ever been put forward. He acknowledged the court was breaking new ground and, if one imagined legal liability having boundaries, that they were 'moving the boundary stone'. The judge did not think, moreover, that it would rest there; he had a 'presentiment that it would not be long before a case would arise so compelling in its facts as to cause the boundary stone to be moved to a new and more distant resting place'.

The Attia judgment indicates the ways in which disaster law is changing, and changing fast. It is a complex field of law because it involves negligence, personal injury law, many international transportation agreements and, for the first time for many years, the use of the criminal law, as victims call for transport authorities to be tried for corporate manslaughter. Lawyers and judges are having to respond with appropriate speed and subtlety.

In most personal injury cases, one plaintiff sues for the damage that has been done to him or her. In disaster cases, the first difference resides in the sheer number of plaintiffs; all will have gone through the same event, but the effects will be highly individual.

Edwina Dunn, of the Law Society, explained to me that when the Bradford City fire took place, British solicitors had very little experience of legal actions in which a number of different plaintiffs sued one company after a disaster. America, where the law on compensation is more highly developed, has much more experience of such multi-party suits. In a multi-party suit, victims co-ordinate their tactics to sue the appropriate authority.

The Law Society therefore set up a co-ordinating committee so that solicitors for the bereaved and survivors could agree on tactics. A committee of five solicitors was constituted to direct the progress of the cases. Going to law, as many writers have pointed out, is stressful. The ordinary man or woman becomes embroiled in a mystifying technical process full of high-sounding jargon. People feel they simply cannot comprehend or control the process. A number of studies highlight this stress. Victims of crime often feel that they are at a disadvantage when they go to court and that they suffer great stress in the process (Shapland and Cohen, 1987). Couples going through divorce report that they not only had to suffer the miseries of the end of the marriage but a long, anxiety-provoking legal process (Davis, 1988).

Sheffield solicitor Michael Napier is one of the first in Britain to become something of a disaster expert. He has long had an interest in mental health law, and in 1981, won a case at the European Court of Human Rights on behalf of a Broadmoor patient. This case established the right of mental health tribunals to discharge detained patients. Until then, only the Home Secretary had that power. Napier became involved in two of the major disasters of 1985: the Bradford fire and the Manchester aircraft fire. In both these situations he saw the chance to use his knowledge of mental health law.

From the mid-eighteenth century, a company could be sued for negligence if it failed in its duty of care to its customers. In Victorian times, railway companies were often sued in the wake of disasters like the Armagh crash of 1889, the courts taking the view that a railway ticket constituted a contract, and that the carrying company therefore owed its passengers a duty of care. In Kelly *v*. Metropolitan Railway (1895), the courts upheld this right of injured passengers to sue for negligence.

The law of negligence developed and in 1932, Lord Atkin, a celebrated judge, argued a duty of care existed towards 'persons so closely and directly affected by my act that I ought reasonably to have them in contemplation as being so affected when I am directing my mind to the acts of omission which are called in question'. For litigants to have a good case they had, therefore, to show that the company had been at fault; negligence excludes bad luck. For example, if a train were swept away in a freak flood or an earthquake, then courts would have commiserated, but not compensated. The most prudent railway executive could not be expected to foresee such an 'act of God'. To prove negligence, plaintiffs had to prove that the company had failed to act with foresight and prudence in respect of predictable risks. Improbable risks were not covered, though in many cases, of course, lawyers were able to produce splendid arguments concerning whether a particular risk could, or could not be foreseen.

The law established two kinds of damages for which victims of accidents could expect compensation. The first was for the extent of physical injuries. Technically, these are known as pain, suffering and loss of amenity. Though in theory there is no set price for a particular injury, in practice there is a kind of tariff. In 1986, for example, the Court of Appeal upheld an award of £80,000 as an appropriate sum for an 'average case of tetraplegia', a tetraplegic being severely disabled. Mike Napier argues that the current figure for the pain, suffering and loss of amenity that a tetraplegic suffers is about £100,000.

The second head under which a person could sue was for loss of earnings. Plaintiffs could seek compensation either for themselves or, if they were dependent, for the money that the breadwinner would have earned for them. Such damages had to be calculated realistically: plaintiffs could hope to receive only a sum that would match what they might have earned had they not been injured.

These categories did not allow for much innovative litigation. There were some precedents, however, that suggested that the law might be widened. In 1925, a lorry belonging to Stoken Brothers ran away down a hill. A Mrs Hanbrook saw it career towards her. Her children were on the hill and she was 'immediately stricken with such fear for the children's safety' that she went into 'mental shock', and died weeks later. Her family sued for compensation and won. Curiously, perhaps, this judgment did not open the floodgates. After the tip disaster at Aberfan, for example, no one sued for psychological shock, even though many parents not only lost their children but saw them dead. The official inquiry into Aberfan never even raised the issue of the psychological damage caused.

Lawyers have become aware, however, of the great variety found in the effects of disasters. Since Buffalo Creek in America and since the Bradford fire in Britain, they have, as a result, tried to find more heads of damages under which to claim. At present, there are a number of areas in which there is debate and controversy. The main ones are:

i) Should there be a fixed payment for the death of a relative?

ii) Should there be compensation for psychiatric injuries, treating them, in effect, as being as serious as physical ones?

iii) Should there be compensation for the 'nervous shock' that relatives can sustain if they learn of the death or injury of their relative in a traumatic way?

iv) What is the fairest way of treating international disasters where the levels of compensation that can reasonably be expected under different legal systems are so widely different?

It is clear that this is bound to be a controversial and contentious area of law. Powerful vested interests want low damages; sympathy for the bereaved and survivors should not blind one to economic realities, transportation companies and their insurers argue. There have, therefore, to be sensible limits to compensation. After Bhopal, Union Carbide became an extremely troubled company: its price on the New York Stock Exchange fell drastically. When it managed to bargain the Indian government down to $470 million, however, its fortunes changed. The settlement was seen as a good deal, and so the stock market price of Union Carbide began rising again. Likewise, nationalized corporations like London Transport and commercial companies like P&O have similarly seen it as their duty to defend claims energetically.

The Death of a Relative

Until 1982, if a relative died, relations who were not dependent got no money at all, and any payments to dependants were calculated on the basis of how much deceased persons would have earned for them if they had not been killed. In 1982, a new Act established a minimum sum of £3,500 which had to be paid to any close relative if someone died in an accident or disaster. The passage of this law was not easy. Some argued that to price someone's life like this was morally wrong. Speaking personally, the then Lord Chancellor Lord Hailsham stated that there could be no value placed on someone's death, that to put what was, in effect, a price on their head was an insult both to them and their families. Despite this objection, the Act was passed. But it has not, since, kept pace with freshly arising problems. Napier believes, for instance, that the £3,500 limit is woefully inadequate: 'Public perception has shifted. There are great expectations. Much bigger damages are being awarded.' Napier acknowledges that people have been influenced by American examples and that some cases, like the disaster involving *Piper Alpha*, have attracted what are known as mid-Atlantic settlements. In the cases of both Zeebrugge and King's Cross, lawyers have managed to obtain settlements of £20,000 for loss of life. But Napier argues that even these sums are not adequate and are somewhat insulting: 'Relatives don't understand that the life of their loved ones is valued at, relatively, so little. There needs to be flexibility for compensation for loss of life.' Napier believes that it may be invidious to leave the decision in the hands of judges rather than juries. It is also widely perceived as an anomaly that damages in libel cases are now higher than damages in personal injury cases. This tends to make the law appear to be 'more of a lottery than usual', as one judge put it to me. The government, however, has now agreed to a consultation process, after Lawrence Cunliffe MP presented a private member's bill which argued that the limit ought to be raised to keep pace with inflation.

Compensation for Psychiatric Injuries

The most noticeable legal change in this area perhaps concerns psychiatric damages. British commentators tend to assume that Americans, with their boundless zeal for psychology, have long been able to sue for psychological damages. In fact, the concept is recent there too, dating back only to 1973, when the American sociologist Kai Erikson, from Yale University, investigated the Buffalo Creek disaster's effects on survivors, so that lawyers could ascertain what course might be open to them in suing for a new sort of damages. Like British law until then, American law recognized that transportation carriers had a duty of care, but any damages had to be either for physical injury or loss of earnings. Erikson came back from Buffalo Creek 'so awed and depressed' by what he had seen that he volunteered his own services. He admitted, too, that as a sociologist he had found surprising advantages in going into a traditionally tight west Appalachian community on behalf of its lawyers. Survivors and families were often wary of professional researchers, and so, as he was, in effect, likely to help them in their legal battle, Erikson met none of that reserve with which sociologists and psychologists are usually met. In addition, Arnold and Porter hired Robert Jay Lifton, who had studied the Hiroshima victims, and, finally, they also hired psychologists from the University of Cincinnati. The federal judge eventually ruled that each of the 650 victims be individually assessed. In Chapter Two, I described the subsequent research in some detail. As a result, by 1976, the principle of claiming for psychological damages had been accepted and a legal precedent was set.

The American ruling in the Buffalo Creek case affected what lawyers – and their clients – saw as being possible. British lawyers began to explore the possibility of asking for psychological damages in disaster cases. Michael Napier told me, 'I was already interested because of my background in mental health. I knew the American work on Vietnam veterans and on Buffalo Creek.' When he began to tackle disaster cases, therefore, Napier added psychological damage to the conventional heads of claim.

The concept of psychological damage was not totally unknown in British law, as the cases I mentioned earlier show. Additionally, some of the reasons for damages that are given in personal injury cases are fundamentally psychological: pain, suffering and loss of amenity. The law has also used the concept of nervous shock. Defining nervous shock, however, is not easy. The Court of Appeal in 1983 had to consider the case of McLoughlin *v.* O'Brien, in which Mr McLoughlin and three children were involved in a serious accident with a lorry. Two hours after the accident, Mrs McLoughlin was told about it by a neighbour, who took her to the hospital. There, she found out that her younger daughter had been killed, and she saw her husband and how bad her family's injuries were. Mrs McLoughlin sued for damages for nervous shock. She claimed that seeing her relatives so close to death had triggered an episode of depression.

In giving judgment, Lord Bridge noted that nervous shock was a tricky concept: 'The Common Law gives no damages for emotional distress which any normal person experiences when someone is killed or injured. Anxiety and depression are normal human emotions. Yet an anxiety neurosis or a reactive depression may be a recognizable psychiatric illness with or without psychological symptoms. So the first hurdle which a plaintiff claiming damages of the kind in question must surmount is to establish that he is suffering not merely grief or distress, or any other normal emotion, but a positive psychiatric illness.' In the McLoughlin case, this was established, and so the plaintiff won.

Soon after Lord Bridge set this test, the American Psychiatric Association *Diagnostic and Statistical Manual*, in its 1986 edition, accepted that post-traumatic stress syndrome was a psychiatric illness. From now on, as a result, lawyers could argue that the cluster of symptoms afflicting disaster victims were not merely ordinary human emotions and pain but a properly defined illness.

In America, after the Buffalo Creek disaster, the concept of post-traumatic stress syndrome has been widely accepted by the courts. It is now routine for disaster victims, whether they be survivors or the bereaved families, to get substantial psychological damages in millions of dollars.

British courts, however, have been slower to accept the concept. Survivors of the Bradford fire, for example, did not succeed in getting psychological damages. In the settlement of the claims of the victims of the *Herald of Free Enterprise*, Napier and his fellow lawyers argued powerfully that some clients had suffered severe post-traumatic stress. The Zeebrugge cases went to arbitration. The three arbitrators, Sir Michael Ogden QC, Michael Wright QC and William Crowther QC, all have long track records in personal injury law. In their decision, they accepted the principle that plaintiffs could receive damages for post-traumatic stress. The report of the arbitration of ten cases was published in June 1989 in the *Personal and Medical Injuries Newsletter*. It is worth setting out some of the personal histories.

One case involved a twenty-two-year-old single woman. She had been frightened of water before the disaster. Everyone she was travelling with survived, and she suffered relatively minor physical injuries: bruising to her back and chest, right leg, arms, hands and left index finger. Where her leg had been bruised, she developed an irritable skin condition. Twenty-four hours after the event, however, she reacted. For two or three days, she wept uncontrollably. She became so terrified of water that for some months she could not take a bath unless someone was there to encourage her. Many of her symptoms were the classic ones associated with post-traumatic stress: she had nightmares, loss of appetite, loss of libido, feelings of guilt and intrusive thoughts about the sinking. She could not help remembering the incident. She could not face a trip to Sweden in 1987, but in 1988 she did manage to fly to Corfu and to enjoy her holiday, although she was unable to face swimming. The arbitration award set out that there should be a fixed payment of £5,000 for all those who had survived. As a result, she received, in addition to this fixed payment, damages for psychiatric injuries of £1,750; for physical injuries of £1,250; and special damages of £1,135:75 pence.

The heaviest award of damages was to a fifty-four-year-old married man who worked at a main railway terminal. His wife, mother, daughter and ten-month-old grandchild were all killed. The physical injuries he sustained were fairly severe: a whiplash injury of the spine, injuries to the right elbow and the right middle finger. His neck continued to feel uncomfortable. He still cannot lift things easily and as a result finds it hard to do even DIY jobs. But these injuries were as nothing compared to the emotional and psychological impact of the disaster. Its effect on him has been catastrophic: his life has simply been destroyed. The arbitrators here faced a macabre dilemma. Under common law, there is, as Lord Bridge observed, no remedy for ordinary human grief and pain. In their judgment, the arbitrators noted that it would be normal for anyone who lost four relatives in a disaster to suffer terribly. In assessing damages, they therefore had to measure how much more than this kind of normal, but intense, suffering this man was experiencing. The psychiatric reports were powerful. The arbitrators were told that, two years after the capsize, the victim was still very depressed. He had thoughts of suicide. He was still suffering pathological grief and severe post-traumatic stress. The arbitrators found him to be demoralized, bitterly unhappy and unable to reconstruct his life. Their judgment was that he would never be able to work again. As a result, the damages that he received were substantially higher than those awarded to the twenty-two-year-old woman. In addition to the fixed payment of £5,000, he was given damages for psychiatric injuries of £30,000; for physical injuries of £5,500; for loss of earnings of £19,026; for future loss of earnings of £65,880; for the cost of DIY £2,000; in addition to fixed payments for lost relatives of £20,000 and special damages of £3,708. The award for psychiatric damages was the largest ever, but Napier suggested to me that 'perhaps £30,000 isn't really that much for this kind of catastrophic collapse'. He would like to see higher limits given for damage which can stop someone's life in its tracks in this way.

Arbitration awards do not create binding law; the Zeebrugge case, however, does provide a strong precedent. Napier argues that the arbitration has established a number of important principles. First, he points out that post-traumatic stress is now a recognized psychiatric illness. Second, pathological grief is a recognized psychiatric illness. Third, since some survivors had other psychiatric illnesses, such as depression, the arbitrators accepted that a survivor can suffer from more than one psychiatric illness. Fourth, it may be quite reasonable for survivors to refuse psychiatric treatment. Finally, any arbitration award should take into account how vulnerable victims are to future psychiatric illness.

The legal procedures have also improved somewhat. The two sides are no longer supposed to surprise or ambush each other with dramatic new evidence, each side being required to put all its cards on the table so that justice can be arrived at fairly. Napier is sure that this has made the process a little less tense. Nevertheless, going through litigation is undoubtedly still stressful. Some clients' eagerness to see the end of it may make them unwise: they want to settle quickly so that they can put the whole nightmare behind them. 'Being a disaster lawyer is very much a matter of timing,' Napier told me. For post-traumatic stress can take a long time to appear. Some of the Falkland Islands soldiers, for example, did not begin to show any symptoms of distress until five years after the campaign.

Napier does not recommend waiting that long; nevertheless, he says, 'If you settle too soon before the symptoms have fully appeared, there is a risk that you'll undersettle.' There is also the opposite risk: 'If you wait too long, the client can end up in a state of limbo. We take instructions from our clients, but often I do advise them to wait.'

It will be interesting to see how the Zeebrugge arbitrations affect the settlement of other cases that are pending.

If the compensation available to survivors and families has improved in recent years, it has hardly begun to take into account the question of what to do for those who help, and suffer resultant psychological damages. In much of this book, I have referred to the stress that dealing with disaster causes. Michael Napier himself has found that being a disaster lawyer is stressful because he has constantly to deal with clients who are extremely angry and emotionally charged. There is also a body of research, and some anecdotal evidence, suggesting that rescuers can suffer stress, as in the aforementioned research from the Antarctic dealing with the Air New Zealand plane crash on Mount Erebus in 1979. Much legal ground remains unexplored.

Compensation for 'Nervous Shock'

Michael Napier also points out that the high level of coverage disasters get in the media may also have unanticipated consequences. He asked me to imagine the wife of a lorry driver. Her husband rings her at seven o'clock from Zeebrugge to say that he is getting on the ferry. Two hours later, in her sitting room, she watches the TV news and sees that there has been a terrible disaster there. If she now goes into shock, should it not be possible for her to seek compensation? Napier is not suggesting that media coverage of disasters should be curtailed, but that it ought to be possible for her also to sue. In the McLoughlin *v.* O'Brien judgment, Lord Wilberforce said that, for a case to succeed at present, 'The shock must be through sight or hearing of the event or its immediate aftermath.' He went on virtually to invite new litigation, adding, 'Whether some equivalent of sight or hearing, e.g. through simultaneous television, would suffice may have to be considered.' Napier is sure such cases will arise, and that they will have the additional effect of raising questions about how the media cover disasters.

International Disasters and 'Mid-Atlantic Settlements'

The level of compensation awarded to victims is determined by a number of factors which have nothing to do with the severity of the injuries they receive. In shipping law, the level of compensation is limited by a number of international agreements like the Hague Convention. In aviation accidents, the Warsaw Convention sets a limit of 16,000 international currency units, worth about £12,000. The UK airlines have a voluntary aggreement which raises the maximum to £60,000. Michael Napier adds that these limits are, of course, modest; most of the signatories to these conventions are worried by American levels of settlement.

The crucial factor in determining the level of damages victims receive has turned out to be a geographical one. In Europe, lawyers look enviously at the levels of damages awarded in America. In Britain, a typical settlement for multiple injuries in a crash is £100,000 for pain and suffering; in America, the average figure is $750,000. In the last few years, there has been a tremendous, and quite unfair, variation in the levels of damages that British people have received for similar injuries. These variations have depended very much on, first, whether the carrier was American and, second, on whether any of the victims have also been American. In either case, if Americans are involved, it becomes possible for lawyers to press for much larger damages. As a result, lawyers speak in an almost melancholy manner of disasters like Zeebrugge, in which American damages are out of the question, since there was absolutely no American connection.

In a settlement in which there is an American element, the lawyers make a calculation. Going to an American court is expensive. British clients would also have to pay lawyers contingency fees, which would take up to 30 per cent of any settlements they won. Under British law, plaintiffs can often get legal aid. The legal aid authorities are studying how to deal with cases involving multiple plaintiffs, but so far, in disaster as opposed to some medical cases, no one has complained about cost making it impossible for them to press for their rights.

Lawyers are understandably reluctant to reveal the levels of damages they manage to obtain. If the issue comes to trial, the damages will be revealed in open court, but often, the issue is dealt with under arbitration, as at Zeebrugge, or by settlement before the parties come to court. Nevertheless, it is possible to piece together some interesting facts about the degree of damages awarded in the last few years in cases that have involved what Napier calls 'mid-Atlantic settlements'.

The first case in which British lawyers pressed for mid-Atlantic settlements was the 1985 Manchester Ringway Airport runway fire; some settlements in that case were reported to be over £500,000. Such figures would be much larger than might be anticipated from a purely British disaster. In the *Marchioness* disaster, for example, and at King's Cross, some survivors were offered sums of £1,000 to £2,500 as interim payments to tide them over six to nine months. Only public demonstrations in the case of the *Marchioness* led to an agreement to consider interim payments of £5,000. The Zeebrugge settlements show how difficult it is to get really high sums in the UK.

In 1988, when the *Piper Alpha* disaster took place, Occidental did its best to press for quick settlements. Its lawyers accepted that, as it was an American company, it could not get away with the normal low level of British settlements. The victims' lawyers and those of the company waged a considerable battle of nerves. Victims threatened to sue in the American courts and, though many cases were settled in July 1989, a number of families may yet start litigation in Louisiana, not only against Occidental but against the manufacturers of the platform jacket, McDermott, a company with its world head-quarters in New Orleans. In the July settlement, Occidental and the lawyers for the *Piper Alpha* Action Group reached an agreement for settling claims. The group represents 136 deceased and fifty survivors. Occidental set aside $106 million to meet all claims. It has been said that the families of each of the deceased will get somewhere between £500,000 and £1.2 million; the average settlement will be £600,000. In May 1989, the Court of Sessions in Edinburgh confirmed settlements of that sort to adults who agreed to the division of the total sum of $106 million. The court did not rule, however, on cases involving children under eighteen. Under Scottish law, the court has to appoint an independent curator *ad litem* to look after the interests of children.

Occidental denied that the prospect of litigation in American courts had prompted them to offer fairly high settlements; to the sceptical observer, however, it seems evident that the high level of damages obtained after the *Piper Alpha* disaster by comparison with the Zeebrugge cases, for example, owes a great deal to the prospect of victims going to court in America.

It is understandable, of course, that both the bereaved and survivors should seek to get the best level of damages available, but the question of the fairness of different settlements is left open. It is simply bad law which allows people to receive widely differing amounts for similar injuries. Victims need compensation to enable them to put their lives back together. Even high levels of compensation do not, however, meet with a basic human need: the need to feel that justice has been done.

Corporate Manslaughter

Until 1988, it was assumed that the most that a company could suffer, as the result of a disaster would be to pay high damages for negligence. In fact, since companies usually insure themselves against this risk, they generally emerge relatively unscathed financially from such events. The real burden therefore devolves upon their insurers, though companies like P&O and London Transport do play hard. In 1988, however, the jury sitting on the inquest on the dead of Zeebrugge returned a verdict of unlawful killing, despite having been advised by the coroner in the strongest possible terms not to bring in that verdict. There was much evidence that P&O had failed to take proper note of safety warnings that the jury ignored that advice. There was also the blatant fact to be borne in mind that the master of the ship had sailed with the bow doors open and without verifying that they had been closed. These mistakes prompted the jury to return a verdict of unlawful killing, implying that someone was guilty of breaking the law, that it was more than an accident, however negligent the company had been.

The coroner had assumed that British law did not have such a concept, but he was mistaken. Legal precedents were found: corporate manslaughter was first considered in 1920. Lord Denning said that in any company there had to be directing minds and hands. The directing minds must be capable of intentional action and so must be capable of committing manslaughter. The Kent police therefore sent the papers to the Director of Public Prosecutions, who decided to proceed. P&O have now been charged with corporate manslaughter, a case due to come to trial as this book goes to press. Clearly, the authorities have decided, as a matter of public policy, to examine this avenue open to the law.

There have been some interesting consequences. Rita Valco, representing the King's Cross family victims, told me that they were upset and angry when the police did not press criminal charges as a result of the fire. Then, in the Clapham rail crash, the police decided to investigate the possibility of criminal charges before the inquiry. In the *Marchioness* tragedy, too, there was an immediate pre-inquest police investigation into whether something had gone wrong. The driver of the Purley train who went through a series of signals at red has been charged with reckless driving/manslaughter. These moves can only be welcomed, because they emphasize the fact that people are responsible for those whom they are transporting though, so far, P&O has been the only public prosecution. In the *Marchioness* disaster, the captain of the *Bowbelle* has been charged for not keeping a proper watch but the company that owned the dredger has not been indicted. Some survivors are campaigning for that company also to be charged.

The Law Society, apart from becoming adept at setting up co-ordinating panels, has also started to offer general help to members of the public involved in disasters. According to Edwina Dunn of the Law Society, they have been overwhelmed by requests for help after each major disaster, and they have applied the techniques they have learned from these cases to other groups like those enmeshed in the Barlow Clowes case, where investors lost a great deal of money instead of suffering injury or trauma, but where there were many other similarities to physical disasters. The growing interest in this aspect of the law by solicitors is likely to improve the compensation and treatment victims receive. Michael Napier believes, however, that there is still a long way to go before people who, through no fault of their own, find their lives irredeemably altered by a disaster, achieve proper and just settlements under the law.

10

Lessons of Disaster

In September 1989, Bradford University set up a Disaster Prevention Unit. It drew heavily on the work various Bradford academics and agencies had done into the causes of the Bradford City fire. The unit surprised the press by claiming that a study of over a thousand disasters since the nineteenth century showed that over 60 per cent could have been prevented. In this final chapter, I want to draw together some of the themes I have dwelt on and also to suggest ways in which disaster prevention could be encouraged. Often, people seem to suggest that the number of accidents is bound to increase as technology becomes more complex and people travel more. There is no reason, however, why we should not use both technological advances and our greater psychological knowledge about how people think – and refuse to think – to prevent disasters. It will never be possible to prevent them all, but the Bradford unit's audit of past tragedies suggests that we should not be too defeatist.

Vigilance and Magical Thinking

In many disasters, the eventual inquiries, whether official or investigations by the press, reveal many early-warning signs. Similar, but not as grave incidents frequently preceded the tragedy itself. A year before the King's Cross fire, for instance, there was a blaze at Oxford Circus tube station. One person died. London Transport did not ignore this event: there was an inquiry, after which smoking was banned on tube trains. Yet many recommendations of that internal inquiry, especially those that emphasized the need to train staff to be safety-conscious and to have proper liaison with the fire brigade, were not put into practice. There was no sense of urgency and no attempt to foresee and forestall dangers. Both the King's Cross and Clapham inquiries highlighted this problem: the lack of willingness to learn from clear warnings and to implement appropriate improvements.

Curiously, even when there was a major disaster like the Bradford fire, all the official recommendations made in the subsequent inquiry have not necessarily been implemented. The Disaster Prevention Unit announced, for example, that if all the Popplewell recommendations had been carried out, Hillsborough simply would not have happened. The specific Popplewell recommendations which could have prevented the Hillsborough tragedy were many and thoroughgoing. Evacuation procedures should be a matter of police training and form part of the briefing by police officers before a match. Stewards should be trained in how to help the police with evacuation procedures. Football clubs should review both their arrangements for entry and organization of their turnstiles. Popplewell also pointed to the risks inherent in perimeter fences and stressed the need for 'proper exits'. The inquiry was also worried by the lack of consultation between various bodies and urged that 'there should be urgent consultations between the Health and Safety Executive and the fire authorities as to how best to co-ordinate and communicate their inspections and reports'. Finally, Popplewell suggested that the *Green Guide* should be amended to read that 'all exit gates should be manned at all times while the ground is used by the public and be capable of being opened immediately from inside by anyone in an emergency'. This clearly did not happen at Hillsborough.

Even the Popplewell recommendations dealing directly with fire safety were not all implemented. The Bradford City fire turned into an inferno partly because the ground did not comply with the latest fire safety precautions. Popplewell therefore recommended that all football grounds be inspected for fire safety. Yet the Fire Brigades Union claims that brigades have been unable to supply the manpower needed to check fire safety regulations at many sports and other stadia. The Fire

Brigades Union General Secretary, Jim Cameron, estimates that it will take twenty years to do so at present levels of staffing.

The level of government commitment to implementing safety proposals is also open to question. After the Lockerbie air crash, the families of victims have campaigned for airport security to be tightened. A year after the crash, however, evidence continues to filter through which shows that reforms have been piecemeal. Many reasons have been given for this, but one of the main complaints is that government is simply unwilling to provide the necessary resources. I have argued throughout that it is too easy to blame such failures solely on a lack of resources. The *Guardian* recently took John Prescott, Labour's shadow Transport Secretary, to task on the day of the memorial service for the *Marchioness* dead because he seemed to suggest that disasters would cease under socialism, that there would be more investment in safety and the problem would, as a result, disappear. His 'warm heart', sniped the *Guardian*, raised false hopes, and the paper suggested, sensibly, that human error and sheer happenstance would always be contributing factors to disaster, even if their likelihood could be reduced to the lowest level possible.

I have also tried to suggest that another important factor in disaster prevention is that it is hard to be rational about such tragic events: they make us fall back on what I have termed 'magical thinking': if we do not dwell on them, they will not happen. They will never happen to us, and so on. Human beings have an oddly irrational attitude to disasters. They are certainly much written about, yet it seems that, on the ground, people often resist making obvious improvements that stare them in the face. There is a clear psychological paradox here. Given the importance of the issue, however, the immediate point is not to solve this theoretical puzzle but rather to suggest ways in which organizations can implement practical change. There are three ways in which it is possible to deal with this problem: training to look for danger, surprise inspections and a regular safety audit. None of these concepts is wholly new, but it is nevertheless true that none comfortably fits into existing patterns of work.

Training

Training for various jobs, especially in transportation industries and on hazardous sites like reactors and chemical installations, needs to emphasize far more strongly the routine safety risks involved. The accounts given by various victims of disasters, like Stephen Homewood – of work on the *Herald of Free Enterprise* – and Ed Punchard – on practices on *Piper Alpha* – are extremely revealing. There was little emphasis on safety training from their respective companies. Punchard accepts that workers on *Piper Alpha* did carry out safety drills, but claims that these drills never envisaged the massive disaster that occurred. It is also an indication of the low priority that safety receives in the offshore oil industry that workers were required to acquire a survival certificate which involves just four days' study. This requirement has not been altered. Moreover, the press has frequently alleged that training certificates can be bought in bars and pubs.

In the Introduction, I discussed Singleton's ideas on how management can create a safety-conscious climate. Singleton also suggests ways of training people to work better in emergencies. This 'error correction work' is distinguished from 'error reduction'. Singleton argues that effective handling of emergencies requires:

1. Avoiding confusing decision situations where it's not clear who has to authorize what. In a ship or plane, that's easy – the captain commands – but in industrial plants there is not always such an obvious chain of command.

2. Making sure that there is rapid feedback on actions and their consequences. That was not the case at Three Mile Island, Bhopal and the M1 British Midland crash.

3. Making sure that the initial design makes it feasible for errors to be remedied quickly.

4. Replacing continuous control by action selection so that operators aren't totally reliant on automatic back-up systems and have to think about the implications of what they are doing.

5. In the light of the latter, Singleton argues that it is important to have man-to-man monitoring.

One way of countering the human tendency not to focus on danger is to develop scenarios. This idea is not original, as it is used in tasks as diverse as military training and marketing. Most safety drills simply sound an alarm and get people to muster at a prearranged point. There is no attempt to take people through a rehearsal for any real incident. Moreover, the safety drill is often seen as a joke or a chore. Much recent work on the psychology of training stresses the need to catch the imagination of those being trained. Scenario safety training could do this. It would take staff through simulated emergencies, sharpening their responses. Those running the exercise would also have to provide good feedback. After the fire at King's Cross, there was one attempt by London Transport to mount such an exercise, but many of the press were strangely critical. They saw it as a ghoulish exercise, not a precaution. Simulating specific disasters is routine in teaching pilots and air crew their skills, pilots having to go through refresher courses every six months to check that their skills are up to scratch. Possibly as a result, in a number of recent air crashes, there have been many survivors. Over fifty survived the British Midland crash at Kegworth; thirty-eight came out of the Brazilian jungle following a crash where radio contact was lost and the plane disappeared; fifty-eight came out alive from the crash of the US Air jet at La Guardia on 21 September 1989. Pilots are universally perceived as having people's lives in their hands, hence the focus on good training to prepare them to cope with emergencies. Pilots told Sloan and Cooper in *Stress on Pilots* that while there was undeniably a great difference between a real emergency and a simulated one, the practice was nevertheless extremely helpful.

When I was writing this book, I noticed, during a series of flights on British Airways, that passengers themselves tend to pay little attention to safety announcements on planes. Many read their papers or daydream. This blasé attitude may well reflect the fact that we do not want to think about accidents, but it augurs badly for our behaviour in an actual emergency. It seems clear to me that a little preparation would be valuable. Both airports and railway stations offer an ideal area in which to have large-scale safety demonstrations in which passengers could join. The recent findings of a study for the Civil Aviation Authority (CAA) showed that people panicked when trying to get out of an aeroplane, shoving each other mercilessly out of the way. The CAA used these findings to argue, wisely, for larger gangways in planes, but the experiment also suggests that transport authorities which presently use station and terminal space for marketing might more usefully use these for constant safety demonstrations, so that passengers could have some clue as to how to act in a disaster. Such demonstrations, clearly, would not be comforting or, initially, popular, but many passengers might be willing to undergo a little discomfort to know how to behave in an emergency.

Surprise Inspections

It has been possible for many organizations to avoid making safety a key issue because systems of inspections are somewhat haphazard. All too often the inspection is not a real inspection at all: everything has been prepared for, as in the oil industry. The Railways Inspectorate, too, has an essentially cosy relationship with British Rail and does not suddenly descend on stations or trains to make sure everything is in order.

In mental health law throughout the 1960s and 1970s, there were worries about the conditions in which mental patients were detained. The 1983 Mental Health Act set up the Mental Health Law Review Commission. This is a quango made up mainly of doctors, lawyers and a few social workers. Its members have the right to descend, day or night, on any facility where a person is detained under mental health law. The annual reports of the commission have commented on the fact that if they give no warning, they are much more likely to see conditions as they routinely are. The commission does not spring surprise visits too often, since it feels this would destroy valuable trust between it and the hospitals whose care it seeks to improve, but it is a power it uses every year on a number of occasions, to great effect.

The airline with the best safety record with regard to terrorists, El Al, operates in a similar way. El Al inspectors do not reveal who they are. They behave as someone who was a skilful terrorist might behave. They see if they can slip through safety checks. Many witnesses at the *Piper Alpha* inquiry claimed that such surprise inspections would greatly benefit the oil industry. It is telling, too, that in the wake of the *Marchioness* disaster, such a system has been set in motion on the Thames. Sceptics will note, however, that the financial interests operating in the Thames pleasure boat trade are rather smaller than those involved in North Sea oil exploration.

The Safety Audit

It is common for companies to express concern about safety. As their PR skills have increased, many companies have frequently made such statements of policy; they have not simply waited to react to a disaster. Yet the incidents described in this book, and thousands of others, show how hard it is even for genuinely concerned enterprises to translate general concern for safety into an adequate programme of precautions.

One solution may be for engineers, psychologists and health and safety experts to devise a safety audit for particular industries. In manufacturing the notion of quality control is well known. Dollond and Aitchison, a leading maker of lenses, told me, for example, that every single lens that leaves its premises is inspected by people whose aim it is to find faults. At the end of each production batch, therefore, it is possible to see how many lenses are deficient. It would seem to be possible to devise ways of applying these principles of quality control to safety in transportation. It is an area where engineers and psychologists need to collaborate. One starting point for such an audit would be to identify the key elements that need to be checked in regular surprise inspections. The reports of these safety audits would need to be fed back to both staff and customers. Given the increasing public anxiety about safety, it would be a boost to customer confidence if some companies included such independent audits in their annual reports. It is a concept that needs a great deal of development, but it should be possible to create such procedures, and oblige companies to disclose the results.

Controlling One's Fate

The psychological evidence suggests strongly that while there are some similarities between all disasters, researchers are also becoming increasingly aware of the sheer complexity and heterogeneousness of disasters. There is a concept in the psychological literature called locus of control. Research suggests that people can be divided into those who have an *external* and those who have an *internal* locus of control. Externals blame other people, social conditions, the world, for what happens to them whether it is good or bad. Internals blame themselves. No psychologist has yet studied disaster victims in this light. The theory, which is well established in areas like reactions to cancer, suggests some intriguing ideas. Are the people who suffer worst in disasters those who usually have an internal locus of control? Externals expect to be buffeted by the world, and being in an earthquake, flood or fire is the final confirmation of their attitude. I do not mean to suggest that they will be less shocked by a traumatic event but rather that the quality of their shock will be different. It will be transient. Essentially, the trauma confirms their experience of the world and their way of dealing with it. Internals, however, expect to remain in control of their environment. As a result, after a trauma, on top of their shock, their view of how the world works and how they work in relation to it is shattered. Do they, therefore, suffer worse than externals?

I have no empirical proof concerning the above ideas, but the one fact that all the psychiatrists, psychologists and social workers I talked to were struck by was the extent to which it was hard to predict who would cope and who would not cope after a disaster. The locus of control theory offers a possible explanation of these variations, especially since all the accounts survivors and carers give stress the need people feel to reassert some degree of control over their lives and their environments.

Where they fail to do so, as at Buffalo Creek, the results can be devastating.

I have tried to argue that we need to be much more sophisticated in our response to disasters. It is important to understand the variety of consequences resulting from the loss of control that individuals experience. In natural disasters people do not expect to have any degree of control over events. We are at the mercy of nature. There is, therefore, no one to be angry at until the rescue operations start to go wrong. Man-made disasters, on the other hand, are perceived very differently. Most have a comprehensible cause. Bereaved and survivors often become obsessive in trying to pinpoint that cause. Often, the cause reveals a long trail of organizational neglect and error. There is, therefore, something 'safe' for campaigners to be angry at.

I also found that victims and the bereaved need to feel that what they went through was not pointless, and often the only way of making any use of the deaths and suffering was to prevent a similar disaster happening again. One sees, therefore, as for example in the aftermath of the Dutch train hijacks and of *Piper Alpha*, a determined attempt to learn lessons well. It could be argued that individuals who put energy into changing the system that went wrong tend to cope well with disasters. The effort is good for them, giving meaning to the ordeal they went through. Often, too, their efforts can actually lead to considerable reforms, because as a result of their ordeal they do enjoy a certain status. Their suffering, for a while at least, especially if they learn to handle the media skilfully, gives them a right to speak.

The worst psychological impact of disasters seems to occur in situations where people suffer and then feel helpless, where they cannot see what they can do either to make sense of what happened or to use it as a starting point for action to prevent a similar situation recurring. Where people feel unable to make use of disaster as a starting point, they are likely to suffer growing frustration. That may be most true, perhaps, of those who had, before the disaster, an internal locus of control. Counselling therefore needs to take into account how important it can be for victims, if possible, to turn the disaster into something positive. It is significant that a number of survivors have tried to write books about or accounts of what happened to them immediately afterwards, as part of that process. In the September 1989 La Guardia crash, for example, one of the passengers was a CBS news producer. He had a mobile phone with him and, before he was rescued, from inside the cockpit as water was flooding in, he filed a report. He lived. It is perhaps macabre, even a little comic, but it is also more than that: he was fitting his disaster into the pattern of his life. Counselling needs to be sensitive to clients' needs to do this, and so does society in general.

References

Apter, M. (1988): *Reversal Theory*. London: Routledge.

Attia case: reported in *The Law of Tort*, ed. Salmond. London: Butterworths.

Banyard, P. (1989): 'Hillsborough' in *Psychology News*, vol. 2 no. 7.

Bell, J. B. (1978): *A Time of Terror*. London: Jonathan Cape.

Bignell, V., Peters, G., and Pym, C. (1977): *Catastrophic Failures*. Milton Keynes: Open University Press.

Broadbent, D. (1961): *Behaviour*. London: Eyre & Spottiswoode.

Bull, R. (1985): 'Disfigurement' in *Psychology News* no. 25.

Canter, D. (1979): *Cry Wolf*. London: Routledge.

Cohen, D. (1988): *Forgotten Millions*. London: Paladin.

Davidson, L., Baum, A. and Collins, D. (1982): 'Stress and Control Related Problems at Three Mile Island' in *Journal of Applied Social Psychology*, 12, pp. 349–69.

Davis, G. (1988): *Partisans & Mediators*. Oxford: Oxford University Press.

Dohrenwend, B. P., Dohrenwend, B. S., Kasl S. V. *et al* (1979): *Report of the Task Group on Behavioural Effects to the President's Commission on the Accident at Three Mile Island*. Washington, DC.

Erikson, K. (1976): *Everything Fell In*. New Haven: Yale University Press.

The Fennell Inquiry into the King's Cross Fire (1988): Command Paper no. 499, HMSO.

Flynn, C. and Chalmers, W. (1980): *The Social and Economic Effects of the Accident at Three Mile Island*. Washington, DC.: Nuclear Regulatory Commission.

Geiger, J. in *Journal of the American Medical Association*, 20 August 1986.

Hansard, 6 March 1989.

Hardy, T. (1957): 'The Convergence of the Twain' in *Collected Poems*. London: Routledge.

Health and Safety Executive: *The Green Guide*.

Hersey, J. (1946): *Hiroshima*. New York: Knopf (based on articles originally published in the *New Yorker*).

Hidden (1990): Report on the Clapham Train Crash. Command Paper 820, HMSO.

Indian Council on Science (1985): *Report on Scientific Studies on the Factors Related to Bhopal Toxic Gas Leakage*.

Lundin, T. (1984): 'Morbidity Following Sudden and Unexpected Bereavements' in *British Journal of Psychiatry*, 144, pp. 84–8.

McGurk, T. (1989): 'The After-effects of being Taken Hostage'; paper presented to the British Psychological Society Annual Conference.

McLoughlin case reported in *Personal and Medical Injuries Newsletter*, June 1989.

Millais J. (1924): 'Shell Shock' in *Journal of Nervous and Mental Diseases*, 54, pp. 98–104.

Murgatroyd, S. (1986): *Counselling*. Milton Keynes: Open University Press.

Murthy, S. (1984): 'The Karnataka Circus Fire' in *Indian Journal of Psychiatry*, vol. 27, pp. 166–73.

Napier, M. (1989): 'Post Traumatic Stress Disorder' in *Personal and Medical Injuries Newsletter*, May 1989, pp. 29–33.

Personal and Medical Newsletter report (1989): 'The Zeebrugge Settlement' in *Personal and Medical Injuries Newsletter*, June 1989, pp. 37–42.

Popplewell, O. (1986): Report on the Bradford Fire. Command Paper no. 9710, HMSO.

Punchard, Ed (1989): *Piper Alpha*. London: Unwin Hyman.

Raphael, B. (1986): *When Disaster Strikes*. London: Hutchinson.

Raphael Sarason, I. and Sarason, B. (1984): *Abnormal Psychology*. Englewood Cliffs: Prentice Hall.

Singleton, W. T. (1990): *The Mind at Work*. Cambridge: Cambridge University Press.

Shapland, J. and Cohen, D. (1987): 'Victims of Crime' in *Criminal Law Review*, January 1987, pp. 29–39.

Sloan, S. and Cooper, C. (1985): *Stress on Pilots*. London: Routledge.

Taylor, I. (1981): paper presented to the British Psychological Society on the New Zealand Antarctic air crash.

The Taylor Inquiry on Hillsborough interim report (1989): Command Paper no. 765, HMSO.

The Taylor Inquiry on Hillsborough final report (1990): Command Paper no. 962, HMSO.

Tiresias (1984): *Notes from Overground*. London: Paladin.

The Terrific Register (1825).

Voltaire (1984): *Candide*. Harmondsworth: Penguin Classics.

Wolfe, T. (1971): *The Right Stuff*. New York: Bantam.

Wynn Jones, M. (1976): *Deadline Disaster*. Newton Abbot: David & Charles.

Index